Organizational Behavior

INTEGRATED MODELS *AND* APPLICATIONS

Organizational Behavior

INTEGRATED MODELS AND APPLICATIONS

Wm. B. Zachary
San Jose State University

Loren W. Kuzuhara
University of Wisconsin – Madison

THOMSON

™

SOUTH-WESTERN

Australia · Canada · Mexico · Singapore · Spain · United Kingdom · United States

THOMSON

SOUTH-WESTERN

Organizational Behavior: Integrated Models and Applications, 1e
Wm. B. Zachary and Loren W. Kuzuhara

VP/Editorial Director:
Jack W. Calhoun

VP/Editor-in-Chief:
Michael P. Roche

Publisher:
Melissa S. Acuña

Acquisitions Editor:
John Szilagyi

Developmental Editor:
Emma F. Guttler

Marketing Manager:
Jacquelyn Carrillo

Production Editor:
Lora Arduser

Manufacturing Coordinator:
Rhonda Utley

Technology Project Editor:
Kristen Meere

Media Editor:
Karen L. Schaffer

Design Project Manager:
Rik Moore

Production House:
Argosy Publishing

Cover Designer:
John Robb, JWR Design
Interaction

Cover Images:
© Matthew Chattle, Photonica

Internal Designer:
John Robb, JWR Design
Interaction

Printer:
Thomson/West
Eagan, MN

For permission to use material
from this text or product, submit
a request online at
http://www.thomsonrights.com.
Any additional questions about
permissions can be submitted by
email to thomsonrights@thom-
son.com

For more information
contact South-Western,
5191 Natorp Boulevard,
Mason, Ohio, 45040.
Or you can visit our Internet site
at: http://www.swlearning.com

In Dedication

To Mom and Dad, two special parents who frequently created or supported opportunities to engage in higher-level learning.

WBZ

To my wife, Lavina, my son, Daniel, my daughter, Carolyn, and Mom and Dad, with thanks for their long-term support and understanding.

LWK

BRIEF CONTENTS

TABLE OF CONTENTS

PART III: The Group Level 69

PREFACE

After several years of intensive analysis and discussion, members of the College of Business at San Jose State University (SJSU) decided to initiate significant changes in their business curriculum beginning in Fall 1996. A taxonomy of educational learning objectives developed by Bloom and his colleagues played a major role in shaping the new curriculum (see Chapter 1 for an explanation of this taxonomy). The taxonomy of learning also influenced revisions of a number of College of Business courses—including Organizational Behavior (OB).

The previous SJSU course in Organizational Behavior placed major emphasis on *knowledge* and *comprehension*, the two lower levels of learning in Bloom's taxonomy. Students were required to read a substantial portion of a standard—and rather lengthy—OB textbook. Such textbooks definitely provide a great deal of useful *knowledge*. However, because a large number of different topics, theories, issues, and practices are covered by these traditional textbooks, student *comprehension* of the material varied considerably. Few students could absorb all or even most of it. In addition, while attempts were certainly made to incorporate the four higher levels of learning into some of the Organizational Behavior course activities, actual learning at these levels was limited because the lowest levels of learning inevitably remained the major emphasis of the course.

In the revised OB course, the number of different topics, theories, issues, and practices covered has been significantly reduced. But because *knowledge* and *comprehension* are now focused on a few key models or theories in each topic area—many of which *integrate* the best parts of many other models—the *quality* of students' lower-level learning of each topic covered attains a higher level.

A second key advantage of this new approach is that it frees students to focus more of their time and attention on the four higher levels in Bloom's taxonomy than was previously the case with special emphasis on *application* to real-world settings. *Application* of OB knowledge is, after all, the primary concern of both the students who are or will soon be working, and the organizations that are or will soon be employing them. High-quality *application* almost always requires some high-quality *analysis*, if not *synthesis* and/or *evaluation* as well.

This book has been specifically designed for use in an Organizational Behavior course in which the instructor makes a conscious choice to place major emphasis on the four higher levels of learning in Bloom's taxonomy.

DISTINGUISHING FEATURES

Integrated Models: In each chapter, emphasis is placed on a key integrated model that synthesizes multiple models, theories or approaches concerning that particular OB topic into a single, relatively complete package. Hence students focus in-depth on a model that is theoretically sophisticated as well as practically useful.

Application Sections: These sections explain how to actually implement the chapter's primary, integrated model in a real-world setting. In addition, each Application section contains a detailed Application Example that illustrates how to practically apply the implementation guidelines for the relevant integrated model.

Exercises and Other Activities: A variety of Experiential Exercises and other activities are provided to help students practice applying the key integrated models and to develop deeper insights into various aspects of the field by engaging in higher-level learning. Many of these activities will require group interaction, although some can be completed by either individuals or teams. The experiential exercises are designed for classroom or field work.

Higher Level Learning Modules (HLLMs): Students may engage in higher-level learning while reading this text by considering a variety of HLLMs that are distributed throughout each chapter. Each module raises questions that require students to become actively involved in one or more of the four higher levels of learning: *Application, Analysis, Synthesis*, and/or *Evaluation*.

Practical, In-depth Coverage: This text covers a practical number of OB topics, focusing in-depth on a small number of carefully selected models, theories or approaches in each topic area.

ANCILLARIES

INSTRUCTOR'S MANUAL WITH TEST BANK

A comprehensive Instructor's Manual and Test Bank is available to assist in preparing the students for higher-level learning and being prepared to discuss the book's higher-level learning features. Suggested answers for the Exercises and Other Activities plus the Higher-Level Learning Modules are provided, which may also include tips on what to expect and analyses of potential problem areas where appropriate. The Test Bank contains a variety of essay questions to test the quality of the students' higher-level learning. The Instructor's Manual with Test Bank is available as a downloadable file on the text support site.

POWERPOINT SLIDES

Graphics based on the diagrams in the text are supplied as aids to classroom discussions prior to applying that material in an exercise or other higher-level learning activity. The PowerPoint Slides are available as downloadable files on the text support site.

WEB SITE http://zachary.swlearning.com

Organizational Behavior: Integrated Models and Applications provides a multitude of resources. Additional supplementary materials are included on a password-protected site for both students and instructors. Instructor Resources include downloadable Instructor's Manual with Test Bank files available in Microsoft Word 2000 format and Adobe Acrobat format. Downloadable PowerPoint slide files also are available in Microsoft PowerPoint 2000 format.

ACKNOWLEDGEMENTS

The development of this book has been very strongly influenced by the many students who have taken Bill Zachary's courses in Organizational Behavior, both before and after Fall 1996. Their written, oral, and behavioral feedback about the higher-level and lower-level learning aspects of these courses has played a crucial role in shaping this new approach to a fascinating field of study.

Several of Bill Zachary's colleagues at San Jose State University have made important contributions as well. Marlene Turner contributed not only feedback but also valuable suggestions for new directions and additional key integrated models, greatly enhancing the book as well as expanding its original scope significantly. Anne Lawrence provided both feedback and helpful book publication information. Joe Mori brought Bloom's taxonomy of educational learning objectives to the attention of the key task forces charged with making major changes in the College of Business curriculum, thereby serving as the crucial gate-keeping link to the eventual foundation for this book.

Many thanks, too, to the reviewers who offered their feedback:
Joy Benson, University of Illinois – Springfield
Sally Dresdow, University of Wisconsin – Green Bay
John Drexler, Oregon State University
David Hannah, University of Texas – Austin
Nell Tabor Hartley, Robert Morris College
Edwin A. Locke, University of Maryland
Doyle J. Lucas, Anderson University
David Luechauer, Butler University
Kenneth H. Price, University of Texas – Arlington
Anne O'Leary-Kelly, University of Arkansas – Fayetteville
Holly Schroth, University of California – Berkeley
Joe Thomas, Middle Tennessee State University
John Washbush, University of Wisconsin – Whitewater

Wm. B. Zachary
San Jose State University
Loren W. Kuzuhara
University of Wisconsin – Madison

PART I
Introduction

CHAPTER 1
Introduction to Organizational Behavior

INTRODUCTION TO ORGANIZATIONAL BEHAVIOR

Organizational behavior—or OB for short—is a field of study concerned with the behavior of people in work organizations. OB encompasses how people act, what they say, and why they do things. From a managerial perspective, OB deals with how to influence what people will do in the future. In other words, *predicting*, *explaining*, and *managing* the behavior of others are important goals of the field of organizational behavior.[1]

In virtually any job you may hold, you will need to deal with at least some aspects of your colleagues' behavior. Thus, learning about OB is a relevant and useful way to spend some of your valuable time.

You have undoubtedly studied the behavior of other people for quite some time—at home, at school, perhaps at work. After years of experience, you may feel that you are adept at predicting what people will do in any particular situation, and at explaining why people behave in certain ways. If such knowledge and skills are already part of your "common sense," why bother to read a book about organizational behavior?

Perhaps the most practical reason for reading a book about *applied* OB is to improve the quality of your "common sense." The OB concepts and methods covered in this book are, for the most part, results obtained over many years of research, through many studies done on large numbers of people working in a wide variety of organizations. These studies have been conducted by OB experts, who have applied scientific, objective techniques to obtain their results. Your personal observations and experiences may not have led to the same conclusions as these more thorough, larger-scale studies—which puts you at a competitive disadvantage if you choose to simply follow your common sense. Furthermore, some of the insights into people at work that OB experts have developed are not at all obvious.

For example, would you agree that it is common sense to expect happy, satisfied workers to be more productive and high performing than workers who are not particularly satisfied with their jobs? Many people would. Yet a large number of OB research studies conducted over the past 50 years have reached a distinctly different conclusion. These studies[2] have found that the actual correlation between job satisfaction and job performance is in the vicinity of 0.15, which is quite low.

APPLICATION & ANALYSIS — Job Satisfaction and Performance

Common sense would suggest that the correlation between job satisfaction and job performance in real-world *applications* should be considerably higher than it actually is. However, by doing some thoughtful *analysis*, it is possible to uncover several reasons that might help to explain this surprisingly low correlation. Why might a person perform well while doing a job that this person does not really like? Alternatively, why might a person who likes a particular job perform at a level that is only mediocre, or just barely good enough?

Another reason to read a book about organizational behavior is to improve your behavioral skills (also known as interpersonal skills). Application-oriented OB books such as this one provide a solid foundation for good behavioral skills by presenting models and guidelines that will point you in directions that are likely to be right ones. In-class exercises, case studies based on real-world situations, outside-of-class field projects, and related activities provide you with opportunities to practice your behavioral skills while interacting with other class members as well as people outside of class.

With practice, the systematic application of scientifically developed behavioral models and guidelines becomes almost as natural as using your common sense. In fact, after substantial practice, these models and guidelines *do* become your common sense. The likely increase in job performance you can achieve as a result of learning from studies conducted by OB experts and then applying that learning in the real world will pay dividends for the rest of your career.

ORGANIZATIONAL BEHAVIOR AND ORGANIZATIONAL EFFECTIVENESS

Studying organizational behavior is also important because of its influence on the overall effectiveness of an organization. That is, the application of the concepts and behavioral models discussed in this book will increase the likelihood that an organization will achieve its objectives and remain a competitive player in its industry. For example, many organizations are concerned with increasing customer satisfaction because it generates sales, loyalty, and repeat business from customers. These outcomes, in turn, enhance the profitability of an organization. What kinds of strategies can managers use to enhance customer satisfaction? Specifically, managers can use incentives and rewards to motivate their employees (see Chapter 3) to provide outstanding customer service. They can also design jobs so that the employees experience a sense of pride and accomplishment (see Chapter 3) for providing excellent service to customers. In addition, they can provide strong leadership to support customer service by giving appropriate direction (see Chapter 8) and feedback (see Chapter 9) to employees. The bottom line is that the foundation for achieving organizational objectives is the effective management of organizational behavior issues.

Another key organizational objective for many companies is to be creative and innovative. Companies such as Nokia, Sony, Apple Computer, and Pixar Animation Studios (creator of animated films such as *Monsters Inc.* and *Toy Story*) have all earned reputations for being innovators in their respective industries. How are these companies able to think and behave in highly creative ways? The answer, again, is in the systematic management of organizational behavior issues. Generally, creativity is enhanced when teams are composed of a diverse set of individuals (see Chapter 4) in terms of knowledge, skills, experiences, and also personality (see Chapter 2). A work environment or organizational culture (see Chapter 10) that encourages employees to think creatively is also essential. Employees must be given goals and reward incentives (see Chapters 9 and 3) to think creatively, and leaders (see Chapter 8) must maintain an active focus on stimulating creative decision making (see Chapter 7) among employees through constructive rather than destructive conflict (see Chapters 4 and 5). The effective management of OB issues enables an organization to be a better innovator as well.

ORGANIZATIONAL BEHAVIOR AND THE IMPLEMENTATION OF STRATEGIC AND OPERATIONAL PLANS

Organizational behavior is also important to the success of an organization in terms of its ability to implement or execute its plans and strategies. This issue tends to be one of the most overlooked aspects of the management process. Plans and strategies, no matter how well they have been crafted on paper, will not have much impact on the effectiveness of an organization if they are not implemented effectively. In the real world, it is too often assumed that once a plan or strategy has been developed, it will naturally be implemented in accordance with the plan. Nothing could be further from the truth! The execution of a plan or strategy relies on a disciplined approach to the application of organizational behavior principles and methods. Specifically, the implementation of plans and strategies through the effective application of principles of leadership (see Chapter 8), motivation (see Chapter 3), and teamwork (see Chapter 4) is what ultimately determines the winner in a given business or industry.

One example of the importance of organizational behavior in implementing plans and strategies can be seen in a corporate merger or acquisition. Hardly a day goes by without yet another acquisition or merger taking place. On paper, many of these mergers sound like matches made in heaven. However, in reality, a large percentage of these "corporate marriages" end in disappointment, diminished results for the new company, or even a corporate divorce (e.g., the selling off of the company that was acquired). Given the tremendous cost associated with a failed merger or acquisition, why do they occur so frequently? Again, a lack of attention to OB issues is often a major cause of the failure. Sometimes, management underestimates the cultural differences (see Chapter 10) between the two companies. In other cases, management neglects to create and implement the structures, processes, and systems needed to integrate the two companies into a single entity. This often leads to power struggles for control (see Chapter 6), as some groups may feel that they are being left out of the decision making (see Chapter 7). Finally, managers may fail to manage employee resistance to change (see Chapter 10), resulting in conflict (see Chapter 5), low employee morale, reduced motivation (see Chapter 3), and lack of commitment to the new company. Again, the key lesson from the failure of many mergers and acquisitions is that the application of OB principles is critical to the ultimate success of any plan or strategy.

APPLICATION & ANALYSIS

Real-World Examples of the Role of Organizational Behavior in Contributing to Organizational Effectiveness

Use an Internet search engine to identify an example of an article from a business publication or web site that describes the efforts of an organization to enhance its performance in some area (e.g., product quality, customer service, cost reduction, innovation, or speed in product development). Identify and describe the specific organizational behavior issues that are being addressed by management in the company to support the achievement of their objectives.

THE CONTINGENCY THEORY APPROACH

It certainly would be a great deal easier to predict *what* people will do in the future, or to explain *why* they did what they did in the past, if people were all the same. However, different people and different situations tend to be . . . well, *different*.

Early theories of organizational behavior sought to provide answers to key OB issues in much the same way that theories from the so-called hard sciences, such as chemistry and physics, developed mathematical laws describing precisely how the real world actually works. More recently, OB experts have largely given up on such "one best way" kinds of theories and have focused on developing combination models that suggest different responses depending on the situation.[3] Such theories are known as **contingency theories**. This is because which of several possible answers is likely to be the most appropriate is *contingent*—depends on—other factors related to the situation.

Careful readers of the preceding definition of contingency theories will have noted the use of the phrase "which of several possible answers is *likely* to be the most appropriate." Since people and situations are always at least a little bit different, it is virtually impossible to develop a model of people's behavior that provides a perfect answer for every situation that may arise. Realistically speaking, organizational behavior researchers attempt to develop models that will point their users in the right direction much of the time. This book covers a small number of mostly well-known, well-established OB models, theories, and approaches that have proven themselves repeatedly over time.

In actual practice, while many managers tend to have their own preferred ways of doing things, the best managers are those who are flexible. These managers can adjust their management style or way of doing things to better match the current situation. The contingency models and theories covered in this book suggest which styles or ways of doing things are likely to provide the best matches to the various kinds of problems and situations that commonly arise for typical managers. Effectively applying such contingency models or theories usually leads to significantly better results than either guessing or using one's common sense.

A TAXONOMY OF LEARNING

Bloom and his colleagues have developed a classification, or taxonomy, of educational learning objectives.[4] This places various major types of cognitive learning (i.e., the kind of learning done in OB courses) into a hierarchy that ranges from lower levels of learning to higher levels of learning. The higher the level of learning, the more challenging it is to perform effectively. Figure 1-1 depicts the six key elements of this learning hierarchy.

Figure 1-1   Taxonomy of Educational Learning

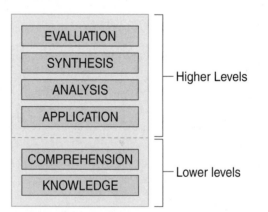

Source: Bloom, B. S., B. B. Mesia, and D. R. Krathwohl. *Taxonomy of Educational Objectives,* Vol. 2. New York: David McKay, 1964.

According to the **Taxonomy of Educational Learning**, the lowest level of learning is **knowledge**. This level of learning consists of taking in new information and remembering it. The second-lowest level, **comprehension**, refers to actually *understanding* the knowledge that has been taken in. This is a more difficult task. Rather than simply repeating back new knowledge, one must make sense of it and be able to explain it.

Both of these lower-level types of learning are fundamental and must occur before higher-level learning can take place. Without a solid lower-level learning foundation, any higher-level learning activity is likely to be flawed.

However, the real excitement begins when one can actually *do something* with that lower-level learning (other than repeat it back on an exam, for example). Of special interest to people who work in the real world is the higher-level type of learning known as **application**, which involves applying knowledge to real-life situations in a useful way.

Application is extremely useful, but what if it is not clear exactly what piece of knowledge should be applied, or in which way? As this chapter has suggested, the best possible solution to any given organizational behavior issue is often not so obvious. To make applications effective, some kind of **analysis** of the situation is usually necessary. For example, analysis might determine which particular OB contingency factors should be applied in a particular situation. Analysis requires using critical thinking and problem-solving skills to take the pieces of a problem apart and examine each of them carefully. Doing such analysis requires significant skill and effort. It also greatly increases the odds of choosing or developing an effective solution.

Even more challenging than analysis is **synthesis**—putting a variety of pieces of knowledge together in a new and more useful way. This book contains a number of synthesized models that combine ideas taken from many previously developed models, theories, or approaches to organizational behavior. Synthesized models may also be strongly influenced by research results obtained through *empirical tests* of those previously developed models or theories. Empirical tests of OB issues are based on data concerning the actual behaviors of relatively large numbers of people. Such data is most often obtained in real-world work organizations. Laboratories at universities or research institutes are another source of data for testing *some* types of OB models or theories.

At the top of the Taxonomy of Educational Learning hierarchy is **evaluation**. Doing a fair, thorough, and impartial job of evaluating such important concerns as the quality of a solution to a problem, or the level of an employee's performance, requires concentration. One must be well aware of goals and standards; the quality of other solutions or performances in the past or present; factors that may affect one's perception of a solution or performance; and so on. All of these concerns must then be kept in mind simultaneously while carefully evaluating the solution or performance currently under review (see Chapter 9).

ANALYSIS

Why Evaluation Is At the Top of the Hierarchy

As is indicated in the preceding section, the types of higher-level learning are application, analysis, synthesis, and evaluation. *Analyze* why evaluation, rather than application, analysis, or synthesis, has been placed at the top of the Taxonomy of Educational Learning hierarchy.

THE PURPOSE OF THIS BOOK

The purpose of this book is to approach the study of organizational behavior from a *non-traditional perspective*. The traditional approach that many OB textbooks take is to cover a wide variety of OB concepts and theories. The basic concept underlying this kind of approach is to provide students with a so-called behavioral "tool kit." In theory, once students have been equipped with such a "kit," they can use any of the "tools" it contains when needed while working in the real world. Since people and situations can be so different, learning about a wide variety of behavioral tools does give industry practitioners many possible solutions to choose from when they are faced with real OB problems, along with some ideas concerninig which tools are more likely to be effective in certain kinds of situations. In other words, the traditional approach does have its merits. However, a major problem with this approach is that when students are presented with a large number of theories, most of those theories are simply read about, perhaps talked about, memorized for test purposes, and then forgotten.

This book takes a more applied approach, recognizing that students must "use it or lose it." It contains useful information about a *reasonable* number—instead of a large number—of important organizational behavior topic areas. Within each topic area, only a *small* number of carefully selected models, theories, or approaches are presented, with preference being given to those that *synthesize* or *integrate* findings of other models, theories, or approaches into a single, relatively complete package. Some combination of activities—experiential exercises, case studies, field projects, and so on—will provide opportunities to practice applying these models, theories, or approaches in ways that mirror how they could be used in an actual work situation.

Another non-traditional aspect of this book is its increased emphasis on the much more exciting (and much more challenging) higher levels of learning in the Taxonomy of Educational Learning hierarchy presented in the previous section. While textbooks must necessarily devote a lot of space to knowledge and comprehension because these lower-level types of learning provide the foundation for higher-level learning activities, this book provides a substantial number of higher-level learning opportunities as well. This will be accomplished in several ways. A variety of application-oriented activities are used, many which require group interaction (although either individuals or groups may tackle some of the case studies, field projects, or certain kinds of exercises). In addition, this book provides opportunities to engage in higher-level learning through the application of a novel concept called "higher-level learning modules." Higher-level learning modules (HLLMs) require engaging in application, analysis, synthesis, evaluation, or some combination of these higher-level types of learning. The types of higher-level learning involved will be noted as part of the title for each HLLM. Some HLLMs require a relatively moderate cognitive effort, while others are more challenging. HLLMs are inserted at various points throughout each chapter in boxes.

The higher-level learning module that appeared near the beginning of this chapter (called Job Satisfaction and Performance) focused on *analysis*. This module asked why the correlation between job satisfaction and job performance is low despite common sense knowledge that happy workers "should" be high performers. If you did not carefully consider this question earlier, think about it now. Why might someone be strongly motivated to perform well even if that person does not really like his current job? This situation arises for a substantial number of college students, especially for those who hold part-time jobs. Conversely, why might someone who really likes his job perform that job at a lower level?

EXERCISES AND OTHER ACTIVITIES
■ *Experiential Exercise: In-Class 1-1*

EFFECTIVE STUDENT STRATEGIES FOR STUDYING AND APPLYING THIS BOOK
The purpose of this exercise is to identify effective, non-traditional strategies for learning and applying the material presented in *Organizational Behavior: Integrated Models and Applications*.

Exercise Process Outline
Form groups of 5 to 6 students.

Carefully review the sections near the end of this chapter entitled "A Taxonomy of Learning" and "The Purpose of This Book." Clearly identify the non-traditional approaches this textbook takes.

Now consider how you will need to modify traditional student strategies regarding how to study for tests, write papers, and so on in order to be effective when taking an organizational behavior course that emphasizes higher-level learning.

In addition to developing several possible strategies, be prepared to explain *why* each recommended strategy would be appropriate by referencing specific phrases in those sections near the end of this chapter.

After all of the groups have developed several different strategies, they will present and explain them. The class will then analyze and discuss these strategies.

The following are several examples of strategies recommended by students who have already taken an OB course based on this textbook:

- The information in this book has to be understood rather than memorized. Students should pay close attention to the Application sections and start studying for an exam early in order to have time to process the information.

- Read the higher-level learning modules; they will help with common sense questions on the tests.

- When writing the papers discussed in the chapters' Experiential Exercises, be sure that you understand the models and Application sections and that you are asking the right questions to people you interview.

■ *Experiential Exercise: In-Class 1-2*

PARTICIPATIVE DECISION MAKING CONCERNING COURSE GRADING

The purpose of this exercise is to empower students to participate in developing solutions to grading-related issues for this class. In doing so, students will develop a set of graded items that will both stimulate high-quality, higher-level learning *and* provide a means for assessing the quality of that learning.

Some Questions Requiring Resolution

What kinds of items (e.g., exams, papers, in-class participation, and so on) should be graded in this class?

How many of each kind of item should be graded?

What percentage weightings would be appropriate for each of these items?

Constraints on Solutions

Your instructor will let you know about any constraints on solutions, based on school regulations, and so on.

Exercise Process Outline

Five student volunteers are needed to serve on a panel, forming a semi-circle at the front of the room.

Your instructor will set a deadline as to when the final vote on a student solution will take place.

The panel will discuss its ideas and present an initial proposal to the class (this will take approximately 10 minutes); everyone else will listen and observe.

Other class members will give feedback to the panel members concerning their initial proposal.

The panel will then discuss the feedback and make revisions to their proposal that take into account the overall concerns of the class; other class members will listen.

The panel will call for a class vote sometime before the instructor's pre-set deadline. If the latest revised proposal is approved by two-thirds of the students enrolled in the class, that plan will appear in the course syllabus. If a plan is *not* approved by the deadline, top management (i.e., your instructor) will develop one instead!

Additional Notes

If class assignments/grades are important to you, volunteer to join the panel.

If desired your instructor can give you feedback about solutions previous classes have liked or disliked, more information about any instructor-required items, and so on.

REFERENCE NOTES

1. Johns, G., and A. Saks. *Organizational Behavior: Understanding and Managing Life at Work*, 5th ed. Upper Saddle River, NJ: Prentice-Hall, 2001.

2. Iaffaldano, M. T., and P. M. Murchinsky. Job Satisfaction and Job Performance: A Meta-Analysis. *Psychological Bulletin*, Vol. 97, 1985, pp. 251–273.

3. Shephard, J. M., and J. G. Hougland, Jr. Contingency Theory: "Complex Man" or "Complex Organization." *Academy of Management Review*, Vol. 3, 1978, pp. 413–427.

4. Bloom, B. S., B. B. Mesia, and D. R. Krathwohl. *Taxonomy of Educational Objectives*, Vol. 2. New York: David McKay, 1964.

PART II
The Individual Level

Chapter List

CHAPTER 2
Personality and Perception

Think about all the people you have worked with in part-time jobs, internships, and group projects in classes. Some of these people were your bosses, co-workers, or even your employees if you were a supervisor or manager. If you tried to describe all of these people as a group, what would you say? The most obvious characteristic of all these people is that they are different from each other. Some may have had a positive attitude, a strong work ethic, and were a joy to work with. Others may have been apathetic about everything and had a "whatever" kind of attitude. These people may have been concerned with doing just the bare minimum to keep their jobs. Unfortunately, you probably have also dealt with people who were extremely abrasive, controlling, or negative about everything that they were asked to do. The point is, each person you have worked with or for is unique. An important part of what makes each person unique is their personality. **Personality** can be defined as the unique and stable collection of psychological traits or characteristics that shape an individual's attitudes and perceptions of other people, issues, and situations. A concept that is closely related to personality is perception. **Perception** refers to the process through which an individual makes sense of her surroundings. In short, a person's personality shapes how she perceives the world.

This chapter will explore two key models that address important factors relating to personality and perception. First, the Big Five Personality Model will be presented and discussed. This model is useful in identifying the most important dimensions of personality. Practical implications of this model will be offered as well. Next, Kelley's Attribution Theory will be discussed. This model helps explain how people interpret the causes of other's actions in a work situation. Practical implications of this model will be discussed as well. Finally, a number of higher-level learning modules have been integrated throughout this chapter to help you develop a higher level of comprehension and skill in relation to the issues of personality and perception.

PERSONALITY AND PERCEPTION: WHO CARES?

Some people are skeptical when they hear that they need to be concerned with personality and perception issues in order to be effective managers. Nonetheless, it is important to consider how personality and perception will matter to people as future individual contributors, managers, and/or leaders of real-world organizations. Some people believe that job success in the real world is simply a matter of who works the hardest and is the most intelligent. However, while these qualities are certainly important, it is also important to be able to understand the "styles" of the people in an organization and how to adapt to these differences in style to achieve desired objectives. For example, suppose someone has a boss who possesses an attitude that the most important consideration in any business situation is costs and how to reduce them. Based on this, what would an employee need to do to work effectively with this boss? Or, imagine that the leader of a task force has a goal to improve organizational effectiveness. Unfortunately, many of the other members of the task force say that they hate working in groups and they don't see any need for change because the current way of doing things is working just fine. What would the task force leader do in this situation? A fundamental understanding of personality and perception will raise awareness of the importance of these issues and help to identify appropriate strategies that can be used to better adapt to different types of people in real-world organizations.

CRITICAL PERSONALITY TRAITS IN ORGANIZATIONAL BEHAVIOR

There are literally hundreds of personality traits that a given individual can possess in varying degrees. These include traits such as dogmatism, locus of control (see Chapter 8), authoritarianism, and so on. However, at a practical level, it is not feasible to try to understand how to deal with such a complex and varied array of personality factors. Thus, this section will focus on the **Big Five Personality Model**, an integrated general model that is widely accepted by academics and practitioners as a valid and useful way of viewing personality.

THE BIG FIVE PERSONALITY MODEL: AN INTEGRATED MODEL OF PERSONALITY

Personality researchers have long sought to determine how the personality of an individual can be described. The challenge for researchers was to distill all of the personality traits that people could possess into a much smaller and manageable set of factors. Based on extensive empirical research, these researchers identified five key dimensions of personality known as the Big Five Personality dimensions. The five dimensions of this integrated framework are:

- **Conscientiousness.** Individuals who are high on this dimension are viewed as careful, dependable, and self-disciplined. Those who are low on Conscientiousness are more careless, disorganized, and irresponsible. High

Conscientiousness is a highly valued quality in today's business environment as many employers claim that they experience tremendous difficulty in hiring and retaining workers who are dependable (e.g., who show up for work when scheduled) and who take some pride in the quality of the work they perform. Individuals who are high on Conscientiousness often become leaders, executives, and high achievers in general.

- **Emotional Stability.** Individuals who are high on this dimension are calm, posed, and secure. Those who are low on Emotional Stability are more depressed, anxious, indecisive, and prone to significant mood swings. A high degree of Emotional Stability is extremely important for any individual who performs a job in a fast-paced, rapidly changing, and stressful work environment, as employers need workers who can maintain their composure under less than optimal working conditions. Individuals who are high on Emotional Stability are well suited for careers as air traffic controllers, airline pilots, finance managers, and engineers.

- **Openness to Experience.** Individuals who are high on this dimension are sensitive, flexible, curious, and creative. Those who are low on Openness to Experience are more resistant to change, less open to ideas, and more set in their way of doing things. An individual with a high level of Openness to Experience is a tremendous asset to any organization that needs to change some aspect of its strategic or operational plan now or in the future. Individuals who are high on Openness to Experience embrace change and view it as a natural and positive force in an organization. These individuals also tend to be attracted to careers as entrepreneurs, artists, and theoretical scientists.

- **Agreeableness.** Individuals who are high on this dimension tend to be caring, good natured, and courteous. Those who are low on Agreeableness are more short-tempered, irritable, and uncooperative. This is a critical attribute for anyone who deals with customers or the public in general. Most of us have had experiences in which we had to deal with a customer service or sales representative who was not agreeable. Individuals who are high on Agreeableness are simply better able to take care of customers. Part of this is due to the fact that being customer service oriented comes naturally to people who are high on Agreeableness. People who are high on Agreeableness tend to pursue careers in teaching and social work, whereas those who are low on Agreeableness are more likely to go into management and the military.

- **Introversion/Extroversion.** Individuals who are high on Introversion are quiet, shy, and cautious. Those who are high on Extroversion are outgoing, talkative, sociable, and assertive. It is not necessarily better to be introverted or extroverted. In a work context, it would depend on the requirements of the job being performed. For example, introverted individuals tend to be attracted to careers in the natural and physical sciences, whereas extroverted individuals tend to be interested in careers in sales and public relations.

Two research studies[2] examined the empirical relationship between the Big Five Personality dimensions and work-related behavior and performance. The following are some of the key findings of this research:

- People who are effective in building support for organizational change (see Chapter 10) tend to possess high levels of all Big Five Personality dimensions.

- Conscientiousness has been shown to be positively related to performance for a wide range of jobs.

- People with high Emotional Stability are better able to work with other people and under stressful conditions.

- People with high Agreeableness tend to be more effective in dealing with customers and in handling interpersonal conflict.

APPLICATION OF THE BIG FIVE PERSONALITY DIMENSIONS

The Big Five Personality dimensions can be used to enhance individual effectiveness in a work context using the following procedures:

1. Conduct a self-assessment of the Big Five Personality dimensions and summarize your results in terms of whether you feel that you are low, moderate, or high on each dimension.

2. Brainstorm examples of specific behaviors that you exhibit in general and in work situations (e.g., based on internships, part-time jobs, group projects, and so on) that reflect your self-assessment.

3. Based on Steps 1 and 2, identify specific aspects of your Big Five Personality dimensions that you feel are strengths for you in terms of making you a more effective worker.

4. Based on Steps 1 and 2, identify specific aspects of your Big Five Personality dimensions that you feel are opportunities for improvement in terms of making you a more effective worker.

5. Summarize your analysis in Table 2-1 (on the next page).

6. Based on Table 2-1, identify some specific action steps you can take to enhance your individual effectiveness. List these steps in Table 2-2.

USING THE BIG FIVE PERSONALITY DIMENSIONS TO ENHANCE INDIVIDUAL EFFECTIVENESS: AN EXAMPLE

Katie Schoen is an undergraduate business student majoring in management and finance. She has a GPA of 3.5/4.0 in her coursework. In addition, she is the president of the Business Student Association at her university. Katie is currently doing an internship with a health care organization in which she helps to plan and implement various customer service and process improvement interventions. Katie completed the steps in the process for using the Big Five Personality dimensions to enhance individual effectiveness. Her results are shown in Table 2-3 and Table 2-4.

Table 2-1   Big Five Personality Dimension Assessment

Big Five Personality Dimensions	Self-Assessment	Supporting Behaviors	Strength/Opportunity for Improvement?

Table 2-2   Steps Toward Individual Effectiveness

Opportunity for Improvement	Action Step(s)

Table 2-3   Example of Self-Assessment, Part 1

Big Five Personality Dimensions	Self-Assessment	Supporting Behaviors	Strength/Opportunity for Improvement?
Conscientiousness	High	I plan carefully and follow through on commitments.	Strength
Agreeableness	Moderate	Sometimes I have a tendency to be defensive and combative with others when they do not agree with me.	Opportunity for Improvement
Emotional Stability	Moderate	Sometimes I can get flustered when things go wrong.	Opportunity for Improvement
Introversion/ Extroversion	Extroverted	I am a people person who enjoys working with and helping others.	Strength
Openness to Experience	High	I am always willing to try new things and explore new ideas.	Strength

Table 2-4   Example of Self-Assessment, Part 2

Opportunity for Improvement	Action Step(s)
Agreeableness	—Be more aware of my tendency to become defensive. —When I feel defensive, pause for 5 seconds before I respond. —Try to see the basis for another person's perspective on an issue. —Ask a trusted co-worker or friend to observe my behavior and to inform me when I am behaving in ways that reflect a low level of agreeableness.
Emotional Stability	—Be more aware of my tendency to become flustered when things are not going well. —Maintain a positive attitude about things to emphasize what is going right as well. —Take a constructive approach to resolving problems that focus on action. —Keep telling myself that "it will be okay."

Katie then used her action plan in Table 2-4 to help her focus on what she needed to work on to enhance her individual effectiveness in work situations. She did a monthly follow-up evaluation to track her progress on implementing the action steps she developed for herself.

PRACTICAL IMPLICATIONS OF THE BIG FIVE PERSONALITY DIMENSIONS

Managers can use the Big Five Personality dimensions to better understand the personalities of their employees and to more effectively manage them. Leadership research often focuses on the importance of "leader-situation match" (see Chapter 8), which emphasizes that an effective leader must understand the situation (the task, employees, and other factors) in order to determine the most effective leadership style. Managers can use the Big Five Personality dimensions as a situational factor to evaluate in establishing a good leader-situation match.

Employers may also choose to assess the Big Five Personality dimensions of potential employees in the hiring process. This helps an organization to better establish "person-job match," which emphasizes the importance of a good match between a person (knowledge, skills, abilities, and other factors such as personality) and a job (the required duties, tasks, and responsibilities of the job).

APPLICATION & EVALUATION

Selecting Executive Team Leaders for a Student Organization

You are the president of a management student organization at your college or university. As the end of the school year approaches, one of your last responsibilities is to decide on the composition of the organization's executive team for the next year. You have the following positions to fill: president, treasurer, secretary, director of fund-raising, director of membership, director of event planning, and director of social events. Based on your knowledge of what these positions entail; the key knowledge, skills, and abilities needed by the individuals who hold these positions; and the discussion of personality in this chapter, develop a specific formal profile of the personality traits needed for an individual to be effective in each of the leadership positions on your executive committee.

Finding Real-World Examples of the Big Five Personality Dimensions

Use a standard web browser (such as Internet Explorer or Netscape) to research business-oriented web sites (e.g., http://www.fortune.com and http://www.businessweek.com) in order to identify an article that provides a profile of a manager or executive who has been particularly successful or unsuccessful. Based on this article, develop a profile (i.e., a list of traits) of the manager or executive. Use the Big Five Personality Model to assess whether you feel the manager or executive is low, moderate, or high for each of the Big Five Personality dimensions.

Self-Assessment of the Big Five Personality Dimensions

Based on the description of the Big Five Personality dimensions presented in this chapter, conduct a self-assessment of your conscientiousness, agreeableness, openness to experience, introversion/extroversion, and emotional stability. Specifically, would you say that you are low, moderate, or high on each of these dimensions? Think about your choice of a major in college. Was this choice consistent with your self-assessment of the Big Five Personality dimensions? Why or why not?

PERCEPTION

As noted earlier, **perception** refers to the process through which people interpret or "make sense" of stimuli in their external environments. Each person perceives the world in a unique way. For example, have you ever met someone who viewed the world in a completely different way than you do? In many cases, this is not an issue of one person being right and the other being wrong. Rather, it is just that you perceive the world differently.

Why does perception matter to a manager? Effective managers need to understand how their employees perceive a variety of issues in order to take appropriate steps to motivate them and to enable them to maximize their job performance. For example, suppose that a manager wants to implement a new management technique (e.g., total quality management) in a work unit in order to enhance the quality, efficiency, and cost-effectiveness of the work that is performed by employees. The manager perceives the use of total quality management as a "no brainer" given the positive results that some other organizations have achieved with it. However, the employees perceive the introduction of total quality management as a negative change, as they see it as a tactic being used by management to make them work harder without increasing their pay. The bottom line is that an effective manager must be able to understand and manage the perceptions of his employees in order to achieve the desired objectives of the work unit and organization.

THE PERCEPTUAL PROCESS

The basic perceptual process is composed of four phases: sensing, selecting, organizing, and translation.[3]

The **sensing phase** of the perceptual process includes all of the stimuli that a person is capable of processing in a given situation. For example, if you are in a busy airport with thousands of people around you and a wide range of activities taking place, all of these stimuli would be part of the sensing phase.

In the **selection phase** of the perception process, an individual makes a conscious (or subconscious) decision to select out certain stimuli for further processing. Selection typically occurs because there is something salient about a stimulus. A good example of this is the hiring process that is used to fill job openings. Why do some applicants get interview offers and then job offers whereas others do not? The reason is that there was something about the job candidates who received interview and job offers that made them stand out.

The **organizing phase** of the perceptual process involves the grouping or clustering of selected stimuli in order to facilitate the efficiency and effectiveness of interpretation. For example, using the job candidates example from above, an employer may group the job candidates he has just interviewed based on the amount of relevant experience they have, their college GPA, or their performance in the interview.

The last stage of the perceptual process is the **translation phase.** This is where an individual derives meaning from the selected stimuli. In many ways, this is the most important stage of the perceptual process as this is where an individual makes sense of what is going on in a given organizational situation. The interpretation of stimuli will influence the individual's reactions to a situation in terms of positive or negative attitudes, work motivation, and so on.

KELLEY'S ATTRIBUTION THEORY

Attribution Theory[4] explains a very important type of perceptual process in which people make judgments or attributions about the causes of other people's behavior. These attributions can be of two types: internal and external. An **Internal Attribution** occurs when a person perceives that the cause of another person's behavior in a situation is due to various aspects of the person such as his personality, skills and abilities, motivation (see Chapter 3), intelligence, and so on. For example, suppose that you go to a restaurant and your server is rude and inattentive. This server makes you wait for 30 minutes before taking your order and then brings you the wrong order. You perceive that the cause of the server's behavior is that he is incompetent and lazy.

An **External Attribution** occurs when a person perceives that the cause of another person's behavior is due to situational factors such as bad luck, timing, unforeseen problems, and so on. For example, the reason why a co-worker is late for a business meeting with you may be that she got caught in traffic (an external factor) as opposed to the person being disorganized and disrespectful of your time.

RULES FOR MAKING CAUSAL ATTRIBUTIONS

Whether an individual makes an Internal or External Attribution in a given situation is a function of three issues:

- **Consistency.** How often has the person acted this way in the past? High Consistency means that the person has acted the same way in the past in similar situations. For example, managers who lose their temper every time an employee reports a problem or concern are acting in a way that reflects high Consistency. Low Consistency exists when an individual who behaves in a certain way in one situation typically does not behave in this manner in other similar situations. An example would be an employee who was late in completing his current project but has not been late in turning in any other projects in the past.

- **Distinctiveness.** How often does this person act this way in other settings? High Distinctiveness means that an individual behaves in a similar manner in other types of situations as well. For example, a manager who is known to be very caring and supportive of her employees tends to behave in a similar manner in dealing with her spouse, children, parents, and friends. Low Distinctiveness exists when a person does not behave in the same way across other kinds of situations. For example, a manager who is very demanding and pushy with his employees is very laid back and carefree when dealing with his spouse and children.

- **Consensus.** How often do other people act this way in similar situations? High Consensus is present when other people behave in the same manner when they encounter a similar situation. For example, if other people have the same problem with using a given software program to complete a project, then this would reflect high Consensus. Low Consensus would exist if other people do not behave in the same way when they encounter a similar situation. For example, if one person complains that she does not receive adequate direction and support from her boss when she works on projects, but other employees do not complain about these issues when they work on similar projects, then this is reflective of low Consensus.

According to Attribution Theory, a person will make an Internal Attribution when a situation is perceived as possessing high Consistency, high Distinctiveness, and low Consensus. Conversely, a person will make an External Attribution when a situation is perceived as possessing low Consistency, high Distinctiveness, and high Consensus. Figure 2-1 presents a summary of these two situations.

PERCEPTUAL BIASES RELATED TO ATTRIBUTIONS

There are two perceptual biases that tend to result from attributions: the Fundamental Attribution Error and the Self-serving Bias.

Figure 2-1   **Internal vs. External Attributions**

High Consistency + High Distinctiveness + Low Consensus = Internal Attribution

Low Consistency + High Distinctiveness + High Consensus = External Attribution

The Fundamental Attribution Error

The **Fundamental Attribution Error** refers to the tendency for people to incorrectly explain the cause of other people's behavior as being due to internal rather than external causes. For example, if a person obtains poor customer service from a flight attendant on an airplane trip, his tendency might be to feel that the poor service received was due to the flight attendant being rude or incompetent. However, in reality, the real cause of the flight attendant's behavior in this situation may be due to situational factors (e.g., the flight is understaffed, another passenger has been causing problems, and so on). It is important to recognize the tendency to exhibit this bias in order to take proactive action to prevent it from distorting a person's perception of a situation or issue.

The Self-serving Bias

A **Self-serving Bias** is the tendency for people to attribute positive outcomes to internal factors and to attribute negative outcomes to external factors. That is, people tend to take credit for good things that happen and to externalize blame for bad things that happen. For example, the manager of a team that just completed a stunningly successful project to develop a new product takes credit for the team's success, but also comments that she had nothing to do with the coordination and internal conflict problems the team experienced during the project.

GENERAL STRATEGIES FOR REDUCING PERCEPTUAL BIASES

The following basic strategies can be used to increase the accuracy of how an individual perceives situations in the work environment:

- **Increase awareness of the tendency to exhibit perceptual biases.** Recognize that everyone exhibits some perceptual biases in certain situations. For example, if a person understands that she has a tendency to form strong impressions of people based on little or no information about them, she can make a conscious attempt to reserve judgment until she has more information about that person.

- **Collect as much information as possible.** Many perceptual biases result from people using too little information (e.g., incorrect attributions) when forming an understanding of a stimulus. One of the most effective strategies for reducing these kinds of perceptual biases is simply to take the time to obtain as much information as possible about the stimulus. In this case, a stimulus could be a specific individual or an issue or problem facing an organization (e.g., low product quality, high costs, inefficient systems of processes). Obtaining as much relevant information about a stimulus as possible will increase someone's ability to accurately understand a person or issue.

- **Obtain information from all the relevant players in a situation.** Different people may hold different views of a given situation. Managers may have one perspective whereas employees, customers, shareholders, the media, and so on may all have different perspectives. Talk to everyone involved in a given issue or problem in order to have the best chance of developing an accurate understanding of the situation.

- **Don't jump to conclusions.** The most problematic influence of perceptual biases is that they can "short-circuit" the perceptual process by causing a person to come to conclusions before she has all of the information necessary to understand a situation. Be aware of the potential risk of jumping to conclusions and make a conscious effort to guard against it.

- **Anticipate how others may perceive things differently and address these concerns.** People often fail to anticipate how others may perceive a given issue in a different way than they do. This problem occurs when an individual assumes that other people will see an issue or situation in the same way as he sees it. To avoid this problem, identify how others may interpret a situation or issue in a different manner and take proactive action to respond to these alternative perspectives.

- **Actively manage the perceptions of others.** Work on an ongoing basis to understand and influence the perceptions of others in ways that will enable them to achieve the organization's objectives. In fact, it should be assumed that one person will not see things in the same way as another and act accordingly.

- **Use empathy.** Empathy is the ability to see things from the perspective of another person. Showing empathy in a work situation might require a person to try and assume the role of another person involved in a situation. For example, a product designer may attempt to assume the role of a customer in order to better understand the customer's needs and preferences.

APPLICATION & ANALYSIS

Finding Real-World Examples of Perceptual Issues

Use a standard web browser (such as Internet Explorer or Netscape) to research business-oriented web sites (such as http://www.fortune.com or http://www.businessweek.com) in order to identify an article that illustrates one of the perceptual biases or strategies for enhancing the accuracy of perceptions. Describe the impact of this perceptual bias on the effectiveness of the individual, group, or organization discussed in the article.

ANALYSIS & EVALUATION — Managing Employee Perceptions in a Real-World Work Situation

Imagine that you are the district sales manager for a team of pharmaceutical sales representatives based in the Midwest. Your company has decided to implement a new computerized customer relationship management system that is designed to help sales representatives better track and manage their clients. You believe that the new system will help your sales representatives to better understand the needs of their customers, to formulate more effective sales strategies, and to increase sales productivity. However, your 20 sales representatives have reacted very negatively to the announcement of the new system as they believe that it is another management tactic to make them work harder. Based on your knowledge of perception, develop an action plan that deals with the issue of how your sales representatives are perceiving the new customer management relationship system. Be very specific and action-oriented.

SYNTHESIS & EVALUATION — The Big Five Personality Dimensions and Kelley's Attribution Theory

Synthesize the elements of the Big Five Personality dimensions and Kelley's Attribution Theory in order to formulate a more integrated overall model of personality and perception. Represent your integrated model in a visual form. This may be challenging, but do your best.

CONCLUSION

This chapter has discussed a select group of the most important models of personality and perception as they relate to the behavior of people in organizations. The Big Five Personality Model was presented as a general model that identifies the most important dimensions of personality. Attribution Theory was discussed as a model of perception that explains how people explain the causality of events they experience in the workplace.

EXERCISES AND OTHER ACTIVITIES
■ *Experiential Exercise: In-Class 2-1*

EMPLOYEE PERSONALITY AND ATTITUDE SURVEY ANALYSIS

Directions

1. Analyze the results of the employee attitude survey shown in Table 2-5 and Table 2-6. These results are based on an actual survey administered to a group of engineers in a real-world organization.
2. Identify what you think are the key results.
3. Develop a set of recommendations for how management should address the key issues raised by the survey.
4. Develop an action plan for implementing the recommendations in Step 3.

Table 2-5   Summary of Responses to Structured Questions: Summary of Personality Scales

Scale	Mean Score (1 = Low to 5 = High)	Range	Comments
1. Conscientiousness	4.6	4.3–5.0	
2. Openness to Experience	3.1	2.1–3.6	
3. Agreeableness	3.5	2.4–3.8	
4. Emotional Stability	3.2	2.0–3.2	
5. Introversion/Extroversion	2.8	1.7–3.3	Lower scores reflect being more introverted; higher scores reflect being more extroverted.
6. Attributional Style— Tendency to Make Internal Attributions	4.5	4.0–5.0	Higher scores suggest a higher propensity to make internal attributions.
7. Attributional Style— Tendency to Make External Attributions	2.5	1.0–2.9	Higher scores suggest a higher propensity to make external attributions.

Note: These results were calculated based on responses of 32 workers to questions from a survey conducted by L. Kuzuhara in 2001.

Table 2-6   Summary of Responses to Individual Questions

Item	Strongly Disagree	Disagree	Neutral	Agree	Strongly Agree	Mean
1. My job provides me with an appropriate level of variety in the duties and responsibilities I perform.	3.2%	6.5%	21.9%	38.7%	29.7%	3.84
2. I receive regular feedback regarding how well I am performing my job.	12.9%	61.3%	16.1%	9.7%	0.0%	2.23
3. My job provides me with an appropriate level of challenge.	6.5%	9.7%	3.2%	45.2%	35.4%	3.94
4. I am given the autonomy I need to perform my job well.	6.5%	12.9%	32.3%	38.7%	9.6%	3.32
5. My job plays an important role in the success of this division.	0.0%	6.7%	0.0%	53.3%	40.0%	4.27
6. I have a clear understanding of the performance standards and expectations associated with my job.	12.9%	29.0%	25.8%	19.4%	12.9%	2.90
7. I am satisfied with the type of work I perform as part of my job.	0.0%	19.4%	9.7%	38.7%	32.2%	3.84
8. I am satisfied with the amount of work I am asked to perform as part of my job.	19.4%	38.7%	19.4%	19.4%	3.1%	2.48
9. I am satisfied with the opportunities for professional development in my division.	29.0%	38.7%	25.8%	3.2%	3.3%	2.13
10. I am satisfied with the work rules that exist in my division.	12.5%	37.5%	28.1%	18.8%	3.1%	2.63
11. I am experiencing stress due to my being asked to perform tasks that require knowledge and skills I do not possess.	0.0%	18.8%	25.0%	31.3%	24.9%	4.23

Table 2-6   Summary of Responses to Individual Questions, continued

Item	Strongly Disagree	Disagree	Neutral	Agree	Strongly Agree	Mean
12. I am experiencing stress due to the amount of work I am expected to perform on my job.	0.0%	18.8%	28.1%	21.9%	31.2%	4.18
13. I am experiencing stress due to a lack of clarity regarding what I need to do to be successful in my job.	0.0%	25.0%	21.9%	28.1%	25.0%	4.53
14. I am experiencing stress due to the conflicting expectations that others have of me.	0.0%	25.0%	21.9%	25.0%	28.1%	4.20
15. I am experiencing stress due to a lack of resources I need to perform my job effectively.	0.0%	18.8%	6.3%	34.4%	40.5%	4.37
16. I am experiencing stress due to the challenges associated with balancing the demands of my job with those of my personal life.	12.5%	43.8%	21.9%	18.8%	3.0%	2.56
17. I am experiencing stress due to interpersonal conflicts I have with others in my work unit.	15.6%	43.8%	21.9%	15.6%	3.1%	2.47
18. I am experiencing stress due to the demands that customers place on me.	0.0%	34.4%	25.0%	34.4%	6.2%	3.13
19. I am experiencing stress due to changes that are being implemented by the division.	3.1%	12.5%	18.8%	37.5%	28.1%	3.75
20. I understand the specific actions I need to take to support the implementation of changes effectively in the division.	12.5%	37.5%	28.1%	18.8%	3.1%	2.63
21. I would like to be more involved in planning changes that affect the division in the future.	0.0%	0.0%	25.0%	31.3%	43.7%	4.19

Table 2-6   Summary of Responses to Individual Questions, continued

Item	Strongly Disagree	Disagree	Neutral	Agree	Strongly Agree	Mean
22. I trust my manager.	9.4%	40.6%	18.8%	18.8%	12.4%	2.81
23. I respect my manager.	3.1%	18.8%	25.0%	31.3%	21.8%	3.50
24. My manager understands the challenges I face in performing my job.	18.8%	43.8%	12.5%	15.6%	9.3%	2.53
25. My manager possesses the knowledge, skills, and experience needed to manage me effectively.	25.0%	31.3%	18.8%	2.5%	12.4%	2.56
26. I understand the short-term objectives of the division.	21.9%	40.6%	9.4%	25.0%	3.1%	2.47
27. I understand the long-term objectives of the division.	28.1%	28.1%	12.5%	28.1%	3.2%	2.50
28. I understand the purpose of a mission statement.	6.3%	9.4%	12.5%	50.0%	21.8%	3.72
29. I am motivated to achieve high job performance.	3.1%	9.4%	15.6%	40.6%	31.3%	3.88
30. I possess a strong sense of loyalty to this organization.	3.2%	3.2%	19.4%	45.2%	29.0%	3.94
31. I intend to remain with the division in the future.	6.5%	0.0%	19.4%	54.8%	19.3%	3.81
32. I am satisfied with my job.	9.4%	15.6%	25.0%	40.6%	9.4%	3.25

Note: These results were calculated based on responses of 32 workers to questions from a survey conducted by L. Kuzuhara in 2001.

■ *Experiential Exercise: In-Class 2-2*

UNDERSTANDING PERCEPTION

Directions

1. Get into groups of two. Try to work with someone you do not know.
2. Answer each of the first five statements in Table 2-7 based on the degree to which you agree or disagree with each statement.
3. Answer the same five statements in terms of how you think your partner will answer each of the statements.
4. When you are done, find out how your partner answered the five statements and calculate the difference between how you thought your partner would respond and how he or she actually responded.
5. Discuss with your partner why you thought he or she would answer the statements in a certain way. What types of biases or causal attributions influenced your perceptions in this exercise?
6. Repeat Steps 2 to 5 above with the second set of five statements in Table 2-8.

Understanding Perception Exercise

Note: Use the following rating scale for responding to the statements below.

1 = Strongly Disagree
2 = Disagree
3 = Neutral
4 = Agree
5 = Strongly Agree

Table 2-7   Round 1: Set of First Five Statements

Statement	Your Score (A)	Your Prediction of Your Partner's Score (B)	Your Partner's Actual Score (C)	Difference Between B and C
1. I like classical music.				
2. My actions control my destiny rather than luck.				
3. Beer is my favorite thing to drink.				
4. I am a Democrat.				
5. I have a great sense of humor.				
Total Difference Score = _____				

Table 2-8   Round 2: Set of Second Five Statements

Statement	Your Score (A)	Your Prediction of Your Partner's Score (B)	Your Partner's Actual Score (C)	Difference Between B and C
1. There is a lack of concern for ethics in business today.				
2. Management is really just a lot of common sense.				
3. Money is the #1 motivator for all employees.				
4. The most intelligent people always become the most successful in the real world.				
5. College GPA is a good predictor of success in the real world.				
Total Difference Score = _____				

REFERENCE NOTES

1. Mount, M. K., and M. R. Barrick. The Big Five Personality Dimensions: Implications for Research and Practice in Human Resources Management. *Reference in Personnel and Human Resource Management,* Vol. 13, 1995, pp. 153–200.

2. Tett, R. P., D. N. Jackson, and M. Rothstein. Personality Measures as Predictors of Job Performance: A Meta-Analytic Review. *Personnel Psychology*, Vol. 44, 1991, pp. 703–742; J. M. Howell and C. A. Higgins, Champions of Change: Identifying, Understanding, and Supporting Champions of Technological Innovations, *Organizational Dynamics,* Summer 1990, pp. 40–45.

3. Dunham, R. B. *Organizational Behavior*. Homewood, IL: Irwin, 1984.

4. Kelley, H. H. *Attribution in Social Interaction.* Morristown, NJ: General Learning Press, 1971.

CHAPTER 3
Motivation, Performance, and Job Satisfaction

From a manager's standpoint, one of the most significant aspects of her job is the extent to which the people she manages are *motivated* to *perform* their jobs in an effective manner. Because how well a manager's subordinates perform plays such a major role in determining the manager's overall success, a manager's ability to create a high degree of motivation is a central concern.

From an employee's standpoint, one of the most significant aspects of our respective jobs is the extent to which each of us is *satisfied* with that job. Because work plays such a major role in most employees' lives, how good employees feel about their jobs frequently has a strong influence on how they feel about their life in general.

This chapter describes two well-established, well-tested, and highly respected models that deal with these key issues of motivation, performance, and job satisfaction. The first model blends together much of the best research that has been done on motivation, job satisfaction, and the relationships between these two factors and job performance. The second model suggests how to strategically redesign jobs to make those jobs more motivating and satisfying to the people who perform them. Both of these models incorporate a contingency approach (see Chapter 1). The chapter culminates with a set of guidelines for applying the first model to any situation in which an employee's performance is not up to par.

THE EXPANDED EXPECTANCY-THEORY MODEL

There are few models in organizational behavior that effectively *synthesize* a sizable number of important OB factors and theories into a single, *integrated* whole in a way that actually makes a good deal of sense to a large number of people. The **Expanded Expectancy-Theory Model** is such a model. Key elements of several different major approaches to motivation, performance, and job satisfaction have been skillfully combined by two OB researchers named Porter and Lawler.[1] Figure 3-1

Figure 3-1   The Expanded Expectancy-Theory Model (slightly modified)

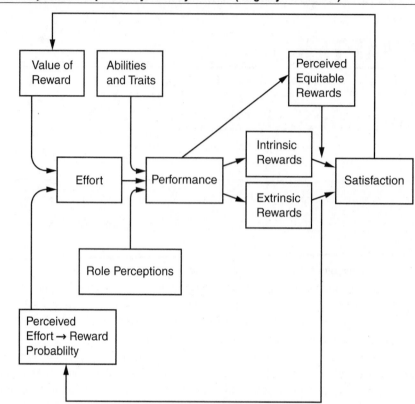

Source: Based on Porter, L. W., and E. E. Lawler III. *Managerial Attitudes and Performance.* Homewood, IL: Irwin, 1968.

shows a slightly modified version of the model resulting from this valuable integration (see also the integrated model in Chapter 9).

The Expanded Expectancy-Theory Model is quite useful for a manager who wants to troubleshoot why a subordinate's performance level has dropped.

PERFORMANCE

From a manager's point of view, the most logical place to begin to explain the Expanded Expectancy-Theory Model is at its center. This is because a primary concern for any manager is subordinate **Performance**. When using this model as a managerial tool for analyzing why the performance of a particular subordinate is not as good as it might be, it makes sense to work backward from the desired result. In other words, follow the arrows in Figure 3-1, but in the reverse direction. These arrows are actually as important as the boxes they link, since they indicate which factors (boxes) lead directly to which other factors (boxes) in this model.

According to the Expanded Expectancy-Theory Model, three key factors lead directly to Performance. These are **Abilities and Traits**, **Role Perceptions**, and **Effort**.

ABILITIES AND TRAITS

Abilities and Traits refer to "relatively stable, long-term individual characteristics," such as intelligence, manual skills, or personality traits.[2] First and foremost, the Abilities and Traits of a given individual play a critical role in determining whether that person should be hired to perform a particular job in the first place. They also have a major impact on the likely *level* of Performance that the given individual can attain. A person with stronger Abilities and more appropriate Traits is likely to perform at a higher level if the job is a good match for those Abilities and Traits.

However, note that further education and training may allow an organization to more fully take advantage of the Abilities and Traits that a subordinate already has. In addition, if a subordinate's job changes in any way, further education and training might provide the subordinate with new skills and capabilities that were not previously necessary, but have become important as the job has evolved.

ROLE PERCEPTIONS

The second factor that directly affects Performance is Role Perceptions. If subordinates do not clearly perceive the work-related roles they are supposed to play—in other words, how they are supposed to *direct* their Efforts to get the job done—it should not be too surprising if their Performance suffers.

Most managers are aware that inaccurate Role Perceptions are a common problem for new employees. However, this same problem also can occur with *experienced* employees. In particular, if a job changes over time, the job that was once well understood may become vague or confusing. Note that if a subordinate continues to perform a key task using an old method when new methods are now necessary to produce good results, performance will suffer even if the old method is still being performed flawlessly. Thus, managers should check on the clarity of a subordinate's Role Perceptions before becoming concerned about an apparently reduced level of motivation.

Role Perceptions deal with an *employee's* perception of how her Effort should be applied to accomplish a job effectively. However, from a practical standpoint, making sure that Role Perceptions are clear is a key responsibility of the employee's *manager*—although subordinates who are professionals should also assume major responsibility for knowing what they should be doing in their jobs.

EFFORT

Should analysis of Abilities and Traits plus Role Perceptions fail to uncover any satisfactory explanations for a significant drop in a subordinate's Performance, then that subordinate's manager may indeed be faced with a motivation problem (see also Chapter 8). The third factor that can directly affect Performance is Effort. It is important to recognize that high Effort means trying very hard, whereas high Performance means doing very well. Effort alone will probably not lead to high Performance unless Abilities and Traits are a reasonably good match for the job and the Role Perceptions of the job are reasonably clear.

ANALYSIS   **Effort and Performance**

There is a common-sense tendency to think that Effort and Performance are the same. Are they? Why or why not? If your *analysis* suggests that they are different, in what kinds of situations might they be fairly equivalent concepts?

VALUE OF REWARD

Moving to the left side of the Expanded Expectancy-Theory Model shown in Figure 3-1, note that Effort, in turn, is portrayed as being strongly and directly affected by two additional factors. These factors are **Value of Reward** and **Perceived Effort→Reward Probability.** Both factors are derived from the *original* **Expectancy Theory of motivation.**[3]

Expectancy Theory fundamentally says that people are likely to be motivated to perform well when they receive rewards that they value in exchange for doing their jobs. This is common sense, right? Unfortunately, it is not quite that simple. Taking a contingency approach, Expectancy Theory recognizes that different people will value different rewards, and that any particular kind of reward will be valued by different people to a different extent. Practically speaking, this means that a manager who wishes to effectively motivate any given subordinate must initially determine the answers to three questions:

1. Which kinds of rewards is the organization capable of giving—and willing to give—to the subordinate if the organization determines that the subordinate's performance is sufficiently high?[4]

2. Which kinds of rewards does the subordinate prefer?

3. How much does the subordinate like each different preferred reward?[5]

It is essential that managers consider all three of these questions for each of their subordinates if the rewards they eventually use are to serve as effective motivators for those subordinates.

Properly performing this kind of analysis requires that managers get to know each of their subordinates quite well, thereby obtaining an accurate picture of each subordinate's needs and desires. Managers must then try to match those needs and desires with whatever rewards the organization is willing to offer. In other words, this is a very personal approach to motivation.

PERCEIVED EFFORT→REWARD PROBABILITY

If an employee perceives that a good Effort on his part is likely to lead to receiving a Valued Reward from the organization, then he will probably be highly motivated. But what if this employee's Perceived Effort→Reward Probability is low? In that case, he probably will not be motivated to make a big Effort—even if a highly Valued Reward is being offered.

Perceived Effort→Reward Probability is a *subjective* perception generated by the subordinate, based on his own experiences and possibly inputs from other employees about their experiences as well. It actually involves considering two different probabilities, not just one.

The first probability is the chance that the Effort the subordinate is able to make will—when combined with the subordinate's Abilities and Traits and the clarity of his Role Perceptions—result in a level of Performance that will be perceived as sufficiently high by his manager.

The second probability is the chance of receiving a particular reward for a level of Performance that is in fact perceived to be sufficiently high. If the subordinate or his co-workers who have performed sufficiently well in the past have actually received a particular Valued Reward—for example, a pay raise—then this second probability is likely to be higher. However, if some employees made a big Effort and did not receive that Valued Reward, this second probability is likely to be lower. Note that the reasons for not obtaining a reward such as a pay raise can vary considerably. For example, one possibility is that the manager may have felt that the employee's Performance was not good enough. Alternatively, there may have been a company-wide freeze on pay raises at that point in time.

Perceived Effort→Reward Probability is thus a combination of:

1. "Can I do it?" (Effort→Performance)

2. "If I do it, will I receive the Valued Reward?" (Performance→Reward).

Hence Perceived Effort→Reward Probability would more accurately be labeled the *Perceived Effort→Performance→Reward Probability*. However, that would be even more of a mouthful to say. Note that any particular subordinate's answers to both of the above questions must be fairly solidly "yes" for that subordinate's Perceived Effort→Reward Probability to be high.

HIGH PERFORMANCE→REWARDS→SATISFACTION

Now consider the right side of Figure 3-1. For many years, the common sense of many a manager has suggested that a very happy, satisfied employee would also be a high-performing employee. Unfortunately, as noted in Chapter 1, this apparent common sense does not hold up in actual practice. The correlation between job **Satisfaction** and job Performance is in the vicinity of 0.15, which is clearly quite low.[6]

However, the higher correlation that many people expect to see between Satisfaction and Performance does result when rewards are taken into account. Instead of positing that Satisfaction with the job will lead to higher job Performance, a revised approach suggests that if high Performance leads to Valued Rewards, then a high degree of Satisfaction is likely to be the result. This fits in very nicely with the ideas from the original Expectancy Theory of motivation that were discussed previously. The right side of Figure 3-1 appends this revised model of job Satisfaction and job Performance to the motivation model that comprises the left side of the diagram, thereby blending these two important pieces of research into an integrated whole.

Before concluding this section, it is worthwhile to elaborate a bit more on the key concept of job Satisfaction (see also Chapter 8). Job Satisfaction is an **attitude** concerning how one generally feels about one's job. Exactly what will create feelings of satisfaction in any given person is usually based on **values** that are developed within that individual at an early age. The Expanded Expectancy-Theory Model makes an assumption that most individuals who work are likely to value receiving rewards for their achievements. In fact, each individual's values will also play a key role in determining which particular kinds of rewards that person will value.

Beyond the link between Rewards and job Satisfaction noted earlier in this section, organizational behavior researchers have also carefully examined linkages between job Satisfaction and both employee absenteeism and employee turnover. Such linkages are of significant interest to managers. The correlation between job Satisfaction and absenteeism is negative and modestly strong, suggesting that satisfied employees are somewhat less likely to be absent from work than are dissatisfied employees.[7] The correlation between job Satisfaction and turnover is also negative and modestly strong, suggesting that satisfied employees are generally less likely to quit their jobs than are dissatisfied employees.[8] However, note that a variety of factors in addition to job Satisfaction play important roles in influencing an employee to stay or leave.

INTRINSIC AND EXTRINSIC REWARDS

The Expanded Expectancy-Theory Model also recognizes that Rewards can be of two general types: intrinsic and extrinsic.[9] **Intrinsic Rewards** are more internal in nature, such as a feeling of accomplishment or the excitement resulting from performing an interesting task. In contrast, **Extrinsic Rewards** are more external in nature, such as a pay raise (money), a certificate of achievement, or a paid vacation. Different people may value either one of these two general types of Rewards more than the other. However, most people prefer to receive some of both.

While some OB experts argue that Intrinsic Rewards are internal, and thus can only be self-administered (i.e., given by the employee to himself), others contend that managers can also give rewards that have a primarily internal effect. It is often easier for managers to help their subordinates obtain rewards that are more intrinsic in nature, as opposed to more extrinsic. This is especially true if the managers are first-level supervisors, who typically have less control over resources (see Chapter 6).

PERCEIVED EQUITABLE REWARDS

Another key contribution from yet another major motivation theory that is blended into the Expanded Expectancy-Theory Model is the concept of **Perceived Equitable Rewards**.[10] It is possible that an employee might not feel satisfaction even when the reward he receives appears to be a reasonably large one. This might occur, for example, if a co-worker performs equally well but receives an even larger reward, or if a co-worker receives a similar reward for what the employee perceives to be a significantly lower level of job Performance. Either of these situations is often perceived as being unfair or inequitable by the employee who receives less or does more—although the same may not hold true for the employee who receives more or does less. Therefore, high performance leads to Rewards, which in turn lead to Satisfaction, but only under the condition of Perceived Equitable Rewards.

FEEDBACK LOOPS

Only two additional aspects of the Expanded Expectancy-Theory Model in Figure 3-1 remain to be explained. These are the two "feedback loops."

One of the feedback loops runs from Satisfaction box up and around to the left, to the Value of Reward box. The logic behind this feedback loop is that what is satisfying at one point in time may become either less satisfying or even more satisfying the next time around. This will have the effect of altering the Value of Reward in the future.

For example, if a new employee's boss gives him the proverbial pat on the back, this may be a nice Intrinsic Reward at first. But eventually, a pat on the back may not mean so much, so its Value of Reward is likely to drop. On the other hand, an experienced employee who performs his job at a high level might really value the esteem given by his boss, co-workers, and other higher-level managers. Over time, this Value of Reward could conceivably increase.

A different way of viewing this particular feedback loop is in terms of satisfying an individual's **needs**.[11] Some needs may no longer motivate once they have been satisfied, such as the need for the safety or security of having a job (from Maslow's Hierarchy of Needs). However, other needs may become even more attractive as a person's performance improves. These might include, for example, the need to achieve (from McClelland's Need for Achievement), or the need to grow (from Alderfer's Existence-Relatedness-Growth Theory) or to be esteemed by others and eventually self-actualize (from Maslow's Hierarchy of Needs). Details concerning these well-known needs theories of motivation are beyond the scope of this book, which focuses on a small number of models and how to apply them. It is important to note, though, that this feedback loop is where these theories fit into this highly *integrated* model.

The second feedback loop in Figure 3-1 starts at a point located *after* the types of rewards and runs down and around to the Perceived Effort→Reward Probability box.[12] Here is the logic behind the slightly revised location of this feedback loop. Assume that an employee has just made a major Effort in hopes of obtaining a desired reward. If the employee actually receives the desired reward, her Perceived Effort→Reward Probability for obtaining future rewards is likely to increase, or at least stay the same. However, what if the employee does not receive the desired reward? Or what if the employee's boss *thinks* the employee has been given a desirable reward for good Performance, but the employee does not view that particular reward as being particularly desirable? In either of the latter two scenarios, the employee's Perceived Effort→Reward Probability will very likely drop. In addition, as was noted previously, the employee will probably monitor co-workers' experiences as well to see whether their Efforts lead them to receive desired Rewards.

While the two feedback loops in Figure 3-1 allow the Expanded Expectancy-Theory Model to provide a much more realistic picture of the various forces that motivate subordinates to perform at varying levels, they also further complicate the jobs of managers who are trying to understand their subordinates. Greater managerial effort is required to take into account these likely changes over time when developing an updated motivation strategy for each subordinate. Thus, it is helpful for managers to communicate frequently with their subordinates, so that the managers will become aware of relevant changes in their subordinates whenever they may occur.

ANALYSIS   **Perceived Effort→Reward Probability**

The concept of Perceived Effort→Reward Probability arises fairly often in employee conversations, even though that particular terminology is unlikely to be used. Think about it: How often have you heard something like "It's not worth it to me," or "There's no way that will happen," or "Hey, I can go for that" when employees are talking with each other? Since this concept is definitely a concern, a key issue for managers is trying to keep each employee's Perceived Effort→Reward Probability as high as possible. How might this be done? A related question to consider is whether most employees are likely to underestimate or overestimate the Perceived Effort→Reward Probability.[13] Analyze why that would be the case.

THE JOB CHARACTERISTICS MODEL

A different kind of approach to motivation essentially focuses on creating jobs that have highly Valued Rewards built into them. The notion of "the work itself" acting as a motivator initially led to a concept called *job enrichment,*[14] and is readily linked to Intrinsic Rewards in the Expanded Expectancy-Theory Model. However, the most widely accepted OB approach to motivation through careful job redesign is the **Job Characteristics Model** developed by Hackman and Oldham.[15] Figure 3-2 indicates the key elements of the Job Characteristics Model and the relationships between those key elements.

CRITICAL PSYCHOLOGICAL STATES

As was the case for the Expanded Expectancy-Theory Model, it makes the most sense to begin analyzing the Job Characteristics Model in Figure 3-2 at its center. This model suggests three conditions under which a high degree of internal work motivation is likely to occur. These conditions are called "**Critical Psychological States**" because they are states of mind that make critically important contributions to feelings of a high degree of internal work motivation and other valued outcomes.

The first of these three conditions is **Experienced Meaningfulness of the Work**. To be motivating, the work being done must be perceived as meaningful by the person who is doing it. It must be seen as important in some way, as having value.

The second condition is **Experienced Responsibility for Outcomes of the Work**. If a person feels directly responsible and personally accountable for the results achieved in a job, there is much greater personal investment and commitment than if that person simply follows someone else's instructions.

The third condition is **Knowledge of the Actual Results of the Work Activities**. This is enhanced when feedback about job performance comes directly to the person doing the work. When an individual can personally confirm how well the work has been done, that person's feelings of satisfaction—or concern—will be stronger than if the feedback is indirect, unclear, mistrusted, or minimal (see also Chapter 9).

Figure 3-2   **The Job Characteristics Model**

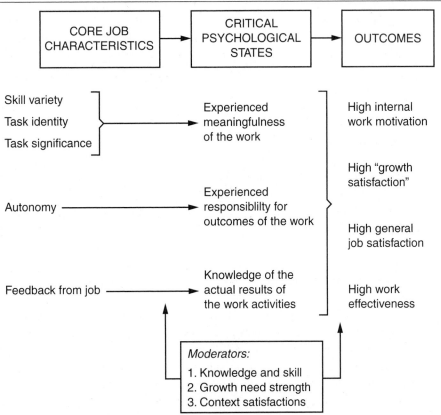

Source: WORK REDESIGN by Hackman/Oldham, ©1980. Reprinted by permission of Pearson Education, Inc., Upper Saddle River, NJ.

CORE JOB CHARACTERISTICS

The points made in the previous paragraphs may sound logical, but they are also very *psychological*. Note that the Critical Psychological States occur *inside* a person. This makes obtaining an accurate picture of them difficult. To cope with this problem, the Job Characteristics Model suggests some **Core Job Characteristics** to build into jobs that are likely to facilitate the creation of the three Critical Psychological States in the people who will be performing those jobs. Unfortunately, there are no guarantees that these job characteristics will definitely create the desired Critical Psychological States in *every* person who might conceivably perform that job. However, the probability that this will happen is high under certain conditions, which arise from factors called **Moderators**. Those conditions will be discussed later in this section.

Of the five Core Job Characteristics appearing on the left side of Figure 3-2, three have a strong impact on the Experienced Meaningfulness of the Work.

The first of these three Core Job Characteristics, **Skill Variety**, is the degree to which a job requires a person to use a variety of different skills to perform different job activities. For example, a painter who plans a job, buys the materials, completes the work, and participates in the final inspection of the work would probably experience a higher degree of Skill Variety than a painter who simply paints walls. Experienced

Meaningfulness of the Work is increased when a person is allowed to apply more of his talents and skills.

The second Core Job Characteristic, **Task Identity**, is the extent to which a job allows a person to perform a "whole" task that therefore has its own identity. For example, a person whose job entails building a "whole" car—or even a "whole" car engine—would very likely experience a high degree of Task Identity. In contrast, a person whose job entails bolting a couple of tires on the right sides of a series of cars moving along an assembly line would probably experience a much lower degree of Task Identity. Experienced Meaningfulness of the Work increases when a job is designed in such a way that the employee has a sense of completing something "whole." This gives that person something to point to proudly and say, "I did that." An automotive worker might point proudly at an engine he built himself, but would be rather unlikely to point proudly at a brand new vehicle and say, "I bolted those two tires onto that car."

The third Core Job Characteristic, **Task Significance**, is the degree to which a job has an important impact on the lives of other people, both inside and outside of the organization. For example, medical doctors and nurses hold jobs that have a high degree of Task Significance. A builder of jet engines also affects the lives of others. Experienced Meaningfulness of the Work is increased if the work being done is important enough to be recognized by other people as being significant.

The remaining two Core Job Characteristics—**Autonomy** and **Feedback from Job**—strongly affect the remaining two Critical Psychological States. A job that provides a high degree of Autonomy, allowing an employee to make many decisions related to his job without constant supervision, leads to much greater Experienced Responsibility for Outcomes of the work. Finally, direct Feedback from the Job supplies employees with the desired Knowledge of the Actual Results of the Work Activities.

Note that the Core Job Characteristics are much easier to look at *objectively*, as compared with the subjectivity involved in attempting to guess the current status of a person's Critical Psychological States. Furthermore, it is possible to analyze how much of each of the five Core Job Characteristics a particular job currently has, and then focus on ways to increase the levels of any of those characteristics that appear to be undesirably low.

OUTCOMES

The **Outcomes** displayed on the right side of Figure 3-2 are very similar to several key factors appearing in the Expanded Expectancy-Theory Model. **Work Effectiveness** is basically the same as Performance, while **General Job Satisfaction** is quite similar to Satisfaction. **Internal Work Motivation** corresponds to the cluster of three factors on the left side of the Expanded Expectancy-Theory Model: Effort, Value of Reward, and Perceived Effort→Reward Probability.

The Job Characteristics Model suggests that all of these important Outcomes are likely to be high if the Core Job Characteristics for any particular job are likewise high. However, this will only be the case under certain conditions (in other words, only if certain contingencies apply). These contingencies will be discussed in depth in the next section.

An additional Outcome that also may be high, **Growth Satisfaction**, should make more sense once the Moderators at the bottom of Figure 3-2 have been explained.

MODERATORS

The Moderator factors incorporate a contingency approach (see Chapter 1) into the Job Characteristics Model. Realistically, *some* people will probably fail to be excited about any job, no matter how special it is. At the other end of the spectrum, however, many people would prefer to have jobs that exhibit a high degree of as many of the Core Job Characteristics as possible. Yet situations exist where even the latter set of people might *not* be highly motivated to perform a particular job—despite its exhibiting a high degree of all five Core Job Characteristics. The Moderator factors provide three major reasons to analyze as a basis for determining why any particular redesigned job might or might not be perceived as motivating by any particular person.

The first Moderator factor to be considered is **Knowledge and Skill**. Jobs that require a lot of Knowledge and Skill are probably going to be much more motivating for people who in fact *have* a lot of Knowledge and Skill. People who are less well educated or less well trained seem much more likely to be intimidated or frustrated by trying to perform a job characterized by a good deal of Skill Variety, Autonomy, and so forth.

The second Moderator factor recognizes that some people have a stronger need to "grow" or improve themselves than do others. Those people who have high **Growth Need Strength** would probably love to work at a job that exhibits a high degree of as many of the five Core Job Characteristics as possible. Conversely, however, people who have low Growth Need Strength might conceivably hate such a job.

The third Moderator factor is the so-called **Context Satisfactions**.[16] Research has suggested that people are often dissatisfied with their jobs when factors *surrounding* the job serve to make them unhappy. Four key job-related factors that are outside of "the work itself" include bosses for whom employees do not enjoy working; dirty, uncomfortable, or unsafe work environments; unfriendly, unhelpful, or even downright nasty co-workers; and inadequate pay. In other words, the "Context" Satisfactions Moderator factor implies that even if the actual job—"the work itself"—is interesting, exciting, and motivating, this might not compensate for other significantly negative job-related aspects that exist within the *context* of the work environment.

ANALYSIS & COMPREHENSION

The Context of the Work Environment

Common sense suggests that "the work itself" should be part of the work environment. Carefully *analyze* what "Context" Satisfactions really means, then use your clearer *comprehension* of this unusual term to explain why "the work itself" is *not* an element of the context of the work environment.

At this point, the "Growth" Satisfaction form of Outcome mentioned at the end of the previous section should also make more sense. People who are high on the Growth Need Strength Moderator will have a good chance of achieving High "Growth" Satisfaction—and quite possibly other positive Outcomes as well—if they work at a job that rates high on most or all of the five Core Job Characteristics in the Job Characteristics Model.

 **The Usefulness of Contingency Factors**

Analyze the Job Characteristics Model described in the previous pages. Then *evaluate* whether this approach to redesigning people's jobs to make them more motivating and interesting would be useful to a practicing manager if it did not include any contingency factors (labeled "Moderators" in Figure 3-2). Why or why not?

APPLICATION: PRACTICAL GUIDELINES FOR IMPLEMENTING THE EXPANDED EXPECTANCY-THEORY MODEL

For managers needing further guidance in applying the Job Characteristics Model, it should be noted that the creators of this model have developed a helpful questionnaire for analyzing jobs called the *Job Diagnostic Survey.*[17] However, because the complexity of the Expanded Expectancy-Theory Model tends to make it the more difficult model to apply, it is the major focus of this section.[18]

BEGIN WITH PERFORMANCE, THEN WORK BACKWARD
A manager's desire to make use of the Expanded Expectancy-Theory Model in a real-world setting is usually triggered by a drop in a subordinate's Performance. Therefore, as was suggested earlier in this chapter, it is best to begin at the "Performance" box in Figure 3-1, and then work backward through the model from that point.

FIRST CHECK FACTORS OTHER THAN LACK OF MOTIVATION
The model suggests that Abilities and Traits, Role Perceptions, and Effort are the three key factors leading to Performance. The question to be answered is, "Which of these three factors probably caused Performance to drop?" A temptation for many managers is to immediately assume a lack of motivation (lack of Effort).

An advantage of using the Expanded Expectancy-Theory Model is that it encourages managers to first consider alternative explanations related to such issues as training—to further sharpen those Abilities and Traits, when necessary—or inaccurate Role Perceptions. Does the subordinate clearly understand what he needs to do to perform the job well? Or, has the subordinate's job recently changed in some way? In today's fast-paced business environment, such change is actually quite likely. If a change has in fact occurred, the manager needs to objectively analyze whether she has done a good job of preparing the subordinate to perform the revised job effectively. Only if that preparation has taken place should the manager move on to a consideration of Effort.

ANALYZE KEY REASONS WHY MOTIVATION MIGHT BE REDUCED
The Expanded Expectancy-Theory Model suggests that Effort is a function of the perceived Value of Reward and the Perceived Effort→Reward Probability. While changes

ANALYSIS & EVALUATION   Dealing with a Drop in Performance

As noted above, many people tend to assume that a drop in Performance is due to a lack of motivation. This is a form of common sense that may be based on direct personal experience, "war stories" heard during conversations with friends and co-workers, or both. Organizational behavior experts on perception have labeled this tendency the **fundamental attribution error** (see Chapter 2).[19] Many people assume that if a problem arises, it is the fault of the person involved—as opposed to a problem due to factors in the situation that are beyond that person's control. Is this assumption fair? Why or why not? Will making this assumption help to motivate a person whose Performance drop is due to factors outside of his control?

in either factor could result in a drop in Effort, changes in the Value of Reward are much more likely to occur as a result of changes in a *subordinate's* needs or desires. In contrast, the Perceived Effort→Reward Probability often drops because of something the *manager* or the *organization* has done, rather than because the subordinate has changed in some way. Thus, an argument could be made that it is fairest to consider the Perceived Effort→Reward Probability *first*.

From a manager's standpoint, because the Perceived Effort→Reward Probability is a subjective perception on the part of the subordinate, it may be difficult to pin down precisely. However, it can be helpful for managers to determine whether any given Perceived Effort→Reward Probability may have shifted significantly *downward* for some reason—even if the actual before and after probabilities cannot be estimated very accurately.

To do this, managers must look at the rewards that have been given to the subordinate in the relatively recent past and analyze how these compare with the rewards that the subordinate has received in the more distant past. Are the recent rewards lower, or less appealing? Also managers must determine if there have been any relatively recent cases where other subordinates—or other employees holding similar jobs in other departments—did not receive rewards that they were expecting to receive. In addition, managers must determine whether the subordinate has recently made a big Effort to do well on some critical aspect of the job, but unfortunately performed significantly below her personal expectations. Any of these events could conceivably explain a drop in the subordinate's Perceived Effort→Reward Probability.

At this point, it is helpful to consider the possibility that a perceived inequity in the way Rewards have been distributed recently might provide an alternative explanation for a drop in the subordinate's Perceived Effort→Reward Probability. In other words, managers must work backward from Perceived Effort→Reward Probability via the lower feedback loop in Figure 3-1 to check on Perceived Equitable Rewards. It is important to bear in mind that a perceived "inequity" might possibly be the result of an inaccurate perception that can appear completely unrealistic to the manager—or even to a neutral observer.

The preceding kinds of analysis can lead to an understanding of *why* a drop in the subordinate's Perceived Effort→Reward Probability may have occurred, which usually helps managers develop a practical solution to that problem. If other subordinates—or other employees holding similar jobs in other departments—have been recently denied rewards they were expecting to receive, one possible solution might be for the manager to make a greater effort to provide deserved rewards as immediately as possible. Promises should be made clear, and then kept. Alternatively, if organizational changes have resulted in new limitations on rewards that were available in the past, new forms of valued rewards may need to be explored (i.e., move on to an examination of the "Value of Reward" box in Figure 3-1). For a subordinate who has recently made a major Effort to do well but failed, a possible solution is for the manager to engage in some counseling to jointly decide whether such performance below expectations can best be dealt with through further training or through a change in job assignment to better match the subordinate's Abilities and Traits. Possible solutions to perceived inequities include taking steps to correct them or rationally explaining why they are much more equitable than initially perceived.

If analysis of the subordinate's Perceived Effort→Reward Probability produces no likely explanations for a drop in Performance, managers must ask some questions to determine to what extent the rewards currently being offered to that subordinate are currently valued by that subordinate. In other words, they must check on possible changes in the Value of Rewards.

For example, a subordinate may have previously valued receiving feedback about performance while in the process of learning how to do a new job, but now understands that job well. Hence that subordinate might currently place much greater value on receiving bonuses for high performance. Thus, feedback about performance—and verbal recognition—may well have become less valued rewards over time.

Should offering different rewards appear to be the most appropriate solution in response to a change in rewards preferences, it is very worthwhile for managers to think *creatively* about other rewards that *realistically* could be provided—within the constraints of the organizational context—and that might appeal to the subordinate. Managers must think broadly about Intrinsic and Extrinsic Rewards, or perhaps combinations of both. Some possibilities managers may choose to carefully consider include cross-training to learn how to do a variety of different jobs, special projects, training on new equipment, more desirable work hours, more flexible work hours, opportunities to work with admired or respected people, and so on.

Practically speaking, of course, it would be much more effective for managers to engage in activities that serve to *prevent* drops in Performance. Ideally, managers should keep track of subordinates' rewards preferences as part of maintaining contact with subordinates on a regular basis rather than in response to a Performance drop. Also note that managers can do a great deal to make the Perceived Effort→Reward Probability less subjective by being honest, accurate, and clear about what kinds of rewards are available to each subordinate, and what level of Performance is necessary to obtain them. This can help to clearly answer the question, "Will I receive a valued reward?" Encouragement and support, providing further training to improve Abilities and Traits when appropriate, and clarifying Role Perceptions can all help to increase a subordinate's confidence. This should enhance a feeling of "I can do it!" In general, building a high degree of trust between manager and subordinate is fundamental to boosting a subordinate's Perceived Effort→Reward Probability.

APPLICATION EXAMPLE

Troubleshooting a Drop in Performance by an
Engineer in a Manufacturing Company

To illustrate the essentials of actually *applying* the Expanded Expectancy-Theory Model to a real-life situation, the following is an example involving a manufacturing manager at a mid-sized manufacturing company. The manager has noticed a drop in the performance of a promising new employee named George who works as a manufacturing engineer. The manager initially analyzes George's Abilities and Traits as well as his Role Perceptions. No changes have occurred in George's job recently, and his Role Perceptions have been clear for some time.

Presuming that lack of Effort is the probable source of the problem, the manager next considers how George may view his Perceived Effort→Reward Probability. George recently received a very good six-month performance review and seems likely to be a strong candidate for a sizable raise at the end of his first year of work. Initially, that does not appear likely to create a problem. However, the manager also realizes that George's best friend Alberto had joined the firm a year ago as a design engineer. The manager places a call to his counterpart in product design, where George's friend works. "Yes," the product design manager states, "Alberto has performed very well. In fact, I bent a company rule and gave him a raise after only his first six months here, because I was afraid I might lose him."

Based on this information, the manufacturing manager decides that the probable cause of George's performance drop is a reduction in his Perceived Effort→Reward Probability, and very likely a concern about Perceived Equitable Rewards as well. George appears to be comparing his friend Alberto's positive experience with his own recent failure to receive a raise after six months. Alberto's experience had led George to expect that a raise would be forthcoming, but that did not happen. As a result, George's manager has been placed in a difficult position, through no fault of his own.

To develop trust, the manufacturing manager will probably have to be honest with George and explain how his counterpart in product design actually broke an organization rule by giving Alberto a raise after only six months. The manager then needs to clearly indicate that George is on track to receive a sizable raise at the end of the year—if he continues to perform as well as he has in the first six months.

continues

To bridge the expectation gap with respect to the delay of the *extrinsic* reward of more pay, the manufacturing manager may need to explore some alternative *intrinsic* rewards for George. One possibility might be some training on using new equipment or new techniques, perhaps at an interesting off-site location. Another might be offering George a special project, such as a chance to act as a manufacturing link to product design on an upcoming new product (and see Alberto more often). Such special training or such a special project would be contingent, however, on George's performance returning to its previous high level.

CONCLUSION

Motivation is an important issue for all managers due to its close ties with performance. One of the models discussed in this chapter provides a basis for creating jobs with high motivational potential. This model can be valuable for getting a new employee off to a good start, or for encouraging a more experienced employee to expand his skills and capabilities. The other model discussed in this chapter supplies a systematic approach for analyzing a drop in job performance due to reduced employee motivation or important alternative factors. The application section provided insights about ways to build on the information derived from the performance drop analysis to create practical solutions to such problems.

EXERCISES AND OTHER ACTIVITIES
■ *Experiential Exercise: In-Class 3-1*

APPLYING THE EXPANDED EXPECTANCY-THEORY MODEL TO ARNOLD
The purpose of this exercise is to apply the Expanded Expectancy-Theory Model to a simulated real-world situation in which a subordinate's performance is not up to expectations. The class will provide some advice about motivating employees to the new sales manager of the appliances department at a local department store.

Background Information
The new sales manager had worked in the appliances department on a part-time basis while completing his degree in management at a nearby college. After graduating two years ago, he shifted to full-time work and continued to perform well. Two weeks ago he got a break: his boss of the past four years was promoted to store manager at a store in another part of the state and recommended him as the most suitable candidate for the appliances department sales manager position at the local store.

Before the former sales manager left at the end of last week, she reviewed the major elements of the sales manager position with the new sales manager. However, she didn't spend much time on issues related to motivation because she knew that her protégé had taken a course in organizational behavior as part of his college course work. The new sales manager is highly motivated to show that he can perform well as a manager, but is a bit concerned because it has been more than three years since he took that OB course.

The sales manager is aware that all of his employees—not to mention his new boss—will be watching what he does very closely for the first month or so. In other words, this is important to his career, and he will greatly appreciate any help this class can give him.

The sales manager currently has 12 employees working under him. Eight of the employees are full-time, and four are part-time.

One of the sales manager's concerns is that an employee named Arnold is currently perceived to be performing below his potential. Arnold previously had a good track record as a full-time employee with the men's wear department within the same department store. After spending three years in men's wear, he requested a transfer to the appliances department so that he could "try something different." His transfer came through two weeks ago. The sales manager's former boss had high expectations for Arnold due to his experience and good track record, but Arnold has yet to perform as well as anticipated.

Exercise Process Outline
Form groups of 5 to 7 people.

Each group should develop an answer to the following question: How should the sales manager apply the Expanded Expectancy-Theory Model to Arnold to determine how to improve Arnold's performance? In other words, each group should work its way backward through the model in Figure 3-1 from the Performance box to determine which branch (or branches) of the model make the most sense in Arnold's case. Each group should determine which boxes in the model seem most likely to apply in this situation, and then be prepared to explain why.

When all of the groups have prepared an answer to the concerns outlined above, they will be presented and then discussed by the class as a whole.

■ *Experiential Exercise: In-Class 3-2*

APPLYING THE EXPANDED EXPECTANCY-THEORY MODEL TO DON
The purpose of this exercise is to apply the Expanded Expectancy-Theory Model to a simulated real-world situation in which a subordinate's performance has dropped. The class will be providing some advice about motivating employees to the new sales manager of the appliances department at a local department store.

Background Information
The new sales manager had worked in the appliances department on a part-time basis while completing his degree in management at a nearby college. After graduating two years ago, he shifted to full-time work, and continued to perform well. Two weeks ago he got a break: his boss of the past four years was promoted to store manager at a store in another part of the state, and she recommended him as the most suitable candidate for the appliances department sales manager position at the local store.

Before the former sales manager left at the end of last week, she reviewed the major elements of the sales manager position with the new sales manager. However, she didn't spend much time on issues related to motivation because she knew that her protégé had taken a course in organizational behavior as part of his college course work. The new sales manager is highly motivated to show that he can perform well as a manager, but is a bit concerned because it has been more than three years since he took that OB course.

The sales manager is aware that all of his employees—not to mention his new boss—will be watching what he does very closely for the first month or so. In other words, this is important to his career, and he will greatly appreciate any help this class can give him.

The sales manager currently has 12 employees working under him. Eight of the employees are full-time, and four are part-time.

Of great concern to the new Sales Manager, at the end of his first week as manager, is Don. It seems that not only has Don's performance dropped to a drastically lower level during just the past two days, but he is also upsetting other employees with his visible moodiness and some occasional caustic remarks about other sales-people, customers, the department, and life in general. What is especially disturbing is that this is so unlike Don, who has been an enthusiastic and popular full-time employee in the appliances department for several years. He had even been known to go out of his way to mentor new employees and to make his fellow employees feel upbeat and positive about their work. To the best of the sales manager's knowledge, Don has not been experiencing any personal problems outside of work, and another salesperson who gets along well with Don told the sales manager that he does not know of any outside problems either. However, when the sales manager asked Don to stop by his office "sometime today, whenever it is convenient for you," Don ignored the request, and never showed up.

Exercise Process Outline
Form groups of 5 to 7 people.

Each group should develop an answer the following question: How should the sales manager apply the Expanded Expectancy-Theory Model to Don to determine how to improve Don's performance? In other words, each group should work its way backward through the model in Figure 3-1 from the Performance box to determine which branch (or branches) of the model make the most sense in Don's case. Each group should determine which boxes in the model seem most likely to apply in this situation, and then be prepared to explain why.

When all of the groups have prepared an answer to the concerns outlined above, they will be presented and then discussed by the class as a whole.

■ *Experiential Exercise: In-Class 3-3*

APPLYING THE EXPANDED EXPECTANCY-THEORY MODEL TO MIRIAM
The purpose of this exercise is to apply the Expanded Expectancy-Theory Model to a simulated real-world situation in which a subordinate's performance has dropped. The

class will be providing some advice about motivating employees to the new sales manager of the appliances department at a local department store.

Background Information

Relevant background information for this exercise has already been provided in Experiential Exercises: In-Class 3-1 and 3-2.

Imagine that a couple of weeks after the class helped the sales manager analyze how to improve the performance of Arnold and Don, the sales manager calls asking us for some additional advice. He is now concerned about a drop in Miriam's performance. Miriam has been employed full-time in the appliances department for the past eight years. Based on conversations with his former boss—as well as his own impressions over the past several years—the sales manager knows that Miriam is a steady but not spectacular performer as a salesperson. However, during the past two weeks, her performance has been significantly below its normal level, and she has been observed complaining to other full-time employees about something whenever the sales manager is not in a position to hear what she is saying.

Exercise Process Outline

Form groups of 5 to 7 people.

Develop some possible explanations for this change in Miriam's performance.

Think of some ways that the sales manager might obtain the information needed to determine which of the possible explanations is the correct one.

When all of the groups have prepared an answer to the concerns outlined above, they will be presented and then discussed by the class as a whole.

After all of the groups have developed and discussed their answers, your instructor will tell you the *actual* reason for Miriam's performance drop. Based on this information, provide a recommendation to the sales manager about how to deal with the situation—after once again working backwards from the Performance box in Figure 3-1.

When all of the groups have prepared their new recommendations, they will present and discuss them with the class as a whole.

■ *Experiential Exercise: In-Class 3-4*

APPLYING THE EXPANDED EXPECTANCY-THEORY MODEL IN GENERAL

The purpose of this exercise is to develop some generalizations for applying the Expanded Expectancy-Theory Model to a real-world situation in which a subordinate's performance has dropped. The class will be providing some advice about motivating employees to the new sales manager of the appliances department at a local department store.

Background Information

Relevant background information for this exercise has already been provided in Experiential Exercises: In-Class 3-1, 3-2, and 3-3.

Exercise Process Outline

Form groups of 5 to 7 people.

As a follow-up to any of the previous three exercises, consider what the sales manager would need to do in general to obtain the kinds of information about his other nine employees that would allow him to perform an accurate Expanded Expectancy-Theory Model analysis of each of these employees. Some key questions to consider follow:

To *whom* should he speak? In what *sequence*?

What kinds of *questions* should he ask?

To *whom* should he ask them?

In what *sequence* should those questions be asked?

What *observations* should he make, and when?

Should observations be made *before* or *after* asking questions?

When all of the groups have prepared their answers to the preceding questions and the overall issue, they will present and discuss them with the class as a whole.

■ *Experiential Exercise: In-Class 3-5*

PREDICTING PREFERRED REWARDS

The purpose of this exercise is to focus on a key aspect of the Expanded Expectancy-Theory Model: rewards. You will predict the reward preferences of other members of the class, based on a list of rewards (below) that have previously proven to be of significant interest to people working in real-world organizations.

A LIST OF INTERESTING REWARDS

Job with More Responsibility

Profit Sharing

Private Office

Company Stock or Stock Options

Formal Recognition of Achievement

Personal Time Off with Pay

Opportunity to Develop New Skills

Vacation Trip

Boss Gives You More Freedom to Make Decisions

Company Car

Feedback about Performance

Money

Flexibility in Time Off Work

Paid-Up Insurance Policies

Exercise Process Outline

Carefully consider the preceding list of 14 interesting rewards.

Make a list of those rewards that you would include in your personal Top 5.

Make a second list of those rewards that you predict will be included in the Top 5 for the entire class.

When all of the students have completed their two lists, your instructor will read each item on the list, in turn. When an item that appears on your personal Top 5 list is called, raise your hand. Your instructor will count the number of hands for each item and record this number on the board or a flip chart.

After this data has been collected, the entire class can easily determine the five items receiving the most votes from the class as a whole. Has anyone predicted all five of the Top 5 correctly? How many people identified at least half of Top 5 (i.e., three or more)?

OPTIONAL FOLLOW-UP ACTIVITIES

Please see Case Studies 3-1 through 3-7 to compare the data obtained in your class with data collected from a large number of other classes as part of a longitudinal study (long-term, over time) of students' rewards preferences.

■ *Experiential Exercise: In-Class 3-6*

DETERMINING "REALISTIC" REWARDS

The purpose of this exercise is to apply the results developed in Case Studies 3-1 through 3-7 to a real-world situation. (These results are also related to Experiential Exercise: In-Class 3-5).

A LIST OF INTERESTING REWARDS

Job with More Responsibility

Profit Sharing

Private Office

Company Stock or Stock Options

Formal Recognition of Achievement

Personal Time Off with Pay

Opportunity to Develop New Skills

Vacation Trip

Boss Gives You More Freedom to Make Decisions

Company Car

Feedback about Performance

Money

Flexibility in Time Off Work

Paid-Up Insurance Policies

Exercise Process Outline

Form groups of 5 to 7 people.

Assume that you have just been hired as new first-level supervisors. Your boss has recommended that you carefully consider the preceding list of 14 interesting rewards, and then discuss in your group how this information might help you determine the best rewards with which to motivate your subordinates to perform their jobs effectively. In particular, your boss has suggested that you develop a Top 5 list of "realistic rewards" for these subordinates. You may further assume that your subordinates are all recent college graduates.

When all of the groups have developed their Top 5 lists of "realistic rewards," the class will discuss these lists and why certain rewards would be preferable for new first-level supervisors to use with recent college graduates.

■ *Experiential Exercise: In-Class 3-7*

APPLYING THE JOB CHARACTERISTICS MODEL TO ENHANCE JOB DESIGN

The purpose of this exercise is to develop some practical ideas for applying the Job Characteristics Model to a real-world situation.

Exercise Process Outline

Form groups of 5 to 7 people.

Assume that all of you are working as first-level supervisors at a car, truck, or motorcycle manufacturer. How might you apply the Job Characteristics Model to enhance your employees' jobs and make them more motivating?

When all of the groups have prepared their answers to the preceding question, they will present and discuss them with the class as a whole.

■ *Experiential Exercise: In-Class 3-8*

APPLYING THE JOB CHARACTERISTICS MODEL TO ENHANCE JOB DESIGN

The purpose of this exercise is to develop some practical ideas for applying the Job Characteristics Model to a real-world situation.

Exercise Process Outline

Form groups of 5 to 7 people.

Discuss the various jobs at which some members of your group are currently working. Choose one of these real-world situations as a basis for conducting the following analysis. Look at the chosen situation from the manager's—or supervisor's—point of view. How might the manager or supervisor apply the Job Characteristics Model to enhance his or her employees' jobs and make them more motivating (assuming that the Moderator factors indicate that doing this would make sense)?

When all of the groups have prepared their answers to the preceding question, they will present and discuss them with the class as a whole.

■ *Case Study 3-1*

ANALYZING DATA CONCERNING STUDENTS' REWARDS PREFERENCES: 1987–1991

The purpose of this Case Study is to practice analyzing some organizational behavior data related to the issue raised by the Value of Reward box in the Expanded Expectancy-Theory Model in Figure 3-1.

Empirical Data for Rewards Preferences Survey Results: 1987–1991

Rank	Rewards
1	Money
2	Personal Time Off with Pay
3	Vacation Trips
4	Private Office
5.5	Job with More Responsibility
5.5	Company Car
7	Profit Sharing
8	Formal Acknowledgement of Achievement
9	Feedback about Performance
10	Verbal or Nonverbal Recognition or Praise

Note: These survey results were based on a list of 60+ rewards that appeared in an OB textbook used in OB classes taught by Bill Zachary at San Jose State University in the early- to mid-1980s.[20] Initially, the number of students who included each reward in their personal Top 5 was determined; see Experiential Exercise: In-Class 3-5 for a similar exercise based on an updated and more focused list of popular rewards. The total votes have been replaced by a rank ordering in this table to simplify the analysis.

Activity Process Outline

As a class, discuss the empirical data provided in the preceding list. What information tends to stand out? How might this list be useful in determining the Value of Reward information covered in the section concerning the Expanded Expectancy-Theory Model in this chapter? What does it suggest regarding Intrinsic Rewards versus Extrinsic Rewards?

■ *Case Study 3-2*

ANALYZING DATA CONCERNING STUDENTS' REWARDS PREFERENCES:
1991–1994 VERSUS 1987–1991

The purpose of this Case Study is to practice analyzing some organizational behavior data related to the important issue raised by the Value of Rewards box in the Expanded Expectancy-Theory Model in Figure 3-1.

Empirical Data for Rewards Preferences Survey Results: 1991–1994 Versus 1987–1991

1991–1994 Rank	1987–1991 Rank	Reward
1	1	Money
2	2	Personal Time Off with Pay
3	3	Vacation Trips
4	5.5	Company Car
5	7	Profit Sharing
6	5.5	Job with More Responsibility
7	12	Paid-Up Insurance Policies
8	4	Private Office
9	8	Formal Acknowledgement of Achievement
10	14	Stock
11	9	Feedback about Performance

Note: These survey results were based on a list of 60+ rewards that appeared in an OB textbook used in OB classes taught by Bill Zachary at San Jose State University in the early- to mid-1980s.[20] Initially, the number of students who included each reward in their personal Top 5 was determined; see Experiential Exercise: In-Class 3-5 for a similar exercise based on an updated and more focused list of popular rewards. The total votes have been replaced by a rank ordering in this table to simplify the analysis.

Activity Process Outline

As a class, discuss the empirical data provided in the preceding list. In comparing the two sets of rankings, what information stands out? How might this data be useful in determining the Value of Reward information covered in the section concerning the Expanded Expectancy-Theory Model in this chapter? Has anything changed with regard to Intrinsic versus Extrinsic Rewards? (Hint: What happened during the period 1991–1994?)

■ *Case Study 3-3*

ANALYZING DATA CONCERNING STUDENTS' REWARDS PREFERENCES:
FALL 1995

The purpose of this Case Study is to practice analyzing some organizational behavior data related to the important issue raised by the Value of Reward box in the Expanded Expectancy-Theory Model in Figure 3-1.

Empirical Data for Rewards Preferences Survey Results: Different OB Sections in Fall 1995

Reward	Ranking		
Old Items From Top 10: 1987–1994	10:30 a.m. Class	3:00 p.m. Class	6:00 p.m. Class
Money	3	3.5	1
Personal Time Off with Pay	2	2	7
Vacation Trip	1	1	9
Company Car	—	—	—
Private Office	9.5	8	9
Job with More Responsibility	7.5	9	3.5
Profit Sharing	9.5	7	5.5
Formal *Recognition* of Achievement	4	10	9
Paid-Up Insurance Policies	—	—	—
Feedback about Performance	—	—	—
New Items Now in Top 10			
Company Stock *or Stock Options*	6	5.5	2
Opportunity to Develop New Skills	7.5	5.5	3.5
Flexibility in Time Off Work	5	3.5	5.5

Note: These survey results are based on a pilot version of a survey instrument developed by Bill Zachary and Matt Griffin. (Matt Griffin has since received a Ph.D. in Industrial/Organizational Psychology.) The new survey included all of the popular rewards from the prior list, plus added some new items taken from the more recent literature on rewards (the wording for three of the prior rewards was modified; two changes are shown in italics, plus the "s" was removed from Vacation Trips). A 1–5 rating scale replaced the earlier Top 5 approach, with 5 being the highest rating. However, the average ratings have been replaced by a rank ordering in this table to simplify the analysis.

Activity Process Outline

As a class, discuss the empirical data provided in the preceding list. What information stands out? In particular, to what extent do the results vary depending on the kinds of students that typically take courses at 10:30 a.m., 3 p.m., or 6 p.m.? How might these differences be explained?

■ *Case Study 3-4*

ANALYZING DATA CONCERNING STUDENTS' REWARDS PREFERENCES: A MAJOR SURVEY IN 1996–1997

The purpose of this Case Study is to practice analyzing some organizational behavior data related to the issue raised by the Value of Reward box in the Expanded Expectancy-Theory Model in Figure 3-1.

Empirical Data for Rewards Preferences Survey Results: A Major Survey (N=343) in 1996–1997

Rank	Reward
1	Money
2	Personal Time Off with Pay
3	Vacation Trip
4	Flexibility in Time Off Work
5	Boss Gives You More Freedom to Make Decisions
6	Profit Sharing
7	Opportunity to Develop New Skills
8	Company Stock or Stock Options
9	Company Car
10	Private Office

Note: These survey results are based on a survey instrument developed by Bill Zachary and Matt Griffin. (Matt Griffin has since received a Ph.D. in Industrial/Organizational Psychology.) This new survey included all of the popular rewards from the original list (with a few modifications, noted in Case Study 3-3), plus added some new items taken from the more recent literature on rewards. A 1–5 rating scale replaced the earlier Top 5 approach, with 5 being the highest rating. However, the average ratings have been replaced by a rank ordering in this table to simplify the analysis. The students responding to this major survey were taking either a more basic or more advanced OB course, in either large or small sections, and at a variety of times, day and night.

Activity Process Outline

As a class, discuss the empirical data provided in the preceding list. What information stands out? How do preferences for Intrinsic versus Extrinsic Rewards compare in this major survey that includes a number of new types of rewards?

■ *Case Study 3-5*

ANALYZING DATA CONCERNING STUDENTS' REWARDS PREFERENCES:
1996–1997 MAJOR SURVEY VERSUS 1987–1994
The purpose of this Case Study is to practice analyzing some organizational behavior data related to the issue raised by the Value of Reward box in the Expanded Expectancy-Theory Model in Figure 3-1.

Empirical Data for Rewards Preferences Survey Results: 1996–1997 Versus 1987–1994 (Excluding Newly Added Rewards)

1996–1997 Rank	1987–1994 Rank	Reward
1	1	Money
2	2	Personal Time Off with Pay
3	3	Vacation Trip
5	4	Company Car
6	5	Private Office
8	6.5	Job with More Responsibility
4	6.5	Profit Sharing
7	8	Formal Recognition of Achievement
9	9	Paid-Up Insurance Policies
10	10	Feedback about Performance

Note: These survey results are based on the same sources as those provided in the notes for Experiential Exercises: In-Class 3-2 and In-Class 3-4.

Activity Process Outline
As a class, discuss the empirical data provided in the preceding list. What information stands out? What is similar and what is different?

■ *Case Study 3-6*

ANALYZING DATA CONCERNING STUDENTS' REWARDS PREFERENCES: 1996–1997 MAJOR SURVEY VERSUS 1987–1994

The purpose of this Case Study is to practice analyzing some organizational behavior data related to the issue raised by the Value of Reward box in the Expanded Expectancy-Theory Model in Figure 3-1.

Empirical Data for Rewards Preferences Survey Results: 1996–1997 Versus 1987–1994 (Including Newly Added Rewards)

1996–1997 Rank	1987–1994 Rank	Reward
1	1	Money
2	2	Personal Time Off with Pay
3	3	Vacation Trip
9	4	Company Car
10	5	Private Office
13	6.5	Job with More Responsibility
6	6.5	Profit Sharing
12	8	Formal Recognition of Achievement
16	9	Paid-Up Insurance Policies
19	10	Feedback about Performance
4	—	Flexibility in Time Off Work
5	—	Boss Gives You More Freedom to Make Decisions
7	—	Opportunity to Develop New Skills
8	—	Company Stock or Stock Options

Note: These survey results are based on the same sources as those provided in the notes for Experiential Exercises: In-Class 3-2 and In-Class 3-4.

Activity Process Outline

As a class, discuss the empirical data provided in the preceding list, to which the newly added rewards now appearing in the new Top 10 have been added. What information stands out? What is similar and what is different?

■ *Case Study 3-7*

ANALYZING DATA CONCERNING STUDENTS' REWARDS PREFERENCES:
1996–1997 MAJOR SURVEY VERSUS 2000–2003
The purpose of this Case Study is to practice analyzing some organizational behavior
data related to the issue raised by the Value of Reward box in the Expanded
Expectancy-Theory Model in Figure 3-1.

Empirical Data for Rewards Preferences Survey Results: 1996–1997 Versus 2000–2003

1996–1997 Rank	2000–2003 Rank	Reward
1	1	Money
2	2	Personal Time Off with Pay
3	8	Vacation Trip
9	—	Company Car
10	—	Private Office
13	—	Job with More Responsibility
6	7	Profit Sharing
12	—	Formal Recognition of Achievement
16	—	Paid-Up Insurance Policies
19	—	Feedback about Performance
4	3	Flexibility in Time Off Work
5	5	Boss Gives You More Freedom to Make Decisions
7	4	Opportunity to Develop New Skills
8	6	Company Stock or Stock Options

Note: The 2000–2003 results were based on the number of students in each class who included each
reward in their personal Top 5, using Experiential Exercise: In-Class 3-5. The total votes have been
replaced by a rank ordering in this table to simplify the analysis.

Activity Process Outline
As a class, discuss the empirical data provided in the preceding list. What information
stands out? How much have student preferences for the most popular rewards changed
over the five or so years between the time the first and second sets of data were
obtained?

Considering the data presented in Case Study 3-5 and/or Case Study 3-6 in addition to the data presented above, how much have student preferences for the most popular rewards changed over the approximately *15-year period* for which similar types of data have been obtained?

If your class has already completed Experiential Exercise: In-Class 3-5, how do the data for your class compare with the 2000–2003 San Jose State University OB classes data? If any major differences appear to exist, how might they be explained?

Overall, how generalizable are these reward preferences survey results to the real world? For which kinds of employees might these survey results be especially useful to a practicing manager?

REFERENCE NOTES

1. Porter, L. W., and E. E. Lawler III. *Managerial Attitudes and Performance*. Homewood, IL: Irwin, 1968.

2. Porter, L. W., and E. E. Lawler III. *Managerial Attitudes and Performance*. Homewood, IL: Irwin, 1968.

3. Vroom, V. H. *Work and Motivation*. New York, NY: Wiley and Sons, 1964.

4. This first point is based on three points made in Porter & Lawler, p. 35. Porter, L. W., and E. E. Lawler III. *Managerial Attitudes and Performance*. Homewood, IL: Irwin, 1968.

5. The second and third points are based on the concept of valence in Expectancy Theory. Vroom, V. H. *Work and Motivation*. New York, NY: Wiley and Sons, 1964.

6. Iaffaldano, M. T., and P. M. Murchinsky. Job Satisfaction and Job Performance: A Meta-Analysis. *Psychological Bulletin*, Vol. 97, 1985, pp. 251–273.

7. Scott, K. D., and G. S. Taylor. An Examination of Conflicting Findings on the Relationship Between Job Satisfaction and Absenteeism: A Meta-Analysis. *Academy of Management Journal*, Vol. 28, 1985, pp. 599–612.

8. Tett, R. P., and J. P. Meyer. Job Satisfaction, Organizational Commitment, Turnover Intention, and Turnover: Path Analyses Based on Meta-Analytic Findings. *Personnel Psychology*, Vol. 46, 1993, pp. 259–293.

9. Dyer & Parker (1975) have presented strong evidence that different organizational behavior experts define "intrinsic" and "extrinsic" in different ways. However, the definitions presented in this section are reasonably consistent with the definitions found in many organizational behavior texts. Dyer, L., and D. F. Parker. Classifying Outcomes in Work Motivation Research: An Examination of the Intrinsic-Extrinsic Dichotomy. *Journal of Applied Psychology*, Vol. 60, 1975, pp. 455–458.

10. Adams, J. S. Inequity in Social Exchange. In L. Berkowitz (ed.), *Advances in Experimental Social Psychology*, Vol. 2. New York, NY: Academic Press, 1965, pp. 267–299.

11. Maslow, A. H. *Motivation and Personality*, 2nd ed. New York, NY: Harper and Row, 1970.; Alderfer, C. P. *Existence, Relatedness, and Growth: Human Needs in Organizational Settings*. New York, NY: The Free Press, 1972.; McClelland, D. C. *Human Motivation*. Glenview, IL: Scott, Foresman, 1985.

12. In the original version of the model, Porter & Lawler (1968) have the second feedback loop beginning from a point after Performance but *before* the two types of Rewards. Porter, L. W., and E. E. Lawler III. *Managerial Attitudes and Performance*. Homewood, IL: Irwin, 1968.

13. Lawler, E. E. III. Secrecy and the Need to Know. In H. L. Tosi, R. J. House, and M. Dunnette (eds.), *Managerial Motivation and Compensation*. East Lansing, MI: Michigan State University Press, 1972.

14. Herzberg, F. *Work and the Nature of Man*. Cleveland, OH: World, 1966.

15. Hackman, J. R., and G. R. Oldham. Motivation Through the Design of Work: Test of a Theory. *Organizational Behavior and Human Performance*, Vol. 16, 1976, pp. 250–279. Hackman, J. R., and G. R. Oldham. Work Redesign. Reading, MA: Addison-Wesley, 1980.

16. Herzberg, F. *Work and the Nature of Man*. Cleveland, OH: World, 1966.

17. Hackman, J. R., and G. R. Oldham. Motivation Through the Design of Work: Test of a Theory. *Organizational Behavior and Human Performance*, Vol. 16, 1976, pp. 250–279.

18. Adapted from Porter, L. W., and E. E. Lawler III. *Managerial Attitudes and Performance*. Homewood, IL: Irwin, 1968. The original authors developed a model that synthesizes several different major models of motivation and includes the linkages between Performance and Satisfaction (with Rewards as a key intervening variable). Note that the linkages in that model flow *forward*. In contrast, this section is based on a slightly modified version of the original model (see Note 12) but uses the model as a diagnostic tool by working *backward* from Performance to determine one or more likely causes of a performance drop.

19. Ross, L. The Intuitive Psychologist and His Shortcomings. In L. Berkowitz (ed.), *Advances in Experimental Social Psychology*, Vol. 10. Orlando, FL: Academic Press, 1977.

20. Reitz, H. J. *Organizational Behavior*, rev. ed. Homewood, IL: Irwin, 1981, p. 76.

PART III
The Group Level

Chapter List

CHAPTER 4
Group Dynamics and Team Effectiveness

In most modern organizations, a significant proportion of the work being accomplished is performed by groups. Hence, it is worthwhile to analyze and interpret the interactions that take place within a group, and then use this information as well as other group-related information as a basis for taking actions that will enhance team effectiveness.

This chapter begins by discussing a number of issues that often arise in group dynamics.[1] **Group dynamics** refers to the developing relationships and constantly changing interactions between members of a group. Once an understanding of some important aspects of group dynamics has been attained, a model is presented concerning the stages that a typical group is likely to go through over time. In a sense, this model provides a "big picture" view of the general trends in a group's dynamics that will take place from the time a group is created until the time it is disbanded. Next, an in-depth integrative model indicates which key factors lead to team effectiveness. At the end of the chapter, practical guidelines are presented for applying an action model version of the integrated model to actual group situations. These guidelines outline a series of steps that a manager or self-managed group can follow to increase the chances of group or team success.

ANALYZING GROUP DYNAMICS

Activities in groups at work typically involve two key factors: performance of the group's task and maintenance of the group's interactions.[2] In most work-related situations, group members tend to focus their attention on the task that the group is supposed to perform. Since accomplishing this task is usually the main reason why the work group was formed in the first place, this is not too surprising. However, if members of the group are unable to work together effectively, the group's task performance is likely to suffer. Thus, maintenance of the group's interactions deserves more attention than it typically receives.

Maintenance of the group's interactions generally involves observing group dynamics, analyzing what is occurring in the group and why, and then taking some actions that will help group members to feel good about the group and their contributions to it. Any person who engages in this kind of maintenance activity is said to be *facilitating* the group *process*.

It is amazing how often group process is neglected even when process-related problems are clearly the primary reasons why a group is unable to perform its task effectively. This is a compelling argument for devoting more of a group's time to process-related issues.

Developing sensitivity to the process that is taking place in a group will allow group members to better determine what is not working and what to do about it. The ability of at least some—if not all—group members to improve the process of their group is likely to make working in that group a more enjoyable experience for everyone. In addition, to the extent that the group's task performance is enhanced by such process facilitation, the individual performance evaluation of each process facilitator is likely to be boosted as well.

What follows are some guidelines to help in the analysis of various important aspects of group dynamics within any group one might be observing—as either an outside observer or an inside participant. While other aspects of small group behavior are also interesting and worthwhile to know, the key aspects presented in this chapter are common concerns and often have noteworthy effects on a group's performance.

COMPOSITION AND SIZE

The **composition** of a group refers to the members of which the group is composed. A key issue related to group composition is the group's diversity, or the extent to which group members are diverse or different from one another. On one hand, greater group diversity creates greater opportunities for those differences to create conflict (see Chapter 5). Such conflict has the potential to cause major group process problems and hamper group performance. On the other hand, greater group diversity often leads to greater group creativity, which may result in higher group performance.[3] Interestingly, both desirable and undesirable outcomes—creativity versus group process problems—can result from the conflict that greater group diversity engenders. The difference is that the creativity-enhancing kind of conflict is *constructive*, while the process-inhibiting kind of conflict is *destructive*. Careful process monitoring and process facilitation play important roles in making a diverse group more likely to be a success rather than a failure. Given the extent of diversity in the modern era, this is a critical aspect of group process that merits special attention. Note that diversity within a group in a business setting can include differences in functional specialization (e.g., marketing vs. finance vs. human resources, etc.) as well as gender, ethnicity, age, educational background, and so on.

Group **size** also significantly affects how smoothly the group process will flow. Relatively large groups are likely to experience difficulties with their group process. One process problem that typically becomes immediately obvious in large groups is that it is difficult for every group member to have a chance to contribute when many group members have something they would like to say. Less aggressive group members may seldom or never be heard, thereby costing the group the benefit of their potentially good ideas and probably their motivation and enthusiasm as well. Organizational behavior research suggests that the *optimal* group size is five to seven people.[4]

The reduction in motivation and enthusiasm associated with relatively large groups can also contribute to a phenomenon known as **social loafing**, in which group members tend to contribute less to not only the group process, but to the completion of the group's task as well. The extent of social loafing has been shown to increase as the size of a group increases.[5]

ANALYSIS   **Social Loafing**

The social loafing phenomenon is commonly observable in the workplace—and also can be seen in group projects required in college classes. *Analyze* some of the key factors that cause social loafing to occur. [Hint: One key factor is diminished responsibility for the group's performance.] Based on the set of key factors developed in response to the preceding question, *analyze* how social loafing effects might be reduced.

Group members who desire to contribute but are frustrated in their efforts due to the large size of their group may resort to creating *subgroups*. Such subgroups typically involve people who are located near one another. However, subgroups may also form because certain group members like each other, or because they perform the same work roles, and so on. Some subgroups may be temporary, but others may evolve into fairly permanent subgroups that can substantially disrupt the process of the entire group.

ROLES

A **role** is a set of behaviors that a person is expected to perform. Every person in a group will play one or more roles. Some roles are assigned, whereas others may be taken on voluntarily. Roles related to task completion are more common, but roles that affect group process are also important.

When observing and analyzing group process, it is helpful to consider which roles are most important to the group, and who is chosen to perform which roles. Of special interest is which people voluntarily take on so-called **emergent** roles,[6] either because they want to perform such a role or because they feel that someone in the group *needs* to play such a role.

A role that most group members will play is a **contributor** role. A task-related role that commonly emerges is making suggestions concerning how to solve a problem. A process-related role that commonly emerges in effective groups is facilitating the group process. A **facilitator** role is frequently an assigned role in a business setting but an emergent role in a classroom setting.

VERBAL PARTICIPATION

Perhaps the most obvious indicator of the extent of personal involvement in a group's activities is the degree of **verbal participation**, or how much each group member talks. In most groups, some members are likely to participate more actively than others. Thus, a worthwhile question to answer during any analysis of group dynamics is, "Which group members are highly active verbal participators, which are somewhat active, and which are relatively inactive verbal participators?"

It is important to recognize that any categorizations of group members' verbal participation activity levels may change over time, as someone who has been more active becomes quieter, or someone who has not been talking very much suddenly becomes more vocal. It is worthwhile to note such *shifts* in verbal participation. Figuring out why such shifts occurred can suggest how to best facilitate the group's process in the future. For example, one quiet person may simply be thinking things through carefully before speaking up. Another quiet person may have some great ideas, but prefer—due to her cultural background—to wait until others have had their say. Obviously, these two different explanations for the same kind of shift in verbal participation would suggest distinctly different approaches to facilitating that person's verbal participation in future group interactions.

Another useful way to analyze verbal participation is to determine to which people in the group any particular group member tends to communicate. For example, some people prefer to talk to the entire group, some may talk mostly to people who are located nearby or directly across from them, some may talk more to people who have similar ideas, some may talk mostly to the people who are very active participators, and so forth. Therefore, when trying to explain why certain patterns exist, look at where people are located in the group, what they have in common, and so on, as well as how actively they are verbally participating.

FACILITATION

A group member who facilitates a group's interactions is applying techniques that help the group to work together more effectively. There are a variety of techniques that facilitate task completion and a different set of techniques that facilitate the group process.[7] Both task facilitation and process facilitation are *critically* important to the success of a group.

Some groups are assigned, elect, or accept a group leader, who then assumes the role of facilitating the group's activities. Other groups have two people who play the facilitator role: one who deals mostly with task accomplishment, and one who primarily seeks to create and maintain relatively harmonious relationships among group members to ensure high group morale and effective teamwork. In still other groups, many or all group members take turns acting as group facilitators, providing help when it appears to be needed to complete a task or to make other members feel valued.

Task Facilitation

Task facilitation techniques involve taking actions that help a group to get the job done.

Note that activities such as "contributing good ideas" provide *individual* answers that help a group to solve a problem, as opposed to helping a group to work *together* to solve a problem. While both are important to group success, the focus here will be on facilitation techniques that help a group to work together to solve a problem or complete a task. In other words, a distinction will be made between playing a facilitator role versus playing a contributor role.

One common and important task facilitation technique that focuses on helping the group as a whole to complete the group's task is **summarizing.** A group member might summarize the highlights of a recent group discussion, summarize what the group has accomplished and what remains to be done, or summarize decisions or goals that have been agreed upon in the past.

Evaluating how well the group is performing is another key task facilitation technique. It involves asking fundamental questions, such as "How are we doing?" and "What needs to be improved?" Evaluating is sometimes a sensitive issue, but one that must be dealt with to achieve a high level of performance.

Some other task facilitation techniques include **pushing for action to be taken, helping the group stay focused on the task at hand, and so on**.

Process Facilitation

In contrast, **process facilitation techniques** help group members to feel good about their group and what they are contributing to it.

One of the most valuable process facilitation techniques is **drawing out** some of the quieter group members in an effort to get them more involved in the group's discussion. Quieter group members often have ideas that would help the group perform its task better, but do not feel comfortable jumping into the discussion to present them. Such reticence or hesitation is especially likely when the group is large or when a few of the group members are participating extremely actively and focusing very intensely on achieving the group's *task*.

Sometimes all that is needed to facilitate the participation of quieter group members is to give them a chance to say something. This approach is most likely to work when a less verbally active person is making attempts to speak up but is being cut off by more aggressive or confident group members. In these cases, process facilitators can say something like "Pete, how do *you* think we should deal with this situation?" or "Juana, let's hear your ideas on this issue." An alternative approach is to talk with a quieter person individually, ask what that person thinks the group should do to solve a particular problem, and then help to create an opportunity for that person to speak up in the group if he has an idea to contribute.

Complimenting other group members on their contributions to the group is another helpful process facilitation technique. Most people appreciate the recognition that compliments provide. This often encourages them to contribute again in the future.

Clarifying facilitates the group process by clearly explaining another member's idea when other group members do not understand it. People who do not understand what is happening in the group are unlikely to feel good about being in it. Furthermore, because of their lack of understanding, they will not be in a position to help make someone else's good idea even better.

A common technique for clarifying another person's idea is to say it in a slightly different—and hopefully clearer—way. **Paraphrasing** involves restating in your own words what the speaker has just said, while using any key words supplied by the speaker. It is best to present this revised version of the idea to its originator in the form of a question.[8] This is a good way of checking with the person who originally presented the idea to the group, giving him the credit he deserves for having a good idea, while at the same time re-phrasing the idea so others can more clearly understand it. An advantage of paraphrasing is that it results in *both* complimenting and clarifying at the same time. Another possibility is to clarify some ideas while summarizing the important ideas recently discussed. This would result in both process facilitation (clarifying) and task facilitation (summarizing) at the same time.

To summarize, people are likely to feel good about being in a group if other group members show interest in them by drawing them into the group discussion, complimenting them on making helpful contributions, or helping them to more clearly understand the contributions of others. However, what if someone presents an idea that is not very good? Ignoring the idea or stating that it is not a very good one obviously will not make the person who had the idea feel good about being in the group. Therefore, another important process facilitation technique is **recognizing effort**. After all, that person's next idea may be outstanding, so at least nod, smile, or say something that will encourage further contributions.

Note that a person who uses a facilitation *technique* can also be said to be playing that type of *role*. For example, any person who uses the task facilitation technique of summarizing would be playing a summarizer role; any person who uses the process facilitation technique of clarifying would be playing a clarifier role, and so on.

ANALYSIS & APPLICATION   Process Facilitation

In many groups, some form of *task* facilitation is likely to occur without much effort, probably because at least some group members have had quite a bit of practice in doing this sort of thing. However, it is often more difficult for group members to engage in *process* facilitation, even when it is clear that such facilitation would help the group to work together more effectively. *Analyze* this phenomenon. How might it be explained? What could group members—and especially those members with good facilitation skills—do to ensure that an appropriate amount of process facilitation will be *applied* in the future?

NORMS

Groups typically develop their own standards of behavior to which they expect their members to conform. These are called **norms**. Unlike rules, which are explicitly developed to control behavior, norms typically evolve to control group behavior *implicitly*, or without people necessarily being consciously aware of how they came into being.[9] For example, an explicit rule might state that no eating or drinking is allowed in the room where the group meets. However, an implicit norm might develop that it is acceptable to break that rule if group members are careful and agree to clean up anything they drop or spill.

A variety of norms can be observed in most groups. One common issue is how group members should interact with other group members. Interactions in a group that has a strong politeness norm will be quite different than those in a group that emphasizes honest and direct confrontation. Another important type of norm concerns the degree of effort that will be directed toward task performance. Some groups will have a norm to try very hard to perform well, while other groups will develop norms that encourage group members to relax and perform well *below* their capabilities. The question of how much verbal participation is appropriate for any member of a group is also affected by the norms of that group.

When analyzing group dynamics, it is helpful to identify the norms that are operating in a group, especially those that seem to have the strongest impact on the group's behavior. In particular, since norms that inhibit group effectiveness are typically implicit, bringing them out in the open in a tactful way and taking a careful look at their effects on the group can lead to the development of new norms that can enhance group performance. Often, this process will cause group members to recognize that different members have different personal goals (see Chapter 9). Such differences can then be dealt with through various conflict management techniques (see Chapter 5).

STATUS

Status deals with where each group member stands in a formal or informal ranking of group members based on whatever reasons or criteria the majority of the group feels are important. A person's status often affects the degree to which that person will verbally participate in a group. People of higher status are frequently given the opportunity to participate quite actively, as many group members tend to prefer communicating with people of equal or higher status rather than people of lower status.[10]

Some common criteria that are used to determine a person's status include level in the management hierarchy, occupation, skill, experience, and personality. Multiple criteria are often used to determine status. For example, a person of high status may have developed a considerable amount of skill as a result of hard study and a great deal of practice over many years of experience, plus have an engaging personality that makes it easier for that person to apply that skill effectively.

Status generally has a greater impact in groups in which people are aware of each other's track records within a particular organizational setting, as well as their respective positions within that organization's hierarchy. For example, a respected and successful professional in a well-established business organization would likely be accorded higher status. On the other hand, status is generally less important in groups where members have little knowledge of other members' past accomplishments and do not occupy formal positions. This is often the case for students meeting in a classroom setting.

INFLUENCE

An influential group member is an individual to whom the rest of the group carefully listens and responds. In other words, when an influential person talks, people listen.

Some people may assume that **influence** is basically the same thing as verbal participation. While it is often the case that active verbal participants have a great deal of influence as a result of providing many ideas, just because someone is talking a lot does not mean that other people will necessarily listen to that person. However, if other group members perceive that person's ideas as being good ones, influence and verbal participation are likely to be highly correlated. As was earlier implied, a person's status also affects the degree to which that person will have influence. People of higher status are usually more influential.[11]

NON-VERBAL INVOLVEMENT

Verbal participation is one obvious indicator of group involvement that has been discussed earlier in this section. However, there are also some interesting **non-verbal** indicators of the extent to which any given member is involved in the group's activities.

For example, involved group members are more likely to lean forward *into* the group, make strong or quick gestures with their hands, and so on. In contrast, less involved or frustrated group members may lean backward *out of* the group, look away, cross their legs, fold their arms across their chests, and so on. By analyzing such non-verbal indicators, a group member can better select appropriate process facilitation techniques to get the entire group working together again.

COHESIVENESS

A relatively long-term group in which all members are highly involved, work well together, and express a strong desire to stay together is said to be a *cohesive* group.[12] Research on cohesive work groups indicates that a high degree of **cohesiveness** typically results in a high level of task performance—but only when the goals of the cohesive work group match the goals of the organization.[13]

A cohesive group is likely to try hard to meet its goals. Therefore, if one of its goals is to relax and take it easy, that is probably what the group will do. Managerially guided goal-setting activities (see Chapter 9) that allow group members to participate in a meaningful way can help to make carefully nurtured cohesive groups become a major organizational strategic advantage, as opposed to a major organizational problem.

ANALYSIS & EVALUATION

Are Cohesive Work Groups Really a Good Idea?

Common sense suggests that cohesive work groups should perform better than work groups that are not cohesive. However, the results of organizational behavior research indicate that this is not always the case. Specifically, while a cohesive work group is more likely to accomplish what that group wants to accomplish, this will not lead to higher performance if there is a mis-match between the goals of the cohesive work group and the goals of the manager or organization.[14] This match versus mis-match concern raises a key question: Are cohesive work groups really something that a manager should encourage? *Analyze* and *evaluate* whether the best answer to this question is a single statement or one based on a contingency approach.

THE STAGES OF GROUP DEVELOPMENT MODEL

The general nature of the task- and process-related activities of small groups over time served as the focus of two important studies spearheaded by a researcher named Tuckman.[15] The results of those studies suggest that most small groups appear to go through a particular set of stages during the course of their existence, beginning when each group is formed and ending when that group disbands.

The five stages in the **Stages of Group Development Model** have been cleverly labeled as Forming, Storming, Norming, Performing, and Adjourning.[16] Each of these stages is described in the following subsections.[17]

FORMING

The first stage in the Stages of Group Development Model is **Forming**. When a small group is initially formed, its members tend to be unsure of exactly what the group is about, what their roles within the group should be, how they are supposed to behave in the group, and so on. Therefore, group members typically engage in what might be called **testing behavior**. In other words, members test the limits on how they can behave and what tasks they can perform.

Note that if some forms of standards already exist concerning behavior and group task-related activities, these standards provide quick answers to any testing behavior. For example, if an organization has already developed a code of ethics, any new group formed within that organization is likely to follow that code of ethics during its interactions. In addition, if a group is explicitly formed for the purpose of developing a new product, group discussion is much more likely to focus on product development than on finding new suppliers, revising the criteria for giving employees pay raises, or organizing an after-work party. However, the members of a cross-functional team will typically have a great deal of flexibility regarding the tasks they perform as members of that group. This is in stark contrast to a work group at a bank composed of a supervisor and eight tellers, whose jobs are described in detailed job descriptions.

Another important source of answers about appropriate group behavior and activities is an assigned facilitator or leader, or any *emergent* facilitators or leaders among the group members. Group members often come to depend on these assigned or emergent facilitators or leaders to state or suggest what should be taking place within the group. Uncertainty about what group members should be doing in a group may create discomfort for many members, so facilitators or leaders who act to reduce that uncertainty will tend to increase the comfort levels of those members.

STORMING

The second stage in the Stages of Group Development Model is **Storming**. Not surprisingly, some group members may object to the directions in which preexisting standards, assigned facilitators or leaders, or especially emerging facilitators or leaders are attempting to move the group. Therefore, some degree of conflict at this stage of group development is highly likely (see Chapter 5). Various individuals within the group may have strong opinions about what group task-related activities or group behaviors are most appropriate based on their past experiences, their personal values and priorities, and so on.

For example, students who are working on a group project are likely to have some disagreements about what needs to be done, who is going to perform which tasks, the value of being on time to group meetings, the importance of completing tasks in a timely manner, and so forth. A group of nurses and its manager might have conflicting opinions regarding the relative importance of providing high-quality patient care versus increasing productivity by seeing as many patients as possible each day. A conflict that often arises in groups occurs when two or more members compete for the position of group leader.

NORMING

In most small groups, conflicts that arise during the Storming stage are eventually worked out to a significant extent. During the course of the third stage of group development, referred to as **Norming**, the group develops norms concerning how members should behave in the group. In addition, the group determines which roles group members must play and who is going to play them. Furthermore, the group develops plans regarding which tasks must be accomplished and who will be responsible for performing them. Hence—for the Stages of Group Development Model only—the definition of Norming includes task as well as process concerns related to getting group members organized and prepared to both act and interact.

In general, as a result of this stage of development, group members become more comfortable with each other and with the group's overall task.

PERFORMING

Once all of the hard work of resolving differences between group members and making a lot of important planning decisions has been largely completed, the group is now capable of actually doing what it was formed to do. During the fourth stage of group development, referred to as **Performing**, the energy of the group members becomes focused on performing the group's task.

This is not to say that further conflict will never arise within the group. Some group members may perform their tasks or roles more effectively than others, and actual implementation of a plan is frequently even more difficult than developing it. However, at this stage of group development, the trend is to accomplish—or at least partially accomplish—whatever the group has set out to do.

ADJOURNING

This fifth and final stage in group development, referred to as **Adjourning**, was added to the first four after it became clear that the disbanding or adjourning of a group was often of great significance for its members. This is particularly true in groups that have become cohesive, have a well-liked and respected facilitator or leader, or include members for whom the group is a key source of stability and comfort. However, even in instances where a group simply breaks up with little or no reaction on the part of its members, there is no question that the group has moved on to a different stage in its life cycle. It no longer exists, so its life as a group has ended.

**Moving Through the Stages
of Group Development**

From a manager's point of view, the Norming and Performing stages in group development seem likely to be a great deal more productive than the Forming and Storming stages, during which the members of a group will be preoccupied with testing behavior and interpersonal conflicts. Thus, most managers would probably prefer to "fast-forward" through these first two stages as rapidly as possible in real-world *applications* of this model. *Analyze* this issue to determine what kinds of actions a manager might take to facilitate a group's movement through these initial stages expeditiously, but without going so fast that additional problems will likely arise at a later stage. [Hint: Reading the rest of this chapter will help you develop answers to this HLLM.]

THE NORMATIVE MODEL OF GROUP EFFECTIVENESS

The **Normative Model of Group Effectiveness,** created by Hackman,[18] deals with the design of *work teams, (i.e., focused, synergistic groups)*. It prescribes which characteristics should exist for a team to be able to perform its task effectively. It is also an integrative model in that it brings together ideas from a variety of organizational behavior research efforts related to groups and teams, and considers factors both within the group and in the group's surrounding environment. Because Hackman's own preference was to use the term "group" rather than "team," so will most of this chapter.

Several points should be kept in mind when use of the Normative Model of Group Effectiveness is being contemplated. The model is designed to apply specifically to work groups in organizations: real, ongoing groups with members who play particular roles, operating within an organizational context and performing one or more tasks that lead to clear and measurable group outputs. Thus, for example, the model would be useful in the case of a group of production workers. Note that it might also aid a group of students working on a group project. However, the model is not designed to apply to a social group, a department in which there is little interaction between workers, or a group that is not part of an organization.

Figure 4-1 shows a complete diagram of the Normative Model of Group Effectiveness.

GROUP DESIGN

The design of a group centers around three key elements: the structure of the task, the composition of the group, and group norms about performance processes.

The **structure of the task**—in other words, the *task design*—may be designed to be highly motivational by applying the Job Characteristics Model (see Chapter 3). As is readily evident in the discussion in Chapter 3, the Job Characteristics Model proposes that skill variety, task identity, task significance, autonomy and feedback from the job are five key factors that can make a job more motivating for many—but not all—employees. The Normative Model of Group Effectiveness basically applies the

Figure 4-1   The Normative Model of Group Effectiveness

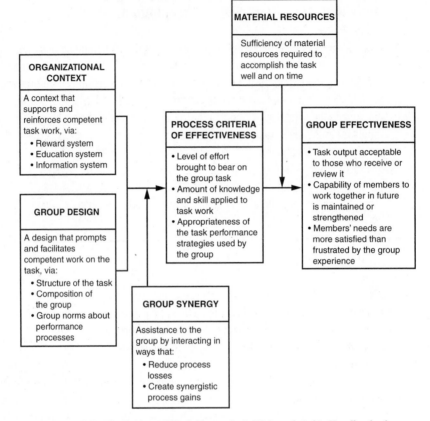

Source: Hackman, J. R. The Design of Work Teams. In J. W. Lorsch (ed.), *Handbook of Organizational Behavior.* Englewood Cliffs, NJ: Prentice Hall, 1987.

Job Characteristics Model of work design or redesign to a *group task* instead of an *individual job.*

Composition of the group appeared as a topic in the subsection on group dynamics earlier in this chapter. An important group composition issue concerns how a group's members should be chosen to best enhance that group's effectiveness. The Normative Model of Group Effectiveness suggests four key criteria for choosing group members:

1. Group members should have expertise that is relevant to the task to be performed. For example, a group that is writing a report needs members who are skilled at performing research and writing up their results.

2. Large groups are inefficient, as noted in the discussion on social loafing earlier in this chapter. Therefore, small groups are better. In fact, some research contends that groups slightly smaller than necessary to accomplish the task are the most effective (e.g., use four people if five people would be a reasonable group size for a particular task).

3. Group members need to have at least moderate interpersonal skills. Otherwise, they will most likely create group process problems.

4. A *moderately* diverse group creates a good balance between valuable variety and the ability to work together effectively. Major differences often create problems. However, so does substantial member similarity, as there is not enough diversity to develop an adequate level of creativity or to ensure that helpful, constructive conflict occurs.

Which of the many possible **group norms about performance processes** is optimal for any given task in any given organization is difficult to predict. However, the Normative Model of Group Effectiveness contends that certain *kinds* of group norms increase the group's chances of developing good strategies for performing its task and then actually implementing those strategies effectively.

One property of good group norms is that the norms support self-regulation. In other words, if things get out of hand, the group has developed norms that are sufficiently clear and well supported by group members that they can readily be used to bring the group back on track. Self-regulation norms may apply to individual members of the group or to the group as a whole.

Another property of good group norms is that the norms support situation scanning and strategy planning. This means looking carefully at what needs to be done, at what opportunities are available, and then developing a number of possible strategies before finally deciding on the best approach. Research shows that groups in which a member says, "this looks like something I've done before, and here is how we did it," are likely to produce *less* effective performance strategies for dealing with the *current* problem.

ORGANIZATIONAL CONTEXT

The Normative Model of Group Effectiveness argues that good group design alone does not guarantee group effectiveness. The organizational context for the group—in other words, aspects of the environment *surrounding* the group (see Chapter 3 for a related discussion of "context" satisfactions)—must also be supportive of the group. The three most important forms of support involve the organization's Reward System, Education System, and Information System.

A supportive **Reward System** begins with challenging, specific performance objectives or goals (see Chapter 9). Next, there must be positive consequences, or rewards, for excellent performance (see the integrated models in Chapter 3 and Chapter 9). Groups, like individuals, tend to focus more strongly on performing activities for which they are rewarded. One additional essential element of the Reward System, according to the Normative Model of Group Effectiveness, is to make sure that the goals are group goals and that the rewards are group rewards for group behavior. Ideally, all group members will make a serious effort to contribute to the achievement of the group's goals, and no social loafing will occur. Thus, all members will deserve any group rewards received.

The organization's **Education System** is the back-up system when the knowledge and skills needed to effectively complete a task do not exist within the group. Methods for providing whatever education may prove necessary range from creating easy access to an expert outside consultant—for answering quick questions that may arise—to full-scale training in new knowledge and skills.

Without adequate information, a group's plans are unlikely to be effective. Just as managers need a management information system to keep on top of what is happening in the organization, groups also need some sort of **Information System** that can supply useful, timely information. Note that just having computer resources available does not create an effective information system. Solid information about a group's *customers*—for example, bosses or other higher-level managers, end-users, other departments, and so on—is crucial. These are the people who will eventually evaluate the adequacy of the group's output, be that a product or a service. Other key information needs include which material resources will be made available, as well as details regarding the task itself and any potential constraints on how the task can be achieved.

GROUP SYNERGY

In a really good group, 2 + 2 = 5 rather than 4. This is a mathematical analogy to the concept of **synergy**, in which the effects of the group working together lead to an outcome that exceeds the sum of the individual group members' contributions. Achieving positive group synergy is easier to describe than to actually do. The Normative Model of Group Effectiveness suggests that for a group to attain **group synergy**, it is necessary to both **Reduce Process Losses** and **Create Synergistic Process Gains**.

Process Losses occur each time group members must coordinate with one another, since such coordination reduces the time and effort the group can focus on accomplishing its task. Some degree of coordination is essential, but too much gets in the way. Forming smaller groups is one way to reduce the amount of coordination that will be required.

A second common source of Process Losses results when some group members lack motivation to put forth a good effort, so they let the rest of the group do most of the work. The research on social loafing presented earlier in this chapter indicates that this type of Process Loss is especially likely in larger groups. This is yet another reason why the Normative Model of Group Effectiveness recommends smaller groups to obtain the best possible group performance.

Process Losses will also arise when the group ignores or downplays the inputs of a group member in the area of his expertise, due to some reason that is not relevant to effective completion of the group's task. This might happen, for example, when a group member talks too much or acts in ways that other members find obnoxious. Alternatively, it might happen when a member has good ideas but lacks the verbal communication skills needed to present those ideas effectively. Note that at least some degree of these kinds of problems is bound to exist in virtually all groups. Hence, the idea is to try to *reduce* Process Losses as much as possible.

Process Losses also occur when implementation of the group's plans slips. Perfect implementation is difficult to accomplish, particularly if a plan is either unclear or not well accepted by some group members. However, quick recovery from any implementation slip is essential for high group performance.

In contrast, it is possible to Create Synergistic Process Gains by building shared commitment to the group and its work. Such shared commitment is easier to facilitate when people value their membership in the group, enjoy working with their fellow group members, and so forth. Helping each other to learn more of the required knowledge and skills—through cross training, for example—is another approach to causing synergistic effects. Developing creative ideas as a result of group members working together and pooling their best ideas and insights constitutes a third helpful and positive way to Create Synergistic Process Gains.

PROCESS CRITERIA OF EFFECTIVENESS

According to the Normative Model of Group Effectiveness, there are three criteria or standards against which the effectiveness of a group process should be compared. These are:

1. The Level of Effort Brought to Bear on the Group Task

2. The Amount of Knowledge and Skill Applied to Task Work

3. The Appropriateness of the Task Performance Strategies Used by the Group.

At this point, the thoroughness of the Normative Model of Group Effectiveness can be made clearer. Each of the three **Process Criteria of Effectiveness** corresponds to particular factors included in Figure 4-1 under the Group Design, Organizational Context, and Group Synergy boxes, respectively.

A high **Level of Effort Brought to Bear on the Group Task** is likely to result under four conditions. The first condition, from the Group Design box in Figure 4-1, is when the Structure of the Task—i.e., the task design—for the group as a whole is highly motivational. This means that the task is designed to involve a good deal of skill variety, task identity, task significance, autonomy, and feedback from the job. The second condition (from the Organizational Context box in Figure 4-1) is when the Reward System provides positive consequences, or rewards, for good performance. The third condition (from the Group Synergy box in Figure 4-1) is when the group Reduces Process Losses caused by the need to coordinate between group members or a lack motivation on the part of some group members. And the fourth condition (from the positive side of the Group Synergy box), is when shared commitment allows the group to Create Synergistic Process Gains.

The appropriate **Amount of Knowledge and Skill Applied to Task Work** similarly depends on four key factors. The first, (derived from the Group Design box in Figure 4-1) is a Composition of the Group that is based on choosing group members who have expertise that is highly relevant to the task to be performed. The second (from the Organizational Context box in Figure 4-1), is an Education System that provides the necessary knowledge and skills when those needed to effectively complete a task do not currently exist within the group. The third (drawn from the Group Synergy box in Figure 4-1) is Reducing Process Losses by making sure that rather than choosing to ignore or downplay the inputs of a group member in the area of his expertise, each member's area of expertise is in fact *used*. The fourth, taken (once again) from the Group Synergy box in Figure 4-1, is Creating Synergistic Process Gains by encouraging members to help each other to learn more of the required knowledge and skills, thereby enhancing the group's overall capabilities.

Finally, the **Appropriateness of the Task Performance Strategies Used** by the Group will likewise be increased under four conditions. The first condition (from the Group Design box in Figure 4-1) is if Group Norms About Performance Processes both enable self-regulation of the group members' behavior toward task completion and support situation scanning and strategy planning. The second condition (from the Organizational Context box in Figure 4-1) is if the group can develop or access an Information System that can supply useful, timely information—especially regarding the group's customers, the resources that will be available to the group, further details regarding the group's task, and potential constraints on completion of the group's task. This allows the group to evaluate alternative strategies before choosing the best one. The third condition (from the Group Synergy box in Figure 4-1) is if minimizing the times when implementation of the group's plans slips allows the group to Reduce Process Losses. The fourth and last condition (also from the Group Synergy box) is if developing creative ideas as a result of group members working together and pooling their best ideas and insights leads to innovative performance plans, thus Creating Synergistic Process Gains.

ANALYSIS, SYNTHESIS & EVALUATION

The Level of Integration in the Normative Model of Group Effectiveness

Looking back over the preceding several pages, *analyze* the sets of key factors covered under each aspect of Group Design, the Organizational Context, and Group Synergy, and then compare them with the key factors that have been integrated in the Process Criteria of Effectiveness section. How many of the key factors were left out of the *integration*? Are any parts of the key factors missing? Next, consider how the few missing elements might also be integrated (*synthesized*) into the Process Criteria of Effectiveness. Finally, *evaluate* the overall quality of the original integration that has been labeled the Process Criteria of Effectiveness. Does this integration seem likely to be helpful to practicing managers who are attempting to design new groups in such a way that the groups will be as effective as possible? Does this integration appear likely to be helpful to practicing managers who are scrutinizing existing groups to determine why they are not as effective as originally planned or hoped?

MATERIAL RESOURCES

Material resources refer to resources other than the resource-like items already included as part of the Organizational Context. Such material resources are tangible items that can be purchased, including equipment, work space, raw materials, and tools. Without adequate material resources, even the best groups struggle.

GROUP EFFECTIVENESS

The Normative Model of Group Effectiveness suggests that if all of the elements of the model described in this section are carefully created and managed, a significant degree of group effectiveness will result.

Developing high-quality Group Effectiveness standards against which the *actual* group performance can be compared is fraught with difficulty (see Chapter 9). This is likely to be especially true in an ongoing organization, in which group tasks—like many managers' tasks—are often difficult to measure *objectively* (again, see Chapter 9).

The Normative Model of Group Effectiveness provides a set of performance standards that focuses on task output, future group synergy, and group member satisfaction (see also Chapters 3, 8, and 9). Note that the standards suggested by the Normative Model of Group Effectiveness set the group performance bar at a level that emphasizes *essential minimums*. More specifically, the model states that **task output should be at least acceptable; future group synergy should be at least maintained, if not strengthened; and group member satisfaction should be at least somewhat positive, as opposed to negative.** This is not to imply that group performance standards could not be set at higher levels. The point is that group performance standards should be set *at least* this high. In most organizations, the most common scenario is that performance standards will be raised over time.

Implementation of the Normative Model of Group Effectiveness actually requires using an **action model version** of the Normative Model that builds upon concepts developed in the original version of that model. A diagram of the four stages in the action model version of the Normative Model of Group Effectiveness appears in Figure 4-2.

APPLICATION: PRACTICAL GUIDELINES FOR IMPLEMENTING THE NORMATIVE MODEL OF GROUP EFFECTIVENESS

This section supplies some practical details and suggestions for implementing the Normative Model of Group Effectiveness[19] in actual work or classroom situations. To accomplish such an implementation, it is *crucial* to heed the words of Hackman.[20]

Implementation of the Normative Model of Group Effectiveness actually requires using an **action model version** of the Normative Model that builds upon concepts developed in the original version of that model. A diagram of the four stages in the action model version of the Normative Model of Group Effectiveness appears in Figure 4-2.

Note especially that the second factor in Stage 1 focuses on critical task demands.[21] These are determined by analyzing which of the three Process Criteria of Effectiveness are critical for the particular group being created. The first three boxes in the original Normative Model of Group Effectiveness have been used to establish the various pieces that are synthesized in the Process Criteria of Effectiveness (fourth box from the left). Now, in the *action model version* of that original model, all of those key concepts are utilized *very early* in the actual implementation sequence, allowing the manager(s) involved to place special emphasis on the factors most likely to enhance the success of the group being newly created.

STAGE 1: PREWORK

Stage 1 takes place *before* a group is actually formed. Hence, dealing with Stage 1 issues is normally the task of the manager or managers who decide that a team is the

Figure 4-2   Action Model Version of the Normative Model of Group Effectiveness

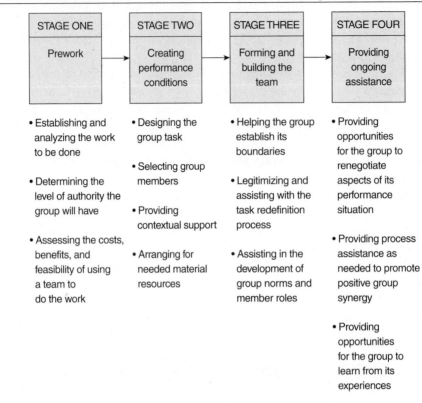

STAGE ONE	STAGE TWO	STAGE THREE	STAGE FOUR
Prework	Creating performance conditions	Forming and building the team	Providing ongoing assistance

- Establishing and analyzing the work to be done

- Determining the level of authority the group will have

- Assessing the costs, benefits, and feasibility of using a team to do the work

- Designing the group task

- Selecting group members

- Providing contextual support

- Arranging for needed material resources

- Helping the group establish its boundaries

- Legitimizing and assisting with the task redefinition process

- Assisting in the development of group norms and member roles

- Providing opportunities for the group to renegotiate aspects of its performance situation

- Providing process assistance as needed to promote positive group synergy

- Providing opportunities for the group to learn from its experiences

Source: Hackman, J. R. The Design of Work Teams. In J. W. Lorsch (ed.), *Handbook of Organizational Behavior.* Englewood Cliffs, NJ: Prentice Hall, 1987.

best way to cope with a particular problem or issue. Because the group does not yet exist, the group's members are not in a position to participate.

Establishing and analyzing the work to be done means that the manager(s) involved must first clearly determine, through careful thought and analysis, what the group task will be. If the group task is not clear and specific, it will be difficult to design a group that is even *potentially* capable of performing well—much less obtain a high level of group performance.

Once a group task has been clearly defined, it is valuable to determine the critical task demands for that particular group task. Again, this requires reviewing the three Process Criteria of Effectiveness and analyzing which of them are likely to be critical to the successful achievement of that task. Greater management attention should then be given to those task demands that appear to be the most critical.

For example, the effectiveness of a group of custodians is likely to be driven by the Level of Effort applied by the group, rather than Knowledge and Skill or an Appropriate Task Performance Strategy. In such a group, the manager(s) involved should focus strongly on creating the four conditions that will specifically support a high Level of Effort. (See the previous section concerning the Process Criteria of Effectiveness for details.) On the other hand, an effective product-marketing group would require substantial Knowledge and Skill plus a very Appropriate Task Performance Strategy—in addition to a reasonably high Level of Effort. Within such a group, the manager(s) involved should focus more broadly on creating all three sets of four conditions described in the prior subsection concerning the Process Criteria of Effectiveness. However, since two of these three process criteria seem to be somewhat more important, then that is where the manager(s) involved should place the greatest emphasis.

Determining the level of authority the group will have means considering the extent to which the group being created should be *empowered*. Should the group be manager-led, self-managing—where group members manage their group in addition to performing the group task—or self-designed *and* self-managing? Often, a manager will decide to begin by giving a group a lower level of empowerment. Later in the group's existence, the manager may increase that group's level of empowerment after it has demonstrated that it has the necessary group knowledge and skills and has created a strong performance track record. Some companies have actually published levels of group empowerment and the criteria for attaining them so that group members are aware of what they need to do to achieve greater autonomy in their jobs. Bear in mind that empowerment plays a major role in determining just how motivational the Structure of the Task will be, as the extent of empowerment determines how much autonomy the group will experience.

Assessing the costs, benefits, and feasibility of using a team to do the work is the final aspect of Prework. This is essentially a means of double-checking to make absolutely certain that creating a new team is the best approach to effectively completing a particular task. Teams are advantageous in numerous ways, but can also require a lot of time, effort, and resources. If it is not possible for the manager(s) involved to create a well-designed and well-supported group, perhaps other alternatives will be better overall choices.

STAGE 2: CREATING PERFORMANCE CONDITIONS

As is the case for Stage 1, Stage 2 takes place *before* a group is actually formed. Hence, dealing with Stage 2 issues is also normally the task of the manager or managers who decide that a team is probably the best way to cope with a particular problem or issue. However, members of *self-designing* teams will become involved in selecting group members as well as managing other aspects of their Group Design. Note that management will always retain responsibility for providing a supportive Organizational Context.

Designing the group task focuses on structuring the task in ways that will likely increase the motivation of future group members. Again, the core job characteristics of Skill Variety, Task Identity, Task Significance, Autonomy, and Feedback from the job can now be applied to the group task rather than to an individual job (see Chapter 3). For example, the degree of empowerment largely sets the amount of team Autonomy, while a group in which members are allowed to perform a variety of different sub-tasks over time will create significant Skill Variety.

Selecting group members is an absolutely *crucial* step. While clearly an important step for any manager of any group, the careful choosing of members is conceivably even more important for a self-designed group. This is because the members of a self-designed group will have to co-exist with their choices every time the members of their group interact—which, in most groups, is quite frequently. As a reminder, the following are four criteria for choosing group members:

1. Members should have expertise that is highly relevant to the task to be performed.

2. The group should be kept small.

3 Members should have at least moderate interpersonal skills.

4. The group should be moderately diverse.

Group member selection should be based on these four criteria with special emphasis on what is needed to respond effectively to the critical task demands determined previously.

Providing contextual support requires developing an appropriate Organizational Context consisting of a Reward System, an Educational System, and an Information System, as discussed in the previous section. Once again, bear in mind that the critical task demands should dictate which of these three systems merit(s) greater managerial emphasis for this particular group.

Arranging for needed material resources—equipment, work space, raw materials, and tools—is similarly relevant in creating appropriate performance conditions for the group before it begins.

STAGE 3: FORMING AND BUILDING THE TEAM

In contrast with Stages 1 and 2, Stage 3 takes place *when* a group is actually formed. Therefore, this stage involves not only the manager(s), but also the members of the group.

Forming and building the team—also known as group formation—is the process of bringing a group together for the first time to develop plans, norms, roles, and so on. The activities that occur early in a group's life set the tone for the duration of the group, so this is a *critical* time. Getting off to a good start helps *immensely* farther down the road. The *action model version* of the Normative Model of Group Effectiveness can supply insights that can make major contributions to successful group formation.

Helping the group establish its boundaries means helping the group to clarify who is or is not a member of the group. If this small but important step is inadvertently ignored, the resulting confusion may have a negative impact on group formation because tasks or roles may be assigned to presumed "group members" who will not in fact be around to complete them.

Legitimizing and assisting with the task redefinition process occurs as group members interpret the results of the initial task definition that took place during Stages 1 and 2. Misunderstandings need to be cleared up, and members may raise some issues that the manager(s) had not considered earlier. Clarifying the group task in greater detail increases the chances of everyone being on the same page, and reduces the chances of the group getting sidetracked and wasting a lot of effort.

From a *process* perspective, it has been noted in an earlier section of this chapter that norms usually develop implicitly. *Assisting in the development of group norms and member roles* during group formation, however, can potentially alter the nature of this development in ways that will improve it. If the group can begin by *explicitly* talking about what kinds of behaviors will be viewed positively by group members, the group is more likely to eventually perform at a higher level. Managers should encourage the creation of such explicit norms. This is particularly true for a self-managing group, since it is responsible for evaluating its own performance on a regular basis.

During a discussion of explicit norms, it is especially appropriate to consider norms that support self-regulation and/or situation scanning and strategy planning, as recommended in the Group Design box in the original Normative Model of Group Effectiveness. As was indicated previously, such norms serve to keep the group on track and to determine the best possible strategy for dealing with the *unique* aspects of the *current* situation.

Members' roles involve both what they will do (task) and how they will do that (process). Discussing the individual members' roles up front, and how they will be combined to result in the completion of the overall group task, also contributes to getting the group off to a good start.

Note that all of these forms of clarification are quite helpful in creating a situation where a manager can let an empowered group take greater control while being clearly headed in the right direction.

STAGE 4: PROVIDING ONGOING ASSISTANCE

Stage 4 takes place *after* a group has been formed. Common sense might suggest that this would be the ideal time for a group's manager to instruct and motivate group members to perform the group task well. However, Hackman suggests that a more effective approach "is to design and manage a group so that task-effective group processes emerge naturally."[22] Hence, the first three stages are arguably the most important aspects of *implementing* the Normative Model of Group Effectiveness because, once again, they get the group off to a good start.

Realistically, though, some aspects of the Group Design or Organizational Context may not work out as originally envisioned. *Providing opportunities for the group to renegotiate aspects of its performance situation* is a logical way to make appropriate adjustments. But rather than having the manager tell the group what is wrong and how to correct that, it is better to hold occasional performance reviews involving the group plus its manager. Such reviews can be used to jointly analyze which aspects of the group and its activities may be hurting the group's performance. Any problem areas identified during the course of such a review should be followed up by determining possible ways for effectively dealing with them (see Chapter 9).

Providing process assistance as needed to promote positive group synergy is another way of saying that it will be helpful to Reduce Process Losses and Create Synergistic Process Gains. Both the manager's and the group members' general awareness of group dynamics (see the initial section of this chapter) will definitely help to accomplish this. In particular, the manager's and the group members' task and process facilitation skills will be especially valuable.

Providing opportunities for the group to learn from its experiences is highly recommended as a way for a group to mature and develop over time, and to assure that the group retains what it has learned so that this knowledge can be used as a basis for performing at a higher level in the future. One possible good time for a typically busy work group to engage in this kind of reflection is immediately after completion of a major phase of the overall group task. The group's manager should encourage and support this learning activity.

APPLICATION & ANALYSIS   Uncovering the Contingency Approach

How is the contingency approach blended into the Normative Model of Group Effectiveness? Carefully review the material covered in the preceding Application section. Which aspects of the implementation process "depend on the situation"?

APPLICATION EXAMPLE

Creating an Effective Team for a Group Project Assignment

To illustrate the essentials of applying the action model version of the Normative Model of Group Effectiveness to a real-life situation, the following is an example involving a group of students working on a group project. Note that this is a general example, not a specific example based on a particular student group.

Effective implementation of the *action model version* of the Normative Model of Group Effectiveness begins with Stage 1: Prework.

The first concern for any group is to clearly determine what its group task will be. In a student group project, this is most often decided by the instructor who assigns the group task.

The next Prework implementation issue is to determine the critical task demands for that particular group task. Is it likely to require a high Level of Effort Brought to Bear on the Group Task? Is it likely to require a high Amount of Knowledge and Skill Applied to Task Work? Is the Appropriateness of the Task Performance Strategies Used by the Group likely to have a strong impact on the group's performance on the group project, or would almost any strategy be appropriate?

continues

In this example, the instructor should have carefully considered these questions. For many student group projects, all three of the critical task demands are likely to affect the group's success. If so, all elements covered in the model will be important, and thus no particular elements should be emphasized more than others. However, if one or two of the critical task demands are clearly more important than the others, then the key elements underlying those critical task demands deserve greater emphasis.

A third Prework implementation issue that the instructor should have considered by this point is the degree to which the student project groups will be empowered. Will the instructor lead the groups or will the groups be self-managing? Many student project groups are designed to be self-managed. However, an even higher level of empowerment results when a group is both self-designed *and* self-managing.

Student project groups often are empowered to deal with the Stage 3: Forming and Building the Team process (to be discussed shortly), which is a very important aspect of getting a group off to a good start. But a key question is whether students will be allowed to participate in the actual *selection* of group members. This is a much more challenging and time-consuming process. It requires careful research on the part of the students, plus some significant opportunities to get to know other students before it is time to make group member choices.

The final Prework implementation issue that the instructor should have considered already is whether using a team is the best possible choice for accomplishing the group task. As this is both a *group* project assignment and a *learning* experience for the students participating in it, the instructor has clearly already decided to use a team approach even if it will *not* necessarily lead to the best possible outcome.

Effective implementation of the action model version of the Normative Model of Group Effectiveness continues with Stage 2: Creating Performance Conditions.

The first element in Stage 2 focuses on structuring the task in ways that will likely increase the motivation of future group members. The instructor—or a self-designed group, if applicable—should look for ways to incorporate Skill Variety, Task Identity, Task Significance, Autonomy, and Feedback from the job. For example, a typical group project requires using a variety of group member skills; produces a "whole" project paper, or a presentation, or both; and gives the students involved considerable autonomy to self-manage their group while completing the task. Therefore, it is often not very difficult to provide substantial Skill Variety, Task Identity, and Autonomy. How might Feedback be incorporated as well?

Actually selecting the group members is the second element in Stage 2. This might be done by the instructor or by the group itself, if the group is self-designed. Regardless of who ultimately determines the composition of a group, the four key criteria for choosing group members are as follows:

continues

1. Members should have expertise that is highly relevant to the task to be performed.

2. The group size should be kept small.

3. Members should have at least moderate interpersonal skills.

4. The group should be moderately diverse.

The second and fourth criteria are generally easier to implement than the first and third, as the latter require doing a lot more homework prior to making good group member choices.

The next implementation element to consider in Stage 2 is providing contextual support. One aspect of the Organizational Context for a group project assignment is explaining the grading criteria for the project (i.e., the Reward System). What must the project cover, both accurately and effectively, to merit a high grade? Another key aspect is indicating how to obtain the necessary knowledge (i.e., the Education System) to complete the project. For example, the instructor might recommend reading the course textbook, taking notes on class lectures, visiting local libraries, searching the Web, and so on. A third key aspect is creating an Information System. Information about customers—for example, bosses or other higher-level managers, end-users, other departments, and so on—is an essential element of a good Information System. In this group project, creating such an Information System might require that some project members eventually visit some local businesses as well as talk with the instructor. Clarifying details about the task and any constraints on its completion, as well as what resources are available, are additional critical elements involved in creating a good Information System. The instructor is the person to speak with regarding these latter concerns.

Finally, Material Resources include equipment, work space, raw materials, and tools. In the case of a group project, computer labs would likely provide applicable equipment. Work space would be supplied by classrooms or meeting rooms. Some examples of raw materials include printer toner and paper.

Once Stages 1 and 2 have been completed, the group can actually be formed. The three key concerns during Stage 3: Forming and Building the Team should involve the establishment of group boundaries, the task redefinition process, and the development of group norms and member roles.

Sometimes it is not always clear who is or is not a member of a project group, as some students may drop out of the class, not show up to meetings, and so forth. It is important to deal with this implementation issue as soon as possible, or it can have a negative effect on group formation.

When a self-managing group is developing plans to complete the group *task* for a group project, it is worthwhile to carefully examine the group project grading criteria. Such an

continues

analysis may lead the group to develop additional questions to ask the instructor, so that members are certain they are interpreting the group task correctly. It may help for group members to write down the results of the group discussion plus the instructor's answers, and to clearly confirm that all group members understand the task in the same way.

Group *process* concerns are frequently a problem for members of student project groups, so it makes sense for group members to talk about them during their initial group meetings. Some common concerns include being on time to group meetings, communicating effectively with other members of the group, meeting deadlines, and so on. Ideally, such concerns would affect the selection of group members in the first place. If that is not possible, it is advisable to work on creating strong explicit norms during early group meetings so that every member of the group knows what everyone else's expectations are. This explicit norms issue may be especially important within a self-managing group, as group members' evaluations may depend—at least in part—on how well they meet the expectations of their peers.

While discussing group norms explicitly, it is worthwhile to discuss norms that support self-regulation and/or situation scanning and strategy planning. Once again, such norms will serve to keep the group on track and to determine the best possible strategy for dealing with the *unique* aspects of the *current* situation. For example, a strong norm about being on time to meetings is self-regulatory.

As another example, carefully consider the possibility that the current group project has *different* requirements for obtaining a high grade than did a successful project completed by one of the group members in a different class last semester. In other words, don't just blindly apply the same approach used last semester to the current group project, or the group's grade on the current project may be lower than anticipated. Instead, scan the new situation and consider a number of possible strategies.

After explicit norms have been developed and the group task has been clearly understood, the individual roles to be played by group members can be decided. To determine who will perform which roles, it can be helpful to create a "responsibility matrix." List all of the sub-tasks to be completed along the left-hand side of a piece of paper, and all of the group members who will be available to perform these tasks across the top. Draw horizontal and vertical lines to create a grid. Then decide which group member(s) will perform which sub-tasks, and fill in the blank spaces in the responsibility matrix to show this. If any confusion should arise, discuss it with the instructor if necessary. Once this responsibility matrix has been completed and approved by the group members, arrange to make copies of it plus the list of explicit norms for everybody in the group. This will minimize later problems concerning who agreed to play which roles, which norms the group agreed to strongly support, and so forth.

continues

Stage 4: Providing Ongoing Assistance is generally a better fit for an industry situation than for a student group project. The instructor will typically be less actively involved in meeting with each of the student groups in a class. Responsibility for consulting the instructor as necessary will therefore fall upon the students, rather than the other way around. This greater degree of empowerment is driven by the instructor's desire to provide opportunities for the group to *learn*—a primary goal within a college setting. In effect, a significant part of any group's grade on a project rests on how well that student group *self-manages* its own group process.

That being said, the same Stage 4 issues should be dealt with, but mostly by the group, rather than by the group's manager. Once group formation has been completed and the project group is well underway, the group should use its members' knowledge of group dynamics—particularly facilitation techniques—to keep the group running as smoothly as possible. It can be worthwhile for the group to occasionally review its performance to identify potential problems earlier rather than later.

CONCLUSION

Unlike most chapters in this book, this chapter presents information on "best practices" before discussing organizational behavior models and guidelines indicating how to apply them. This is because group activities—and hence good group skills—are such critical behavioral concerns in work organizations. A clear understanding of group dynamics is a prerequisite for good task and process facilitation. The latter are essential for guiding a group's development through its various stages, and for minimizing group process losses and enhancing group synergy in particular.

A detailed presentation of a highly respected integrated model of factors that lead to effective teams is a central feature of this chapter. While designed primarily as an aid for work group managers, the Normative Model of Group Effectiveness contains a wealth of relevant material for groups that are self-managing and possibly self-designed as well. Practical guidelines for taking useful ideas from the Normative Model of Group Effectiveness and applying them to a developing group provide some valuable implementation information for members of any work group or any student project group.

EXERCISES AND OTHER ACTIVITIES
■ *Experiential Exercise: In-Class 4-1*

ANALYZING GROUP DYNAMICS: THE RELAY EXERCISE
The purpose of this exercise is to give people in the class an opportunity to work together on a task that requires cooperation and to create some group dynamics.

Exercise Process Outline
Form three approximately equal groups.

Your task in this exercise is to solve a problem related to organizational behavior. Your instructor will provide you with a sheet of paper containing a question concerning an organizational behavior topic. Your instructor will also make available several organizational behavior books, at least one of which will include the correct answer to the question on that sheet of paper.

Groups will have 15 to 20 minutes to develop their strategies for this exercise. Then the exercise will officially begin.

Groups will engage in the problem-solving activity one group at a time. A coin will be flipped prior to the official start of the exercise to determine which group goes first.

To make this exercise more interesting, the organizational behavior books will be located somewhere *outside* the classroom. Your instructor will let you know where the books will be located.

Each group will have 2 minutes during which all group members can get into position before the clock starts and the Exercise Rules to be presented shortly will apply. Your instructor will let you know when your 2 minutes are nearly up.

To officially begin the exercise for each group, your instructor will place the piece of paper containing the organizational behavior question face up on a table at the front of the classroom, while at the same time starting a stopwatch (or noting the current time) **Important:** The paper containing the organizational behavior question must stay on the table—and **please** do **not** write on it!

The exercise for each group will officially stop—and the time taken will be noted—when a **different** sheet of paper containing the group's answer to the organizational behavior question is placed on the table at the front of the classroom. Any group that does not provide an answer within 10 minutes will receive a score of zero.

When one group finishes the exercise, it should return to the classroom. After that group has returned, the next group will have 2 minutes to get into position.

After everything has been completed, your instructor will determine if any member of any group has been observed breaking any of the exercise rules. Then your instructor will determine each group's score using the following formula:

$$\text{Score} = \frac{\% \text{ Correct}}{\text{Time Taken}}$$

Finally, the class will discuss the results of the exercise.

Exercise Rules

No talking or loud sounds.

No use of technology (such as cellular phones, portable computers, PDAs, pagers, and so on). Each group member's feet can move only once per foot per minute.

The three books must remain within a few feet of where you find them.

Groups must stay in the classroom **except** during an actual time trial.

Groups **not** being timed must stay out of the way.

You may **not** use any **elevators.**

Please do **not endanger** the lives of any people nearby!

Please do **not disturb** other classes.

■ *Experiential Exercise: In-Class 4-2*

GROUP DYNAMICS DURING DISCUSSION OF A CURRENT ISSUE: A MORE IN-DEPTH VERSION

The purpose of this exercise is to apply concepts from the In-Class Exercise 4-1, Analyzing Group Dynamics, based on observations of interactions within a small group.

Exercise Process Outline

Your instructor will choose a topic of interest to students at your university or college.

Form a small group in a semi-circle at the front of the classroom, composed of four students plus the instructor. Students who have strong feelings about this topic, or some experience with it, would be excellent choices for inclusion in this small group.

The small group will discuss the topic.

Form groups of 5 to 7 students. The four students who were members of the small group should also form a group to provide an active participant's perspective.

Analyze each of the subtopics in the Analyzing Group Dynamics section of this chapter with respect to what has just occurred within the small group. Each member of your group should be responsible for presenting your group's consensus for at least one of the subtopics. (Some people will need to be responsible for two subtopics.)

After the groups have discussed their observations and developed answers, each group will present its findings and discuss them with the class as a whole.

■ *Experiential Exercise: In-Class 4-3*

GROUP DYNAMICS DURING DISCUSSION OF A CURRENT ISSUE: A SHORTER VERSION

The purpose of this exercise is to apply concepts from the section in this chapter on Analyzing Group Dynamics, based on observations of interactions within a small group when limited time is available for analysis and discussion.

Exercise Process Outline

Your instructor will choose a topic of interest to students at your university or college.

Form a small group in a semi-circle at the front of the classroom, composed of four students plus the instructor. Students who have strong feelings about this topic, or some experience with it, would be excellent choices for inclusion in this small group.

The small group will discuss the topic.

Your instructor will initiate a class discussion. The students who observed the small group dynamics should now analyze each of the subtopics in the Analyzing Group Dynamics section with respect to what has just occurred within the small group.

For some of the subtopics, it may be interesting to contrast the observations of those watching the group in action with the impressions of those who actually participated in the group discussion.

■ *Experiential Exercise: In-Class 4-4*

THE IDEAL GROUP PROCESS

The purpose of this exercise is to develop a profile for an "ideal" group process based on the subtopics covered in the Analyzing Group Dynamics section.

Exercise Process Outline

Form groups of 5 to 7 students.

Using the various subtopics covered in the Analyzing Group Dynamics section as a guide, discuss how a group should ideally conduct its activities with respect to each subtopic. Some examples of the kinds of questions to consider during this exercise include the following: Should any conflict between group members be constructive or destructive? Should everyone in the group participate? What are some good norms for groups in general?

For each subtopic, be sure to designate a different person who will later be responsible for presenting the group's answer to the class if called upon.

When all groups have created profiles for an "ideal" group process, the class will discuss them.

■ *Experiential Exercise: In-Class 4-5*

DEVELOPING CRITERIA FOR CHOOSING PROJECT GROUP MEMBERS

The purpose of this exercise is to brainstorm some criteria for choosing project group members. This exercise will also provide each exercise participant with additional information about other class members who might potentially become members of that participant's project group.

Exercise Process Outline

Form groups of 5 to 7 students.

Brainstorm possible criteria for choosing project group members, then discuss them. Some examples of the kinds of criteria to consider during this exercise include the following: ability to do research, writing or presentation skills, interpersonal skills, time management skills, and dependability. [Tip: Remember to monitor your group's process while you are participating in this exercise. Try to make your process as ideal as possible.]

When all of the groups have developed sets of criteria, your instructor will list them on the board. The class as a whole will then discuss these ideas.

■ *Experiential Exercise: In-Class 4-6*

CHOOSING PROJECT GROUP MEMBERS AND INITIATING GROUP
FORMATION

The purpose of this exercise is to choose project group members and then provide time
to begin the important process of group formation.

Pre-Exercise Activity: Informally Applying Matrix Management Skills

Your instructor will set a deadline date for choosing project group members, at which
time the group formation portion of this exercise will be conducted in class.

In the meantime, you have a choice with respect to choosing project group members.
You may opt to wait until after the deadline and see what you can work out at the
beginning of the group formation portion of this exercise. Or, you may prefer to be
more proactive, and informally seek out other class members with whom you might
have interest in forming a project group.

Should you decide to take a more proactive approach, you will need to think like a
manager (or participant) in a matrix organization. A matrix organization contains functional managers and project managers. Employees within a matrix organization work
directly under the functional managers but also join various project groups that are led
by project managers. Functional managers directly manage, train, and evaluate their
subordinates—just like "normal" managers do. Project managers, in contrast, typically
have less Formal Authority (see Chapter 6) than do functional managers. As a result,
they must try to determine which employees would *probably* make the best project
group members, and then *persuade* those employees to join their project groups.

If you choose to think like a project *manager*, you will need to determine which criteria for choosing group members are most important to *you*; gather information about
other class members abilities, skills and traits *as best you can*; and then try to persuade
the *key people* you have identified to join your group.

If you choose to think like an employee who wishes to join a project group, you will
need to think carefully about which abilities, skills, and traits you possess that might be
of *value* to a project group, then seek out a currently forming group that would *likely be
in need* of at least some of those abilities, skills, and traits. Savvy employees become
aware of the project group leaders for whom they would like to work, as well as which
other employees are more likely to contribute positively to a successful project.

Exercise Process Outline

Depending on what has occurred informally between the time your instructor set the
deadline date for the group formation portion of this exercise and the actual deadline,
some groups will have formed completely, some groups will have formed in part, and
some people may still be looking for a group to join.

If your group is already complete, you now have a large block of time in which to go
through the important process of group formation. [Hint: Ideas concerning what should
occur during group formation (Stage 3) are presented in the Application section of this
chapter.]

If your group is only partially complete, you will need to spend some of that valuable group formation time doing some additional recruiting of people who have not yet joined a group. [Hint: Think about which criteria are most important to the existing members of the group, and also which skill needs the group is still looking to fill. Another key issue to consider is group size.]

If you have not yet joined a group, mentally review your project group skills and then try to persuade others that you will be a valuable addition to their existing or potential group. [Hint: The longer you wait, the fewer the options that are likely to be available to you.]

■ *Experiential Exercise: In-Class 4-7*

FORMING PROJECT GROUPS

The purpose of this exercise is to choose project group members and then begin the important process of group formation.

Exercise Process Outline

Your instructor will ask everyone in the class to take 5 minutes to think carefully about the abilities, skills and traits each of you would *value* in another project group member—and also about the abilities, skills, and traits *you* could *contribute* as a project group member.

Spend 20 minutes informally circulating around the classroom and talking to other people in the class. Ask the people you meet which abilities, skills, and traits they would value in another project group member. Tell them about the abilities, skills, and traits that you could contribute as a project group member. This part of the exercise is purely informational, so try to keep an open mind—and **please do not commit** to forming any groups just yet.

Your instructor will then ask everyone to take a seat and think about what he or she has just learned. Which other people seem like they would be good possibilities for your potential future group members?

Now actual group formation can begin. How this happens is up to you. A common strategy is to form a small group of 2 to 3 members, and then add some additional members until the group is complete. Ideally, the initial members of a group should *significantly* agree on key criteria for choosing group members, and as well as on the eventual size of the group. As you'll recall, organizational behavior research indicates that optimal group size is 5 to 7 people. Some groups may wish to think in terms of a range of numbers, whereas others may decide on a specific number for one or more reasons.

Once your group is complete, focus on the important process of group formation (Stage 3). [Hint: Ideas concerning what should occur during group formation are presented in the Application section of this chapter.]

■ *Experiential Exercise: Field 4-1*

GROUP PAPER GUIDELINES

Purpose and Focus of the Paper

The purpose of this paper is to demonstrate your ability to relate this chapter's Applications section's implementation recommendations based on the *action model version* of the Normative Model of Group Effectiveness to what has occurred in a recently formed work group in a real-world work organization of your choice.

This paper should focus on a work group that has gone through its group formation (Stage 3) process fairly recently (within the past year or so). Analyzing a smaller work group (10 people or less) is highly recommended. Analyzing a very small work group (2 to 4 people) is not recommended because such a small group is unlikely to give you sufficient scope to show your in-depth understanding of how the model should be implemented.

Another key consideration when choosing an appropriate work group to analyze is how well the group's actual performance during its implementation matched what the *action model version* of the Normative Model of Group Effectiveness recommends *should* be done. A group that was essentially perfect will not give you much of an opportunity to display your analytical skills, as there will not be a great deal for you to say other than "this group did everything right." A group that was a total disaster with respect to its implementation would provide you with a huge opportunity to say all kinds of useful and relevant things, but you would never be able to squeeze all of that material into the space available. Thus, your best bet is to analyze a work group that has done some things as recommended, and some not.

Finally, as this book points out, the Normative Model of Group Effectiveness is not designed to apply to a department in which there is little interaction between workers. Choose a work group that spends a significant amount of time working together as a group. A work group within any of a variety of organizations would be an appropriate choice for analysis. Be sure to focus on a work organization, (i.e., one in which the people involved get paid for the work they perform). Examples include business organizations, governmental organizations, and some school organizations. If you do not have direct connections to any such organizations yourself, some of your friends, relatives, or neighbors surely do.

Your paper should provide an answer to the following key question: "How effective was the actual *implementation* of this work group?" In other words, how closely did the actual implementation match what is recommended by the guidelines that are supplied in the Application section of this chapter?

Required Format

Your paper should begin with a title page and contain five sections:

Title Page

1. Introduction

2. Background Information Concerning the Work Group to be Analyzed

3. Implementation Analysis

4. Evaluation

5. Bibliography

The **Title Page** should contain a descriptive title, your name, your affiliation, and the date. The title should provide some indication of the type of organization you are analyzing and should probably include the words "analysis" and "group." In this course, your affiliation is the course number and the name of your university or college.

The **Introduction** tells the reader what the paper will be about. It tells what you are trying to accomplish by writing this paper, *not* what you found. In other words, briefly state the purpose of the paper, not the results or conclusions.

The **Background Information Concerning the Work Group to be Analyzed** section briefly describes the kind of work group being studied and the kind of organization it is housed within. Talk about the organization's products, services, or purpose; indicate how large it is; and so on. Then explain what the work group does and how it fits into the larger organization.

The **Implementation Analysis** section analyzes the effectiveness of the implementation of this particular work group according to the *action model version* of the Normative Model of Group Effectiveness. This requires following the guidelines supplied in the Application section of this chapter, in sequence, and comparing what actually happened with what the guidelines state should have happened. Obtaining accurate information concerning what actually happened is likely to be challenging, so try to talk to a variety of group members to incorporate different perspectives and to compensate for the forgetting factor. Be sure to provide examples and justifications to support why you think each step of the implementation took place—or did not take place—in the way you say it did. To make your analysis much easier for a reader to follow, *use titles rather than names* to identify any people within the organization being analyzed.

The **Evaluation** summarizes your *evaluation* of how well your chosen work group has done with respect to *application* of the implementation ideas prescribed by the *action model version* of the Normative Model of Group Effectiveness, based on the preceding *analysis*. Note that this is not an evaluation of the overall performance of the work group after its formation, but rather an evaluation of how the group was set up (Stages 1 and 2) and formed (Stage 3). Again, the typical work group will have ignored some of the *action model version* of the Normative Model's recommendations, but not others. Your Evaluation should recognize these differences rather than stating or implying that everything went perfectly (highly unlikely).

The **Bibliography**—or the List of References, or simply References—is a list of the literature sources you have drawn upon to write your paper. These sources should be presented in alphabetical order, by the last names of the first authors of each source. However, to save you from having to expend a great deal of extra time and effort doing research in the library, **for this class only** you should base your paper on the key original source (Hackman 1987) that was used as a basis for writing the two sections in this chapter that discuss the Normative Model of Group Effectiveness and its application.

The full reference for Hackman (1987) may be found in the Reference Notes section at the back of this chapter.

Giving Other Writers Credit by Citing Sources

It is very **important to give other writers credit for their ideas when you use those ideas in your paper**. You must do this even when you are not quoting other writers directly, since you are still making use of these writers' ideas. Copying other writers' work is permissible only if you use quotation marks or special indentations, give proper credit, and do not quote extensively. Otherwise, copying other writers' work is considered plagiarism. Plagiarism is both unethical and illegal.

The standard way of giving credit in academic journals that discuss organizational behavior topics is by citing the author(s) and the year of publication. For this paper, credit should be given to Hackman for the ideas taken from his lengthy 1987 book chapter by inserting the phrase Hackman (1987) or the phrase (Hackman, 1987) as appropriate. Virtually all U.S. organizational behavior journals use this technique rather than footnotes or endnotes. A key reason that textbooks such as this one do not also use this citation technique is because they typically contain so many citations that confusion would be created for the reader.

The following are some examples illustrating how this citation technique works:

> Hackman's (1987) Normative Model of Group Effectiveness provides a clear prescription for creating an effective work group.

> The Normative Model of Group Effectiveness provides a clear prescription for creating an effective work group (Hackman, 1987).

These examples illustrate two ways to cite a source. The first method, in which only the year of publication appears in parentheses, can be used anywhere within a sentence as long as the wording makes grammatical sense. The second method, in which both the name(s) of the author(s) and the year of publication appear in parentheses, typically involves inserting the name(s) and date either immediately after the idea for which credit is being given or at the end of the sentence. Either method gives credit where credit is due.

Notice that all citations—such as Hackman (1987) or (Hackman, 1987)—are included *within* the normal sentence structure. It is *not* correct to place citations after the period at the end of a sentence or paragraph. A citation is most commonly placed in the *first sentence* that discusses the ideas obtained from a given author or set of authors, and is presumed to apply until the writer switches to using a different set of ideas, which then triggers the inclusion of a different citation.

The full reference, which includes the title, publisher, and other information about the source, should appear *only* in the Bibliography (List of References) placed at the end of the paper. As was indicated earlier, the full reference for Hackman (1987) may be found in the Reference Notes section at the end of this chapter.

Writing Tips

When writing a paper of this kind, be sure to *avoid an outline format* in your writing style. In other words, *write complete sentences*, put the sentences in standard paragraph form, and so on. Avoid using bullets or numbered lists. They are appropriate for advertisements, and possibly for executive summaries, but not for a paper of this kind.

Proofreading your paper after it has been completed is highly recommended. If at all possible, put your paper aside for a few days (or at least a few hours) before reviewing it. This should greatly increase your proofreading effectiveness.

Finally, just before you print your paper, use a spell-checking program. Such software will not catch all of the mistakes you might have made, but it will spot many of the worst typographical and spelling errors. Such errors are eady tp makr (easy to make), but difficult to understand.

[Tip: A common misspelling is "manger" instead of "manager." Since "manger" is a correctly spelled word, catch it by doing a search-and-replace.]

Paper Length Limits

The length of your paper should be **6 to 8 pages double-spaced, using a 12-point font with 1-inch margins**. Be sure to number each page. This paper length limit does not include the Title Page, Bibliography, or any Appendices.

It is helpful to print the Title Page separately from the body of the paper. The first page with a number on it should be the page *following* the title page.

Grading Criteria

These are the criteria that will be used to evaluate your paper. Read them before beginning to write *or* proofread your paper. If your paper has addressed all of the items listed in the criteria, you are more likely to get a higher grade. [Note that the Application guidelines for the *action model version* of the Normative Model of Group Effectiveness similarly recommend that you carefully review any existing criteria for evaluating performance.]

1. **Overall Grasp of Material.** Based on the information supplied in this paper, does its writer understand how to implement the *action model version* of the Normative Model of Group Effectiveness in a real-world situation?

2. **Effectiveness of Implementation Analysis.** Did the writer effectively compare the Application section guidelines for implementing the *action model version* of the Normative Model of Group Effectiveness with what actually happened during the implementation sequence followed by the work group being studied? Did the writer provide examples and justifications to support why each step of the actual implementation took place—or did *not* take place—in the way the writer claims it did?

3. **Effectiveness of Evaluation.** Did the writer effectively evaluate how well the work group being analyzed performed with respect to applying the implementation recommendations prescribed by the *action model version* of the

Normative Model of Group Effectiveness, based on the preceding analysis? Did the writer realistically recognize that the work group did better in some ways than in others?

4. **Overall Effectiveness of Communication.** In the paper as a whole, is the content organized according to the required format, including required subtitles? Have citations been provided where appropriate in the body of the paper, using the modern citation technique (last name(s) plus year of publication, within the sentence structure)? Is the paper's writing style clear, flowing, and easy to follow? Is the paper written in a more objective third-person format rather than a more subjective first-person format using "I" or "we" (plus "my" or "our," etc.)? Is the paper free of typographical errors or blank spaces? Does the source listed in the Bibliography match the source cited in the body of the paper? Are the pages numbered properly?

REFERENCE NOTES

1. Cartwright, D., and A. Zander (eds.). *Group Dynamics: Research and Theory,* 3rd ed. New York, NY: Harper and Row, 1968; Shaw, M. E. *Group Dynamics: The Psychology of Small Group Behavior,* 3rd ed. New York, NY: McGraw-Hill, 1981.

2. Benne, K. D., and P. Sheats. Functional Roles of Group Members. *The Journal of Social Issues,* Vol. 4, 1948, pp. 42–47.

3. Cox, T. H., Jr. *Cultural Diversity in Organizations: Theory, Research, and Practice.* San Francisco, CA: Berrett-Koehler Publishers, 1993.

4. Shaw, M. E. *Group Dynamics: The Psychology of Small Group Behavior,* 3rd ed. New York: McGraw-Hill, 1981.

5. Karau, S. J., and K. D. Williams. Social Loafing: A Meta-analytic Review and Theoretical Integration. *Journal of Personality and Social Psychology,* Vol. 65, 1993, pp. 681–706.

6. Benne, K. D., and P. Sheats. Functional Roles of Group Members. *The Journal of Social Issues,* Vol. 4, 1948, pp. 42–47.

7. Underwood, W. Roles That Facilitate and Inhibit Group Development. In R. T. Golembiewski and A. Blumberg (eds.), *Sensitivity Training and the Laboratory Approach,* 3rd ed. Itasca, IL: Peacock Publishers, 1977.

8. Robbins, S. P. Training in Interpersonal Skills: TIPS for Managing People at Work. Englewood Cliffs, NJ: Prentice-Hall, 1989.

9. Hackman, J. R. Group Influences on Individuals in Organizations. In M. D. Dunnette and L. M. Hough (eds.), *Handbook of Industrial and Organizational Psychology,* 2nd ed., Vol. 3. Palo Alto, CA: Consulting Psychologists Press, 1992, pp. 199–268.

10. Shaw, M. E. *Group Dynamics: The Psychology of Small Group Behavior,* 3rd ed. New York: McGraw-Hill, 1981.

11. Strodbeck, F. L., R. M. James, and C. Hawkins. Social Status in Jury Deliberations. *American Sociological Review,* Vol. 52, 1957, pp. 713–719.

12. Cartwright, D. The Nature of Group Cohesiveness. In D. Cartwright and A. Zander (eds.), *Group Dynamics: Research and Theory,* 3rd ed. New York: Harper and Row, 1968.

13. Seashore, S. *Group Cohesiveness in the Industrial Work Group.* Ann Arbor, MI: Institute for Social Research, 1954.

14. Seashore, S. *Group Cohesiveness in the Industrial Work Group.* Ann Arbor, MI: Institute for Social Research, 1954.

15. Tuckman, B. W., and M. C. Jensen. Stages of Small-Group Development Revisited. *Group and Organization Studies,* Vol. 2, 1977, pp. 419–427.; Tuckman, B. W. Developmental Sequence in Small Groups. *Psychological Bulletin,* Vol. 63, 1965, pp. 384–399.

16. Tuckman, B. W., and M. C. Jensen. Stages of Small-Group Development Revisited. *Group and Organization Studies,* Vol. 2, 1977, pp. 419–427.

17. Tuckman, B. W. Developmental Sequence in Small Groups. *Psychological Bulletin,* Vol. 63, 1965, pp. 384–399.

18. Hackman, J. R. The Design of Work Teams. In J. W. Lorsch (ed.), *Handbook of Organizational Behavior.* Englewood Cliffs, NJ: Prentice Hall, 1987, pp. 315–342.

19. Hackman, J. R. The Design of Work Teams. In J. W. Lorsch (ed.), *Handbook of Organizational Behavior.* Englewood Cliffs, NJ: Prentice Hall, 1987, pp. 315–342.

20. Hackman, J. R. The Design of Work Teams. In J. W. Lorsch (ed.), *Handbook of Organizational Behavior.* Englewood Cliffs, NJ: Prentice Hall, 1987, p. 332.

21. Hackman, J. R. The Design of Work Teams. In J. W. Lorsch (ed.), *Handbook of Organizational Behavior.* Englewood Cliffs, NJ: Prentice Hall, 1987, pp. 333, 335.

22. Hackman, J. R. The Design of Work Teams. In J. W. Lorsch (ed.), *Handbook of Organizational Behavior.* Englewood Cliffs, NJ: Prentice Hall, 1987, p. 324.

CHAPTER 5
Conflict Management

In an increasingly fast-paced world filled with diverse people with diverse goals and views, the potential for conflict is greater than ever. Three major causes of conflict include communication, structural, and personal differences.[1] Communication-based differences occur when what people hear or read is different than what the communication sender intended. Structural differences result from the division of labor, or specialization, that takes place in the vast majority of modern organizations. Different functions, in particular, are likely to have different goals and concerns. For example, the accounting department's function is typically related to costs and minimizing them, whereas the marketing department often tends to spend money lavishly enroute to achieving its primary goal of pleasing customers. Personal conflicts are due to differences in individual values or personalities (see Chapter 2).

This chapter articulates a variety of ways to manage the kinds of conflicts noted above. A major model that describes several possible styles for dealing with conflict is covered first. Then an interesting joint problem-solving approach to dealing with conflict through negotiation is overviewed. The chapter concludes with guidelines for implementing the major model presented in the next section.

THE CONFLICT MANAGEMENT STYLES MODEL

The **Conflict Management Styles Model** focuses on five different styles of conflict management: Avoiding, Collaborating, Compromising, Forcing (Competing), and Accommodating, as shown in Figure 5-1. From a manager's point of view, these five styles can be categorized according to how much they emphasize the task (getting the job done) or the process (taking care of the people).[2] The concept of creating five conflict management styles based on two underlying dimensions has become very well established, with at least 40 organizational behavior research studies supporting it.[3]

An approach to conflict management that places low emphasis on the **task** and low emphasis on the **process** essentially leads to doing nothing. In other words, the conflict

Figure 5-1   The Five Conflict Management Styles

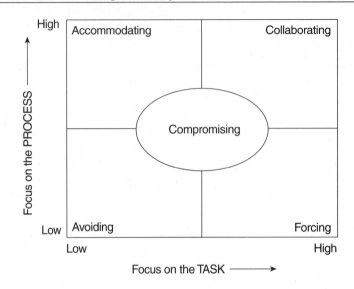

Source: Blake, R. R., and J. S. Mouton. *The Managerial Grid.* Houston, TX: Gulf Publishing, 1964, and Thomson, K. W. Conflict and Conflict Management. In M. D. Dunnette (ed.), *Handbook of Organizational Behavior.* Chicago: Rand-McNally, 1976.

that is taking place is ignored or avoided. Thus, **Avoiding** is an appropriate label for this conflict management style.

An approach to conflict management that is the diametric opposite of Avoiding is much more active, emphasizing both task and process. This style attempts to create a win-win solution that benefits all parties to the conflict. Since everyone works together collaboratively to solve the problem,[4] this style is called **Collaborating.**

Forcing (Competing) is an approach to conflict management that emphasizes the task and largely ignores the process. Forcing occurs whenever a manager steps in and makes the decision about how the conflict will be resolved. In other words, the manager forces a conflict decision. Competing is an alternative term that applies in situations where two parties are involved in a conflict and competing to see which party will win.[5]

An approach to conflict management that is diametrically opposite from Forcing places high emphasis on the process and low emphasis on the task. Its primary concern is with making one of the parties to the conflict happy. The disruption being created by the conflict is smoothed over by accommodating that party's needs.[6] Therefore, **Accommodating** is an excellent label for this style.

Finally, a fifth conflict management style results from taking a middle position on both task and process. This suggests some give-and-take, in which all parties to the conflict obtain at least part of what they desire through some sort of bargaining[7] or negotiating. That kind of activity leads to **Compromising.**

Since four of the five styles of the Conflict Management Styles Model are derived from combinations of extreme positions with respect to emphasis on the task or process, while the fifth style results from a central position on both task and process, these styles are relatively independent of one another. Thus, this particular model does not contain arrows indicating which factors lead to which other factors, as is the case for many of the models presented in other chapters. A more important concern of the Conflict Management Styles Model is how to choose the best style to use in any given situation. Clearly, this is once again a contingency approach (see Chapter 1).

The following sections summarize and describe some appropriate contingencies for each of the five conflict management styles. The summary lists of Contingency Factors are the results of a survey of chief executive officers (CEOs) conducted by an expert on conflict named Thomas.[8] Compromising has been shifted to the third position among the five styles because it is used so often and because it is closely related to Collaborating.

AVOIDING

Figure 5-2 illustrates the various Contingency Factors that suggest situations in which using the Avoiding conflict management style would be most appropriate. In other words, if many of the factors in Figure 5-2 seem likely to apply in any given situation, Avoiding would likely be an appropriate conflict management style to use. Thus, the appropriate style depends on the situation.

Avoiding initially sounds like a terrible "solution" to a conflict problem, but everybody uses it! One major reason for this is that most people do not enjoy participating in conflicts. Another common reason for avoiding conflict is that there may be too many potential conflicts with which to cope. This is often true for managers. Most managers will inevitably experience some degree of conflict with at least some of their subordinates and possibly with their bosses as well. In addition, conflict is especially likely with managers of other departments or functions, since those managers are very likely to have different goals (see also Chapter 9).

Neither of these major reasons is a solid justification for dodging a conflict by avoiding it—particularly for a high-performing manager. However, a more in-depth look at both reasons does suggest a more rational approach. The **"Getting Past No"** approach to conflict management through negotiation[10] that is presented in the next

Figure 5-2   Contingency Factors for Avoiding[9]

Use Avoiding:

When an issue is trivial, or more important issues are pressing

When you perceive no chance of satisfying your concerns

When potential disruption outweighs the benefits of resolution

To let people cool down and regain perspective

When gathering information supersedes immediate decision

When others can resolve the conflict more effectively

When issues seem tangential or symptomatic of other issues

section is a view of conflict that makes being involved in it a much more positive experience. Also, a logical rationale for time management of conflicts certainly exists: the available time should be allocated to dealing with those conflicts that are perceived as being more important.

In fact, choosing to apply the Avoiding conflict management style makes a great deal of sense when the conflict concerns a "trivial" or *un*important issue. The amount of time required to cope with many kinds of conflicts simply cannot be justified. However, from a manager's standpoint, it is worthwhile to recognize that trivial issues can sometimes escalate into major ones, and thus should not be ignored completely.

If more important issues are pressing, it makes sense for a manager to focus on the more important conflicts or other issues first. The remainder will have to be temporarily avoided to at least some extent until the more pressing concerns have been dealt with in some way.

Some conflicts may be so strong or long-lasting that there appears to be "no chance of satisfying your concerns" (achieving a useful solution). In other words, Avoiding may sometimes be a better choice for dealing with a conflict than putting in a considerable amount of time and effort that leads to little or no improvement. Similarly, the Avoiding style is appropriate when the potential disruption outweighs the potential benefits of attempting to resolve the conflict. In other words, if taking action is likely to make a situation worse instead of better, it may be best to simply leave that situation alone.

Sometimes a conflict cannot be resolved or settled immediately, so a *temporary* form of Avoiding will be quite appropriate. This is often the case when at least one of the conflicting parties is in a highly emotional state and needs some time to cool down and regain perspective before an effort to deal with the conflict can be made with a reasonable chance of success. Another common reason for temporary Avoiding is to allow time to gather some information that may help in eventually reaching a better decision regarding how to deal with the conflict.

Avoiding *may* be the best conflict management style choice when others can resolve the conflict more effectively. For example, in some cases, other people in or associated with the organization may better understand the situation. However, it is important that this line of thinking not be used frequently to simply "pass the buck," or as an excuse that prevents one from developing better conflict management skills. For managers in particular, this is a risky rationale unless it is reserved only for special occasions where it is truly appropriate. In fact, research suggests that frequent use of the Avoiding conflict management style is not looked upon favorably by others in business organizations.[11]

Sometimes an issue may be identified as being either tangential or just a symptom arising from other issues. Tangential issues are issues that are not directly relevant. Avoiding therefore makes sense for tangential issues.

An example of a symptom arising from other issues would be when a manager—who perceives another manager as having recently received a undeservedly large raise—attempts to make that manager look bad by delaying the passing of information that affects the work of that other manager's department. A conflict concerning the use

ANALYSIS   **The Many Contingency Factors for Avoiding**

Interestingly, Avoiding has more Contingency Factors associated with it than do any of the other four conflict management styles. *Analyze* why this makes sense—even though Avoiding means doing nothing.

of this information-delay tactic (see Chapter 6) would be symptomatic of the *actual* conflict, which appears to involve Perceived Equitable Rewards (see Chapter 3).

COLLABORATING

Figure 5-3 depicts the Contingency Factors associated with the Collaborating conflict management style.

Collaborating is the only conflict management style that can achieve an integrative or win-win outcome. However, Collaborating does have some serious drawbacks. In particular, effective Collaborating usually requires quite a bit of time to work out a solution that is pleasing—or at least reasonably acceptable—to all parties involved in the conflict.

The time management constraint is best dealt with by applying the Collaborating conflict management style only for the most important issues—especially when the concerns of the conflicting parties are too important to be compromised.

Collaborating is also the best style to use when your objective is to learn. People who are working together toward a common goal will be more open to learning. Similarly, creating an atmosphere of working together can facilitate the merging of "insights from people with different perspectives" (see also Chapter 4).

Since all parties involved in a conflict will participate when the Collaborating style is used, it aids in gaining "commitment by incorporating concerns into a consensus."

Figure 5-3   Contingency Factors for Collaborating[12]

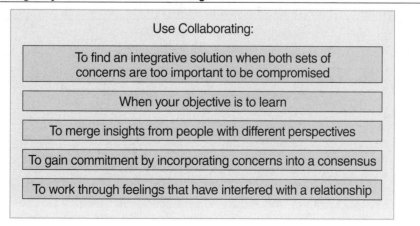

Use Collaborating:

To find an integrative solution when both sets of concerns are too important to be compromised

When your objective is to learn

To merge insights from people with different perspectives

To gain commitment by incorporating concerns into a consensus

To work through feelings that have interfered with a relationship

Organizational behavior research indicates that such cooperation often leads to a higher level of achievement.[13] Collaborating is a particularly good style to use when commitment by others to a conflict solution is critical[14] (see Chapter 7). Collaborating can also help "to work through feelings that have interfered with a relationship" by discussing them openly in a highly participative group setting.

COMPROMISING

Figure 5-4 shows different Contingency Factors to consider for the Compromising conflict management style.

As the only one of the five conflict management styles that is not extreme in some way, the Compromising style tends to be applied quite frequently. When issues or goals are very important, the Collaborating style is the best choice—unless unpopular actions need implementing, in which case the Forcing style is the best choice. However, there may be times when issues or goals are important, but not worth the effort or potential disruption of Collaborating or Forcing styles. Collaborating frequently requires a huge amount of effort, and hence can be highly disruptive of many people's work schedules. Forcing also can be highly disruptive, as many people do not like being forced by another party to do something. Alternatively, Compromising may produce an adequate solution rather than a really good one, but with much less effort and disruption.

Compromising makes the most sense when opponents with equal power (see Chapter 6) are committed to mutually exclusive goals. Mutually exclusive goals exist when the conflicting parties' goals have nothing in common. Because the parties are not at all on the same page, a win-win solution is not possible, and therefore the Collaborating style cannot be used. Furthermore, since the parties to the conflict are equally powerful, one party cannot force a solution on the other(s). Compromising does ensure a *partial* win-win solution, in which all parties to the conflict obtain at least part of what they want.

Compromising is also useful for achieving temporary settlements to complex issues. This means fairly quickly obtaining *some* sort of solution that is at least somewhat acceptable to all parties to the conflict. Such a solution can be changed later when

Figure 5-4   Contingency Factors for Compromising[15]

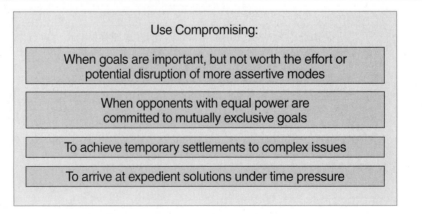

Use Compromising:

When goals are important, but not worth the effort or potential disruption of more assertive modes

When opponents with equal power are committed to mutually exclusive goals

To achieve temporary settlements to complex issues

To arrive at expedient solutions under time pressure

more time is available, or when the complex issues are better understood, or both. Another time-related point is that Compromising usually takes less time than Collaborating. Therefore, Compromising is a good fit when time pressures require expedient solutions (i.e., solutions that can be developed in a hurry but provide a win-win solution to at least some extent).

FORCING (COMPETING)

Figure 5-5 illustrates the Contingency Factors indicating when the Forcing conflict management style is the most appropriate choice.

When applying the Forcing conflict management style, a manager will analyze a conflict and then personally decides how to resolve it. Such decisions typically lead to win-lose outcomes.

Forcing is the best conflict management style to use when quick, decisive action is vital. In a crisis or emergency situation there is no time to sit around and talk (as occurs in the Collaborating and Compromising management styles), yet *something* must be done quickly—which eliminates the Avoiding style. Since Forcing is based on a single person's decision rather than a group decision, it is relatively fast[17] (see Chapter 7).

It also makes sense to use the Forcing style on important issues where unpopular actions need implementing. For example, cost-cutting in a business will undoubtedly be painful and unpopular with those who are affected by the cuts, although Forcing such cuts to occur may be necessary to assure the continued survival of that firm. Likewise, if an unpopular rule or policy states that certain employee actions are not allowed—such as drinking on the job or failing to wear a safety helmet—then the Forcing style is the best way to enforce those rules or policies by initiating appropriate disciplinary action. Because it is quick, Forcing deals with the situation and then hopefully allows people to move on to other things, such as getting work done.

Forcing may be used by *very* high-level managers on issues vital to company welfare when you know you're right. This Contingency Factor appears on the list in Figure 5-5 primarily because the list is based on a survey of chief executive officers (CEOs).

Figure 5-5   Contingency Factors for Forcing[16]

Use Forcing:

- When quick, decisive action is vital—i.e., emergencies
- On important issues where unpopular actions need implementing—e.g., cost-cutting, enforcing unpopular rules, discipline
- On issues vital to company welfare when you know you're right
- Against people who take advantage of noncompetitive behavior

Application of this particular Contingency Factor is not recommended for the vast majority of managers or conflict management facilitators.

Interestingly, the Forcing style can be used against people who take advantage of (other people's) noncompetitive behavior to persuade them to pursue a cooperative rather than a competitive approach. Thus, the Forcing conflict management style can be used to counteract one conflicting party's effort to *Compete* against another.

In the vast majority of cases, only the first two of the four contingencies listed in Figure 5-5 are likely to be applicable for most managers or conflict management facilitators. Savvy managers will tend to reserve the use of the Forcing management style for situations that are truly emergencies or where unpopular actions are truly necessary to deal with a major issue.

ACCOMMODATING

Figure 5-6 shows the Contingency Factors favoring the use of the Accommodating conflict management style.

Unfortunately for a manager who is trying to *facilitate* the resolution or settlement of a conflict, the Accommodating conflict management style can be applied *only* when one of the conflicting parties chooses to use this style.

Figure 5-6   Contingency Factors for Accommodating[18]

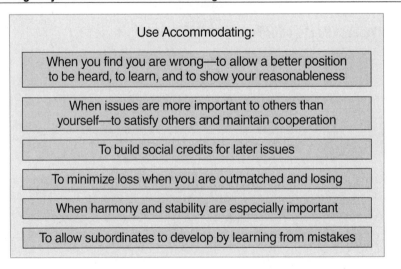

Use Accommodating:

When you find you are wrong—to allow a better position to be heard, to learn, and to show your reasonableness

When issues are more important to others than yourself—to satisfy others and maintain cooperation

To build social credits for later issues

To minimize loss when you are outmatched and losing

When harmony and stability are especially important

To allow subordinates to develop by learning from mistakes

From the standpoint of a party to a conflict that is *directly* involved in the conflict and wishes to do something to resolve it, there are several reasons for choosing to use the Accommodating conflict management style. If, upon reflection, a party to the conflict realizes that he/she/it was wrong, the Accommodating style is both appropriate and fair. It would also show that the individual or group in question is willing to be reasonable—and, in some cases, open to learning a better way of doing things.

For a party to a conflict that feels the conflict issue is more important to others, Accommodating is a good choice of conflict management style. This is because it not only satisfies the needs of the other party, but maintains a spirit of cooperation. However, note that the Accommodating style can also be used in such situations to build social credits for later issues. In other words, the Accommodating conflict management style can be used to create an implicit "you owe me one" future obligation.

Alternatively, the Accommodating style is a useful fallback strategy for a party to a conflict that is outmatched and losing a conflict battle. Smoothing things over may allow that party to minimize his/her/its losses. One of the conflicting parties may note that a particular conflict situation has arisen at a time when harmony and stability are especially important, and hence choose the Accommodating style to resolve the conflict. This kind of selfless gesture can facilitate the long-term success of the conflicting parties' relationship.

A manager may actually choose the Accommodating conflict management style to allow subordinates to develop by learning from mistakes, since in such situations the manager—and each subordinate—is a *direct* party to the conflict. In other words, in such instances, a manager may choose to recognize the value of learning from direct experience and take that into account during the subordinates' performance evaluations (see Chapter 9).

DEALING WITH CONFLICT THROUGH NEGOTIATION: GETTING PAST NO

An **integrative approach**[19] to negotiation views conflict as an opportunity for joint problem solving. This creates the potential for a win-win solution, about which all parties to the negotiation will be reasonably happy.

In contrast, a **distributive approach** views conflict as a confrontation.[20] This creates a win-lose solution, about which only one or a few of the parties to the negotiation will feel happy.

While many real-world negotiations take a distributive approach, an integrative approach makes sense in situations involving ongoing, longer-term relationships. The loser of a past negotiation is much less likely to feel positively about any future negotiations, while a prior win-win solution makes all parties to the past negotiation feel positively about any future negotiations.

A highly acclaimed set of best practices for effective negotiation developed by Ury[21] takes an integrative approach. This approach, labeled "Getting Past No," can turn adversaries into partners. The parties to the conflict jointly attack the problem instead of separately attacking each other.

The key steps in the Getting Past No approach include **Prepare, Prepare, Prepare**; **Go to the Balcony**; **Step to Their Side**; **Reframe**; **Build Them a Golden**

Bridge; and **Use Power to Educate**. Details concerning each of these six steps, plus a variety of tips that suggest how to perform each step effectively in an actual negotiation, are presented next.

PREPARE, PREPARE, PREPARE

Before entering into a negotiation, be sure to do your homework. While this may be perceived as difficult, boring, or time-consuming—or quite possibly all of the above—careful preparation often makes the difference between success and failure. The person or group with whom negotiations are being conducted will be watching every move, so solid advance planning can minimize unintended actions or costly and/or embarrassing mistakes.

Preparation for a negotiation typically begins with consideration of each party's *interests*. Begin by asking the question, "What do I or we want to accomplish in this negotiation?" Be sure to follow up by asking "Why?" There may be several reasons. If so, it is quite valuable to *prioritize* those reasons. For example, a salesperson might realize that getting off to a good start with a potential major customer may be a higher priority than making a lot of money on the first deal with that customer.

When considering the interests of the other party, try to understand the other party's point of view. Putting yourself in the other party's shoes is crucial to effective negotiation.

Next, consider some possible *options* for meeting those interests. This often requires some creative brainstorming, or "thinking outside the box." If the obvious Plan A is likely to be rejected by the other party, are there some options in which *more* may be given in order to obtain a desired outcome *plus* something else? For example, a professional basketball team might trade two or three players to another team instead of just one, to obtain one key desired player plus others.

Another issue to consider is the criteria for deciding who gets what. If some criteria exist that make logical sense *and* support some of the options developed, that can aid later persuasion. Existing standards or precedents can be especially useful criteria to consider.

Yet another critical piece of homework involves thinking about the Best Alternative to a Negotiated Agreement (or BATNA). Each party to a negotiation often has a BATNA, and it is extremely helpful to be as clear as possible in advance about what these BATNAs might be. If negotiations do not go as hoped, what alternative does each party have? For example, when negotiating with a boss for raise, it would be helpful to arrange a BATNA of *already* having a job offer from another company. Sure, there would be costs associated with that BATNA—which is why it is worth the trouble to initiate negotiations in the first place. However, the better the BATNA, the better positioned any given party is to negotiate successfully.

The final major element of doing your homework is to develop proposals for a negotiating settlement that seem likely to be better than each party's BATNA. It may be helpful to develop three sets of proposals:

1. Some more *optimistic* proposals that would be very satisfactory and still meet the other party's basic concerns;

APPLICATION & ANALYSIS

Best Alternative to a Negotiated Agreement

In the example of a BATNA just described, already having a job offer from another company gives a subordinate significant leverage in negotiating with a boss for a raise. What kind of BATNA might the boss create that would provide the boss with a similar level of leverage?

2. Some more *moderate* proposals that would create reasonable contentment and would also seem likely to meet more than just the other party's basic concerns;

3. Some proposals that would be better than your BATNA, if only by a small margin, and that would be the *minimum* necessary to justify trying to achieve a negotiated settlement with the other party.

For example, a high-performing employee who is negotiating a raise with his boss might develop an optimistic proposal involving a 15% raise (plus possibly other requests and perhaps some concessions). A moderate proposal might include a 10% raise (assuming that 10% raises are much more common in the company than 15% raises) and perhaps a concession to do more work on weekends. Finally, a minimum proposal might involve a 6% raise (if, say, the employee's BATNA is a 5% raise for taking a similar job with another company).

GO TO THE BALCONY

"Go to the balcony" means obtaining a broad perspective on what is, or will soon be, occurring on the negotiation *stage*. In other words, step back, become a detached observer, and look at the bigger picture. Note that this will be necessary *during* the negotiation as well as before it.

An essential point to keep in mind is not to get mad, or not to get even, but to focus on *eventually getting at least some of what you want*. In response to any highly emotional or "hardball" negotiating tactics, one might step back and become detached by pausing and saying nothing, summarizing the key points that have recently been discussed, asking the other party to repeat or clarify key points, and calmly refusing to be rushed into making a decision.

STEP TO THEIR SIDE

To jointly solve a problem and create a win-win solution, it is essential to step to the other party's side and work *with* that party, rather than against it. Three key techniques for accomplishing this switch-around include active listening; acknowledging the other party's negotiating points, feelings, competence, status, and so on; and agreeing with the other party whenever reasonably possible.

Active listening requires carefully taking in information, then occasionally paraphrasing the key points (see Chapter 4). In a negotiation, for example, a manager might say "As I understand it, what you are saying is that several other employees that you either outperform or match in performance have received raises recently, so you feel that you also deserve a raise?"

Acknowledging the other party's negotiating points, feelings, and so on essentially recognizes that party as a worthwhile human being or group of human beings. Unless people feel valued, they are not likely to be open to working something out. Note that acknowledging another party's position on some issue does not necessarily indicate *agreement* with that position; it just shows that the other party's point of view has been understood.

Sometimes, an apology on a less important issue can re-open communication. However, there is no need to apologize meekly or to take responsibility for something that the other party did incorrectly or inappropriately. Simply apologize for whatever contribution you might have made to creating the problem, and then use this as a basis for focusing on what might be done to *solve* the problem.

Agreeing with another party creates a point of commonality. Without having something in common, it will be much more difficult to work together and reach an agreement. It helps to say "yes" as often as possible, so try to look for opportunities to do this. However, consider saying "Yes . . . *and* . . ." rather than "Yes, *but* . . ." For example, an astute salesperson might say "*Yes*, you are correct, our company's prices are higher . . . *and* we can provide you with higher quality and better service as a result."

REFRAME

Negotiations typically focus on presenting *positions*. Unfortunately, if the parties' positions do not mesh together well, it is easy to reject the other's position, and possibly become angry or otherwise upset in the process.

An alternative approach is to reframe, or change the nature of the negotiation, by focusing on identifying *interests*. This requires asking some questions to determine more precisely what those interests might be. For example, "I think I understand what you are interested in achieving. Why do you want that to happen? Can you help me to understand more clearly the problem you are trying to solve?" Such reframing has the effect of shifting the focus of the negotiation from positions to interests. Now it may be possible to jointly develop creative options to meet those interests.

Aside from "Why?" other useful questions include "Why not?" "What if?" "What do you suggest?" and "Why would that be fair to both of us?" Open-ended questions are preferable to close-ended questions, which limit the response and tend to put the other party on the spot. Take whatever the other party says and try to reframe it as an effort to *solve* the problem that all parties are facing.

BUILD THEM A GOLDEN BRIDGE

A golden bridge is one that bridges the gap between the two parties' interests while at the same time making this transition a comfortable one. Participation helps. Try to get the other party involved in creating the solution, and be sure to use some of that party's ideas. In addition, seek a critique of current possible solutions. For example, ask "How could we make this solution better for you without making it worse for me?" Try to do

APPLICATION & ANALYSIS

Logrolling in Action

As noted below, logrolling involves making concessions on low-priority items in exchange for concessions on high-priority items. For example, when negotiating with a supplier located in China, a purchasing agent for a U.S. company might agree to pay for the Chinese supplier's products in U.S. dollars rather than Chinese currency if the Chinese supplier is willing to give the U.S. company's orders higher priority to ensure on-time delivery. *Analyze* what other examples might involve logrolling on the part of the parties to such a negotiation *application*.

logrolling by making concessions on low-priority items in exchange for concessions on high-priority items.[22]

If the other party resists these bridge-building efforts, try to give the other party a choice to make a small decision—such as where to meet for the next negotiating session—in hopes that this will re-open communication once again. If necessary, allow the other party to save face by backing away without backing down. Finally, resist the temptation to speed things up by pushing hard. Sometimes, going slower can lead to going faster overall.

USE POWER TO EDUCATE

A successful negotiation following this Getting Past No approach allows all parties to the conflict to satisfy important interests. There is a difference between win-win and winning. Even when one party to a conflict is clearly strong enough to actually win if it should so choose, its long-term interests may be much better served by negotiating a mutually beneficial agreement.

Use power to educate. In other words, use power bases (see Chapter 6) to create a good deal for both parties, rather than to force a victory based on using that power. If resistance is encountered toward the end of negotiations, very calmly and quietly ask what the other party will do as an alternative. It is perfectly acceptable to bring up one's BATNA—but as an indication that alternatives do exist rather than as a threat to break off the negotiations.

Sometimes so-called third parties, such as mediators, mutual friends, or respected peers, can help to forge an agreement by virtue of using their neutrality as a basis for creating an objectively fair outcome that benefits both of the two original parties to a conflict. However, the two original parties should choose the final agreement because each realizes it is the best alternative available—and because each makes a conscious decision to accept that agreement (see Chapter 7).

Make sure that each party has a clear understanding of the final agreement. If appropriate, build in a dispute resolution procedure to cope with any future conflicts during the implementation of the agreement.

APPLICATION: PRACTICAL GUIDELINES FOR IMPLEMENTING THE CONFLICT MANAGEMENT STYLES MODEL

Given a particular conflict situation, implementing the Conflict Management Styles Model requires one to systematically decide which of the five sets of Contingency Factors best matches the current situation.[23] The conflict management style associated with the "best match" set of Contingency Factors is the preferred style to apply (see also Chapter 8).

A STRATEGY FOR ANALYZING THE SETS OF CONTINGENCY FACTORS

There are 26 different Contingency Factors available to analyze. Fortunately, prior experience suggests it is very unlikely that all 26 factors will need to be analyzed to determine the best conflict management style to use in any situation. What follows is a strategy that fairly quickly narrows the *realistic* conflict management style options down to a much smaller number, thereby reducing the number of Contingency Factors that need to be analyzed in any application.

Briefly consider the Accommodating conflict management style first. Choosing Accommodating makes sense *only* if one of the parties to the conflict is willing to accommodate the other(s)—for whatever reason. A manager or other conflict management facilitator could *suggest* that a particular party to the conflict might wish to try Accommodating, but beyond that its usefulness as a choice of conflict management style is limited. In general, when attempting to *facilitate* the resolution or settlement of a conflict, it is better to choose one of the other four styles.

Next, consider the Avoiding conflict management style. Classifying a conflict as trivial serves as a strong indicator that Avoiding should be used. Since the issue is unimportant, Avoiding is the appropriate style. The same line of reasoning applies if the issue seems tangential, or off to the side.

In addition, the two Contingency Factors for the Avoiding style that recommend a *temporary* form of Avoiding may also imply that the Avoiding style should be used—but only in the short term. These factors are to let people cool down and regain perspective or to gather additional information.

In contrast, the three remaining Contingency Factors for Avoiding should be quite carefully scrutinized before deciding to favor Avoiding over the other three more active conflict management styles. This is because the Avoiding style does *not* make any kind of positive contribution toward resolving a conflict. These three remaining Contingency Factors should normally signal the use of Avoiding only as a last resort.

At this point, the possible range of conflict management style alternatives has been narrowed considerably. The three more active conflict management styles are Collaborating, Compromising, and Forcing.

If the issue being resolved is an important one, choosing the Collaborating style is strong suggested. Because the issue is so important, the extra time and effort required is justified. However, if the important issue requires the implementation of unpopular actions, the Forcing style is a more realistic choice. Likewise, if opponents with equal power are committed to mutually exclusive goals, the Collaborating style will not work even if the issue is *extremely* important. This is because the goals have no points of commonality or overlap on which to build a mutually acceptable solution. In such a situation, the Compromising style is the best available alternative.

Unless a conflict situation clearly matches one of the three scenarios just described, the best approach is to perform a detailed analysis of all three sets of Contingency Factors for Collaborating, Compromising, and Forcing. For some conflict situations, which of these three sets of factors provides the best match is immediately clear. In other situations, however, two or possibly even all three sets of Contingency Factors will appear to "fit" equally well. In such cases, look carefully at the factors that do fit, and then choose the conflict management style that appears to have the strongest overall support.

Note that the last two Contingency Factors under Forcing rarely apply for most managers or other conflict management facilitators. Use of the first of these factors makes sense only for CEOs or other high-level managers, whereas the other factor applies to an issue that typically does not come up very often. However, if competing does become a big problem, a manager or other conflict management facilitator should strongly consider the use of the Forcing style to counter it.

Finally, it is very important to recognize that it is *not* appropriate to *reverse* the implementation process that has just been described by choosing a style first and then arguing that some of the Contingency Factors for that style seem to "fit." (Admittedly, this approach is faster—and similar to the Forcing style in other ways as well.) Instead of force-fitting a style to a set of factors, *analyze the Contingency Factors first* to determine which style is the best fit. This approach produces more accurate analyses that are likely to lead to more effective conflict management—*if* that most appropriate conflict management style choice is properly *implemented*.

To facilitate implementation analysis, all five sets of Contingency Factors have been summarized in Figure 5-7.

FALLBACK CONFLICT MANAGEMENT STYLES

Once the conflict management style that best fits a particular conflict situation has been chosen, it should be applied. Fortunately, all is not lost if that initial style fails to resolve or settle the conflict effectively. Each of the five conflict management styles has at least one "fallback" style that a person can fall back on if the prior style fails. In other words, each style has another style to try next.

The fallback style in situations where the Collaborating conflict management style fails is Compromising.[26] Such a fallback usually results when it becomes clear that no common points of agreement exist that can be used as a basis for developing a win-win solution between parties Instead, each party to the conflict wins some and loses some. From a negotiation perspective, if an attempt to reach an integrative (win-win) solution to a conflict based on the Getting Past No approach should fail, it is often possible to fall back to some form of negotiated settlement that at least partially pleases each party.

Figure 5-7   Contingency Factors for the 5 Conflict Management Styles[24]

Use Avoiding:

When an issue is trivial, or more important issues are pressing

When you perceive no chance of satisfying your concerns

When potential disruption outweighs the benefits of resolution

To let people cool down and regain perspective

When gathering information supersedes immediate decision

When others can resolve the conflict more effectively

When issues seem tangential or symptomatic of other issues

Use Collaborating:

To find an integrative solution when both sets of
concerns are too important to be compromised

When your objective is to learn

To merge insights from people with different perspectives

To gain commitment by incorporating concerns into a consensus

To work through feelings that have interfered with a relationship

Use Compromising:

When goals are important, but not worth the effort or
potential disruption of more assertive modes

When opponents with equal power are committed to mutually exclusive goals

To achieve temporary settlements to complex issues

To arrive at expedient solutions under time pressure

Use Forcing:

When quick, decisive action is vital—e.g., emergencies

On important issues where unpopular actions need
implementing—e.g., cost-cutting, enforcing unpopular rules, discipline

On issues vital to company welfare when you know you're right

Against people who take advantage of noncompetitive behavior

Use Accommodating:

When you find you are wrong—to allow a better position
to be heard, to learn, and to show your reasonableness

When issues are more important to others than
yourself—to satisfy others and maintain cooperation

To build social credits for later issues

To minimize loss when you are outmatched and losing

When harmony and stability are especially important

To allow subordinates to develop by learning from mistakes

The fallback style if Compromising fails is Forcing. Note that it can *sometimes* be helpful to make the conflicting parties aware that the Forcing style will be used if Compromising fails. Such awareness may provide additional incentive for the conflicting parties to participatively negotiate a solution rather than be forced to cope with whatever solution a manager might choose to impose on them. However, also note that using this fallback strategy too frequently can make it ineffective. Unless the particular Contingency Factors listed for the Forcing style *strongly* suggest otherwise, the Compromising style is generally a better choice.

In fact, the fallback style if Forcing fails is Compromising.[27] Note that while using Compromising as a fallback style for Forcing makes sense, frequently using Compromising as a fallback style for Forcing may undermine the future effectiveness of Forcing. This is because people will soon learn that if they continue to oppose a manager's or conflict facilitator's Forcing solution, they will probably eventually get at least some of what they want through a Compromising fallback.

When Avoiding fails and the conflict becomes non-trivial, do *something*! The best approach will depend on the remaining sets of Contingency Factors. The Compromising or Forcing styles are the most likely choices unless a previously trivial conflict has by now become very important—which would suggest a Collaborating style. In particular, note that Avoiding is a common strategy for handling conflicts caused by strong personal differences.[28] If the Avoiding style fails in such cases, the fallback style that is often chosen is Forcing. Forcing does not really resolve those personal differences, but may force those in conflict to set their personal problems aside—unless they want to risk losing their jobs or being transferred to different parts of the organization.[29]

Accommodating, by definition, does not normally require a fallback style because the party being accommodated should be quite happy to obtain what that party wants. However, if it should turn out that the party being accommodated wants too much, a possible fallback is the Compromising style, in which the person previously doing the Accommodating also benefits in some way. Otherwise, the likely outcome is limited Accommodating and an unsuccessful settlement of the conflict.

ANALYSIS   How Many Times Can One "Fall Back"?

The preceding section suggests fallback styles for each of the five conflict management styles. This leads to an important question: In any given conflict situation, how many times can a manager fall back to a different style? Why is that particular number the most logical response? What does that answer imply regarding the initial analysis of the various conflict management style Contingency Factors?

APPLICATION EXAMPLE

Choosing A Conflict Management Style in a Student Project Group

A group of five students is meeting to discuss the group project they must complete for another course. The required length of the paper is 30 to 40 pages, and the paper is worth 40% of their course grades.

One member of the group has remembered reading somewhere that the first issue to be dealt with during implementation is to clearly determine what the group task will be.

The instructor has already defined the group task for this project to a significant extent. However, the instructor has also indicated that any one of six major topic areas would be an appropriate focus for the project paper.

Unfortunately, after a few minutes of discussion, it is clear that different students within the group have different ideas about which topic area would be the best choice. There is a conflict.

To choose the most appropriate conflict management style to apply to resolve or settle this particular conflict, begin by considering the Accommodating style first. It is possible that some group members will be willing to accommodate other members, and thus settle the conflict. But what if they do not?

Next, consider the Avoiding style. Unfortunately, the issue is definitely not trivial, as the project paper is worth 40% of the course grade. Obviously, the Avoiding style will not be an effective choice—although temporary use of the Avoiding style might apply to gather more information or to let people cool down.

Now the three more active categories of conflict management styles should be considered. An important issue strongly suggests choosing the Collaborating style, since the extra time and effort required to use this style will be well spent. This *is* an important issue. However, if opponents with equal power are committed to mutually exclusive goals, the Collaborating style will not work even if the issue is *extremely* important. Also, because this particular issue could require the implementation of unpopular actions from at least some group members' points of view, the Forcing style initially sounds like a realistic choice. However, there is one small problem: who will do the forcing?

Hence, the choice of conflict management styles has been narrowed down to two candidates: Collaborating and Compromising. The following is a detailed breakdown of the Contingency Factors for each of these conflict management styles.

continues

Collaborating

+ The issue is important

+ The objective is to learn

+ People do have different perspectives that require merging

? Commitment is needed, and a consensus would be nice—if possible

? If upset, could work through feelings

Compromising

? The issues are important but not worth the potential disruption of Collaborating or Forcing

?? Opponents with equal power committed to mutually exclusive goals

n/a Temporary settlements to complex Issues [n/a = not applicable]

? When time pressures require expedient solutions

While most of the factors noted above either definitely apply or might apply for both styles, the Collaborating appears to be the best overall fit, unless opponents with equal power are committed to mutually exclusive goals. If that is the case, then the Compromising style is the best choice. If it is not initially clear that group members (who presumably have equal power) are committed to mutually exclusive goals, it would make the most sense to begin with the Collaborating style, and then fall back to the Compromising style should that prove to be necessary.

Collaborating might focus on *interests* to determine whether there is a topic that substantially meets all group members' interests in one way or another. Should that prove to be the case, the Collaborating style will be successful. If not, how might the Compromising style be effective when the group can only choose one topic for the paper? Other members might be allowed to choose which tasks they prefer to perform, when and where the group meetings will be held, and so on.

In contrast, note that if the Compromising style is chosen as the initial style, the fallback style would be Forcing. Again, Forcing is not a very realistic style to use in a student project group. Therefore, if the Compromising style is chosen as the initial style, a major effort should be made to reach a reasonable compromise and avoid the need to resort to a fallback style.

Key

+   A good fit.
?   A possible fit.
??   A possible fit that is particularly important to analyze carefully.

CONCLUSION

Much of this chapter has focused on five major conflict management styles. While preferences for particular styles vary across individuals and cultures, some general trends have been noted. Avoiding is used for most potential conflicts, but one of the other styles is likely to be more appropriate when the conflict grows in importance. Collaborating has received strong support as the preferred method for dealing with the most important issues. The Getting Past No approach provides a number of creative ideas to apply when attempting to negotiate an integrative (win-win) solution rather than a distributive (win-lose) one.

Despite these general trends, the best overall approach appears to be to choose the conflict management style that best fits any particular situation. This chapter has provided numerous recommendations for effectively making such choices. Should the initial conflict management style prove unsuccessful, it may be possible to resort to a fallback style with a reasonable chance of eventually settling the conflict.

EXERCISES AND OTHER ACTIVITIES
■ *Experiential Exercise: In-Class 5-1*

THE CARD NEGOTIATION EXERCISE

The purpose of this exercise is to apply negotiation skills and best practices during a series of discussions with several different groups.

Background Information

All of the face cards (kings, queens, and jacks) have been removed from a deck of cards. This leaves 40 cards: four different suits, each with cards ranging from 1 (ace) to 10.

Exercise Process Outline

Form four approximately equal groups of students. Each group should sit in one of the four corners of the classroom.

Using the material on negotiations supplied in this chapter, each group should develop initial strategies for negotiating with each of the other three groups in an effort to score as many points as possible. You may use any negotiation strategies—including any number of negotiators—that you wish . . . **except** for *spying* on the other negotiations.

At the beginning of the strategy development session, 10 cards will be dealt at random for each of the four groups, and subsequently given to each of those groups respectively. In addition, each group will be supplied with an Information and Data Sheet indicating how that particular group can score points during the exercise. *Be sure* to fill out the Initial Numbers for the 10 cards your group was dealt in the appropriate column of your Information and Data Sheet (list the 10 numbers). Toward the end of the strategy development session, "negotiating tables" will be placed at the center of the both the front and the back of the room in preparation for the forthcoming negotiations.

During the actual negotiations, pairs of groups will negotiate simultaneously, in the front and the back of the room. Again, no spying allowed.

Each group will have two opportunities to negotiate with each of the other three groups. Your instructor will provide a schedule that indicates which groups will negotiate when, in addition to how long the negotiations will last.

During the first set of three negotiations, a group may trade a maximum of *one* card during any given negotiation. During the second set of three negotiations, however, a group may trade a maximum of *two* cards during any given negotiation. Any time one or more cards are traded, the groups involved must exchange an *equal* number of cards, so that each group always holds 10 cards. [Tip: While you may exchange a maximum of only *one* card during the first set of negotiations, there is nothing to stop you from talking then about what you might exchange during the second set of negotiations.]

At the end of the second set of negotiations, write the ending numbers for your new set of 10 cards on your group's information and data sheet, and calculate your column totals. After you have completed these calculations, your instructor will examine the information and data sheets to determine which groups will receive bonus points. Your instructor will also supply each group with an overall score sheet. Once you have received the bonus points information, you can make the appropriate calculations on your overall score sheet to determine your group's grand total and improvement scores.

■ *Experiential Exercise: Field 5-1*

CONFLICT ANALYSIS GROUP PROJECT GUIDELINES

Focus of the Project Paper

This paper should focus on conflict situations arising in one to six work organizations plus a group project conducted in a class taken at this university or college. The parties involved in the chosen conflict situations should be either individuals or small groups (10 people maximum).

The key integrated model covered in this chapter presents five conflict management styles and implementation guidelines for when to choose each of those styles. Begin by analyzing one example situation of recent conflicts in work organizations for each of the five conflict management styles, recommending the style that best fits the situation. In each case, your recommendation should be based on a thorough analysis of the conflict management style Contingency Factors, following the implementation guidelines in the Application section of the chapter. Note that your recommendation may or may not match the style that was actually used in the situation. Focus on *past conflicts* that have taken place relatively recently (within the previous year).

Students can use the following for subtitles for their cases:

Example Case 1: Avoiding Style Recommended

Example Case 2: Collaborating Style Recommended

Example Case 3: Compromising Style Recommended

Example Case 4: Forcing Style Recommended

Example Case 5: Accommodating Style Recommended

Next, shift your focus to a likely *future conflict* (within the year following the paper due date). Analyze an example situation involving a different set of people than the ones covered in any of the prior five examples. Choose a case in which your recommended conflict management style will be Collaborating, Compromising, or Forcing (Accommodating and Avoiding cases are less challenging). Again, your recommendation should be based on a thorough analysis of the conflict management style Contingency Factors, following the implementation guidelines in the Application section of this chapter, to determine which of the *sets* of factors best fits the likely future situation. In this case, you must not only recommend a particular style, but also discuss how that *style* should be implemented (i.e., what steps should be taken by a manager or other individual who is attempting to facilitate the resolution or settlement of the conflict). Please note that *telling* a manager how to actually resolve or settle a conflict would constitute forcing. Instead, focus on suggesting how to *facilitate* the resolution or settlement of the conflict.

Students can use the following for subtitle for their case.

> Case 6: Future Case: Collaborating, Compromising, or Forcing Style Recommended

Finally, tap your group's reservoir of experience with group projects in other classes to conduct one further example case analysis. Focus on a *conflict* that is taking place now or seems likely to occur before the project is completed. To give your group a good opportunity to display its depth of knowledge, you should **not** choose an unimportant group project conflict that would best be dealt with through an Avoiding management style, nor should you choose a conflict anticipating that it will be resolved by one or more group members who will agree to use the Accommodating style to smooth over the problem. To show your versatility, it would be preferable to analyze a case that recommends the application of a different style than was recommended for Case 6. As usual, analyze the conflict management style Contingency Factors to determine which of the *sets* of factors best fits this particular situation. Follow up by presenting ideas on how that conflict management style could be *implemented*. Be sure to cover who would be the best person(s) to attempt to facilitate the resolution or settlement of the conflict by applying that style, exactly how the style should be applied to facilitate the resolution or settlement of the conflict, when it should be applied, and why your recommended implementation sequence seems likely to be effective. Again, please note that *telling* people how to actually resolve or settle a conflict constitutes Forcing; instead, focus on how to *facilitate* the resolution or settlement of the conflict.

Students can use the following for subtitle for their case:

> Case 7: Student Group Project Conflict: Collaborating, Compromising, or Forcing Style Recommended

This group project is designed to contribute to your higher-level learning of an important organizational behavior topic by giving you opportunities to *apply, analyze, synthesize,* and *evaluate.* To make this project as applied as possible, it is important for your group to contact people who have direct knowledge of the conflict situations being studied. While conflict is an important issue in most contemporary organizations, it is also a somewhat sensitive issue. Therefore, generally speaking, it is likely to be easier to acquire information about conflict situations when one or more group members have been in a position to directly observe a particular case. For situations in which no members of your group are already associated with the kind of organization or project group you would like to study, try making contact through friends, relatives, or neighbors with whom you have good relationships. Access to knowledgeable sources of information is essential. Be sure to promise confidentiality for all sources, conflict participants, and organizations or project groups involved. Then be sure to live up to that promise! Choose different kinds of examples that will give you the opportunity to show how your group can effectively analyze and evaluate a diverse variety of conflict situations, and synthesize some effective solutions.

Creating a Project Group

Organizational behavior research has found that the optimal size for decision-making groups is 5 to 7 people. Past experience with group projects indicates that groups of 5 to 6 people provide the best balance between sharing the workload and ease of coordination.

Getting Organized

Once your project group has been created, you will need to get organized. As a result of your initial organizational efforts, your group should supply your instructor with the following items:

1. A list of names for all group members

2. A project timeline

3. A responsibility matrix indicating which group members are responsible for performing each of the tasks listed in the timeline

4. A list of explicit group norms that represent the shared expectations of your group members about what behaviors and types of group process will be valued by your group.

Note that items 2 and 3 can be combined into a single matrix if desired.

Required Format

Your paper should begin with a title page and contain seven sections.

Title Page

1. Introduction

2. The Kinds of Organizations and Project Groups to be Analyzed

3. Recent Examples of Recommended Applications of the Five Conflict Management Styles (Example Cases 1–5)

4. Example Analysis for a Likely Future Conflict Within a Work Environment (Case 6)

5. Example Analysis for a Current or Likely Future Student Project Group Conflict (Case 7)

6. Conclusion

7. Appendix (if applicable)

The **Title Page** should contain a descriptive title, your names, your affiliation, and the date. The title should provide some indication of the types of organizations you are analyzing and should include the word "conflict." In this course, your affiliation is the course number and the name of your university or college.

The **Introduction** tells the reader what the paper will be about. It tells what you are trying to accomplish by writing this paper, *not* what you found. In other words, briefly state the purpose of the paper, not the results or conclusions.

The Kinds of Organizations and Project Groups to be Analyzed section presents a fairly brief description of the kinds of organizations and project groups that you will be studying. Talk generally about each organization's major products, services, or purposes; indicate approximately how large each organization is; and so on. For the single project group, discuss what kind of course the group members are taking, the topic and purpose of the project, how many members are involved, and so forth. In other words, give the reader an idea of what kinds of organizations and project groups you will be analyzing, without clearly identifying those organizations by name or by certain unique characteristics.

The **Recent Examples of Recommended Applications of the Five Conflict Management Styles** section provides a work-related case example for recommendation applications of each of the five styles in turn. [Hint: Use five subtitles.]

Some questions to ask when writing this section include the following:

1. Did we briefly remind the reader which kind of work organization is being analyzed in this particular example? [Use "Insurance Firm X" rather than "Company X."]

2. Who was involved in the conflict? [Use generic job titles, not names.]

3. What specifically caused the conflict? Was the conflict a result of communication, structural, or personal differences, or some combination of these? Why?

4. Which conflict management style does the group recommend applying to this particular conflict case? [Analyze the Contingency Factors, following the implementation guidelines in the Application section of this chapter.]

5. Which conflict solution was actually applied within the organization being studied? Was it the most appropriate solution, according to the group's analysis and recommendation?

The **Example Analysis for a Likely Future Conflict** section predicts a likely future conflict within a work environment and makes suggestions for effectively facilitating its resolution or settlement.

Some questions to ask when writing this section include the following:

1. Have we chosen a work-related conflict for which the Collaborating, Compromising, or Forcing conflict management style seems likely to be the most appropriate?

2. Did we *briefly* remind the reader which kind of work organization is being analyzed?

3. Who was involved in the conflict? [Use generic job titles, not names.]

4. What specifically seems likely to cause this conflict? Will the likely future conflict be a result of communication differences, structural differences, personal differences, or some combination of these? Why?

5. Which conflict management style—Collaborating, Compromising, or Forcing—would be the most effective way to facilitate resolution or settlement of the likely conflict situation? [Analyze the Contingency Factors, following the implementation guidelines in the Application section of this chapter.]

6. How should the recommended style be applied in the actual organizational setting, when, and by whom? Why would your approach be the most effective of the possibilities available? [Be sure focus on suggestions concerning what steps the likely facilitator of the conflict resolution or settlement should take to cause a resolution or settlement to occur. Do **not force** a solution that you personally have created on the conflict participants; rather, suggest what steps the conflict facilitator should take to create an environment in which the conflict participants can develop the solution—through Collaborating, Compromising, or even Forcing by the facilitator, if appropriate.]

The **Example Analysis for a Current or Likely Future Student Group Project Conflict** section analyzes a current or likely future conflict within an existing university or college project group and makes suggestions for effectively facilitating its resolution or settlement.

Some questions to ask when writing this section include the following:

1. Have we chosen a group project conflict for which the Collaborating, Compromising, or Forcing conflict management style seems likely to be the most appropriate choice?

2. Did we briefly remind the reader which kind of project group is being analyzed?

3. Which group members are, or would be, involved in the conflict? [Be fair by disguising all of the group members' names!]

4. What specifically caused, or seems likely to cause, the conflict? Was the conflict—or will the conflict likely be—a result of communication, structural, or personal differences, or some combination of these? Why?

5. Which conflict management style—Collaborating, Compromising, or Forcing—would be the most effective way to facilitate resolution or settlement of the likely conflict situation? [Analyze the Contingency Factors, following the implementation guidelines in the Application section of this chapter.]

6. How should the recommended style be applied in the actual project group setting, when, and by whom? Why would your approach be the most effective of the possibilities available? [Be sure to focus on suggestions concerning what steps the likely facilitator of the conflict resolution or settlement should take to cause a resolution or settlement to occur. Do **not force** a solution that you personally have created on the conflict participants; rather, suggest what steps the conflict facilitator should take to create an environment in which the participants can develop the solution—through collaborating, compromising, or even forcing by the facilitator, if most appropriate.]

The **Conclusion** section wraps up the paper by summarizing the major findings and noting some particularly interesting outcomes.

The **Appendix** is a good place to put any supporting materials you may have used to prepare this paper, such as general characteristics of your sources for each example, interview questions, diagrams (including portions of organizational charts if applicable), and so on. An Appendix is **not** required for this paper.

Writing Tips

In longer sections, the use of subtitles can be helpful in keeping the reader organized and on track. Most textbooks—including this one—provide examples of how to use subtitles effectively.

When writing a paper of this kind, be sure to avoid an outline format in your writing style. In other words, write complete sentences, put the sentences in standard paragraph form, and so on. Avoid using bullets or numbered lists. They are appropriate for advertisements, and possibly for executive summaries, but not for a paper of this kind.

Proofreading your paper after it has been completed is highly recommended. If at all possible, put the paper aside for a few days (or at least a few hours) before doing the proofreading. This should greatly increase your effectiveness. It also can be helpful to have more than one group member do proofreading, as different people may pick up different errors or problems.

Finally, just before you print your paper, use a spell-checking program. Such software will not catch all of the mistakes that might have been made, but it will spot many of the worst typographical and spelling errors. Such errors are eady tp makr (easy to make), but difficult to understand. [Tip: A common misspelling is "manger" instead of "manager." Since "manger" is a correctly spelled word, catch it by doing a search-and-replace.]

Paper Length Limits

The length of your paper should be **20 to 25 pages, double-spaced, using a 12-point font with 1-inch margins**. Be sure to number each page. This paper length limit does not include the Title Page or an Appendix (if applicable).

It is helpful to print the Title Page separately from the body of the paper, so that it is not accidentally numbered as page 1. The first page with a number on it should be the page *following* the Title Page.

Grading Criteria

These are the criteria that will be used to evaluate your paper. Read them before beginning to write your paper. If your paper has addressed all of the questions and issues that are spelled out in the grading criteria, it is likely to get a higher grade than a paper for which this kind of checking has not been done. Note that these criteria are closely related to providing good answers to the various questions presented in the prior key sections.

1. **Overall Grasp of Material.** Based on the information supplied in this paper, do the writers of this paper really understand conflict, particularly the Conflict Management Styles Model and how to analyze and apply that model in actual real-world situations? In general, did the writers of this paper *apply, analyze, synthesize,* and *evaluate* effectively?

2. **Effectiveness of Example Analyses of the Five Conflict Management Styles.** Did the writers display a clear understanding of each of the five conflict management styles, especially how to do an in-depth analysis of the Contingency Factors, following the implementation guidelines in the Application section of this chapter, to determine which conflict management style is the best fit for any particular situation? Were the general causes of each conflict clearly presented?

3. **Effectiveness of an Example Future Conflict and Some Recommendations for Coping with It.** Did the writers make—and support—predictions about a likely specific future conflict? Were the general causes of the conflict clearly presented? Did the writers perform an in-depth analysis of the Contingency Factors, following the implementation guidelines in the Application section of this chapter, to determine which conflict management style—Collaborating, Compromising, or Forcing—would be the most effective way to facilitate resolution or settlement of the likely conflict situation? Did their discussion concerning why this recommended style was chosen make sense and do a thorough job of explaining why possible alternative approaches were rejected? Were the suggestions regarding how, when, and by whom the recommended style should be implemented in the actual organizational setting logically presented?

4. **Effectiveness of an Example Current/Future Group Project Conflict and Some Recommendations for Coping with It**. Did the writers provide and support information about a current conflict, or make and support predictions about a likely specific future conflict? Were the general causes of the conflict clearly presented? Did the writers perform an in-depth analysis of the Contingency Factors, following the implementation guidelines in the Application section of this chapter to determine which conflict management style—Collaborating, Compromising, or Forcing—would be the most effective way to facilitate resolution or settlement of the likely conflict situation? Did their discussion concerning why this recommended style was chosen make sense and do a thorough job of explaining why possible alternative approaches were rejected? Were the suggestions regarding how, when, and by

whom the recommended style should be implemented in the actual group setting logically presented?

5. **Overall Effectiveness of Communication.** In the paper as a whole, is the content organized according to the required format, including required and optional subtitles? Is the paper presented in a writing style that is clear, flowing, and easy for the reader to follow? Is the writing style consistent, or does it appear to have been written by a number of different people who are taking different approaches or have different writing styles? Is the paper written in a more objective third-person format rather than a more subjective first-person format using "I" or "we"? Is the paper free of typographical errors? Are the pages numbered properly?

Determining Individual Group Member Evaluations

Individual grades on the Group Project will be based on how well the group as a whole does plus how well each individual member within the group contributes to the group, as rated by the other members of the group. In most cases, each individual project group member's grade on the project will be determined by multiplying the project group's grade by that individual's average rating, as determined by the other members of that project group. In instances where an individual's average rating is significantly below the average (i.e., significantly less than 100% contribution), an even lower grade may be given (see below).

The total points available may be calculated as follows:

Number of people in your group = _____ – 1 = _____ × 100 = _____

For example, a student in a group of six people would have 6 – 1 = 5 × 100 = 500 points to distribute among the other five group members. It would not be wise to give points to oneself. The number you have just calculated for your own group is the number of points you may distribute among your group members during this evaluation. In the spaces provided on the separate evaluation sheet supplied by your instructor, write in the names of the *other* members of your group and the share of the total points available that you feel each group member deserves.

If you feel that everyone in your group contributed equally, give every other group member 100 points each. If all group members do this, each member will get 100% of the group's project grade, or 1.00 × (the numerical equivalent of the group's grade). For example, if the group's grade on the project is a B+ = 3.3, and every group member is rated as contributing equally, every group member's grade will be calculated as follows:

1.00 × 3.3 = 3.30

Every group member will thus receive a grade of B+ on the project.

If you feel that some group members contributed more than others, you may give more than 100 points to the perceived higher contributors and less than 100 points to the perceived lower contributors. **In the interest of overall fairness, the total points given must equal the total points available, so please check that these totals match.**

The **maximum** number of **points** you can give to any individual is **140**.

The **minimum** number of **points** you can give to any individual is **0**.

Anyone whose **average** point total falls **below 60** will automatically receive an **F** on the project.

Anyone whose **average** point total is **between 60 and 69.99** will receive either a **D or** his/her calculated grade on the project (average rating × group grade), whichever is lower.

Anyone whose **average** point total is **between 70 and 79.99** will receive either a **C or** his/her calculated grade on the project (average rating × group grade), whichever is lower.

If at least one member of your group has an average rating below 80, the ratings for all of the other group members whose average ratings are 80 or above will be **normalized** and then re-calculated to determine those group members' average point totals. This means determining what the ratings *would have been* if the person(s) with low average ratings had not been in the group, and then doing the grade calculations. If this were not done, the other members in a group with at least one low-rated member would receive inflated grades compared to groups in which all members contributed approximately equally.

The maximum grade any individual may receive on the group project is an A (= 4.0).

Example Group Member Evaluations
Number of People in Your Group = 6 – 1 = 5 × 100 = 500

Name of Group Member	Points
Nina	120
Fred	110
Ngoc	100
Mario	95
Shanna	75

Check that total points given = total points available   500

Note: When the project has been completed, your instructor will provide blank copies of the above form for each group member to fill out and hand in separately.

■ *Case Study 5-1*

CHOOSING A CONFLICT MANAGEMENT STYLE: THE CASE OF TWO EMPLOYEES IN THE MAIL ROOM DEPARTMENT

The purpose of this case study is to apply the Conflict Management Styles Model and other conflict-related analyses to a real-world case involving members of a department in a public service organization.

The Case

The mail room department, located in a post office, consists of 10 employees plus a departmental supervisor.

It is a busy Monday morning in the mail room department. Unfortunately, in addition to the hectic level of activity, a conflict has arisen between two members of the department. It seems that one employee's favorite football/basketball team lost over the past weekend to another team that had a losing record. One of the other employees is teasing the first employee about that loss.

Activity Process Outline

Form groups of 5 to 7 students.

Use the material provided in the Applications section of this chapter (plus the first page of the chapter) to determine (a) the general cause of the conflict in this case; (b) the most appropriate initial conflict management style to use to deal with this conflict; and (c) the fallback style to use if the initial conflict management style should prove to be ineffective. [Reminder: The general cause of a conflict may be a result of communication differences, structural differences, personal differences, or some combination of these.]

[Hints: Follow the implementation guidelines presented in the Application section, and take advantage of Figure 5-7, which summarizes all five conflict management styles. A section that discusses fallback styles appears immediately after the implementation guidelines. The Application Example also shows how to perform the analysis needed to determine the initial conflict management style.]

After all of the groups have determined the general cause, the initial style, and the fallback style for this case, the class will compare and discuss these findings.

■ *Case Study 5-2*

CHOOSING A CONFLICT MANAGEMENT STYLE: THE CASE OF THE STUDENT PROJECT GROUP

The purpose of this case study is to apply the Conflict Management Styles Model and other conflict-related analyses to a real-world case involving a student project group.

The Case

A group of five students has been meeting to discuss the group project they are required to complete this term. The project, which is due at the end of the term, should be 30 to 40 pages long and is worth 40% of the grade in the course.

The students have already met on the second and fourth Wednesdays of the prior month (i.e., every two weeks). At the end of the last meeting, someone had said "See you at the next meeting at the regular time," and the other members nodded their heads in agreement.

Three of the students in the group showed up at the regular meeting place on the first Wednesday of the new month, two weeks after the last meeting. They waited and waited, but the other two students never arrived. Only one of them could be reached by phone—and he quickly said he thought the meeting was planned for the second week of the month.

Activity Process Outline

Form groups of 5 to 7 students.

Use the material provided in the Applications section of this chapter (plus the first page of the chapter) to determine (a) the general cause of the conflict in this case; (b) the most appropriate initial conflict management style to use to deal with this conflict; and (c) the fallback style to use if the initial conflict management style should prove to be ineffective. [Reminder: The general cause of a conflict may be a result of communication differences, structural differences, personal differences, or some combination of these.]

[Hints: Follow the implementation guidelines presented in the Application section, and take advantage of Figure 5-7, which summarizes all five conflict management styles in one place. A subsection that discusses fallback styles appears immediately after the implementation guidelines. The Application Example also shows how to perform the analysis needed to determine the initial conflict management style.]

After all of the groups have determined the general cause, the initial style, and the fallback style for this case, the class will compare and discuss these findings.

■ *Case Study 5-3*

CHOOSING A CONFLICT MANAGEMENT STYLE: THE CASE OF A DOWNTURN AT COMPANY J

The purpose of this case study is to apply the Conflict Management Styles Model and other conflict-related analyses to a real-world case involving a company that is experiencing a reduction in sales.

The Case

Company J, which had performed quite well last year, is currently facing a drop in demand for its products. The chief executive officer (CEO) of Company J has just e-mailed a memo to the general managers in charge of the company's four divisions. The memo clearly states the current sales levels and the forecasted sales over the next year, which are projected to continue the downward trend. The memo concludes by stating that all divisions must cut costs by 12%. How that cost-cutting is accomplished is to be up to the division managers.

The general manager of Division 2 is very aware that none of his functional managers want to reduce their budgets. In addition, the GM feels strongly that the budgets of certain key revenue-producing functions must not be cut. He also knows in advance that such a policy will make the other functional managers very unhappy.

Activity Process Outline

Form groups of 5 to 7 students.

Use the material provided in the Applications section of this chapter (plus the first page of the chapter) to determine (a) the general cause of the conflict in this case; (b) the most appropriate initial conflict management style to use to deal with this conflict; and (c) the fallback style to use if the initial conflict management style should prove to be ineffective. [Reminder: The general cause of a conflict may be a result of communication differences, structural differences, personal differences, or some combination of these.]

[Hints: Follow the implementation guidelines presented in the Application section, and take advantage of Figure 5-7 which summarizes all five conflict management styles in one place. A section that discusses fallback styles appears immediately after the implementation guidelines. The Application Example also shows how to perform the analysis needed to determine the initial conflict management style.]

After all of the groups have determined the general cause, the initial style, and the fallback style for this case, the class will compare and discuss these findings.

■ *Case Study 5-4*

CHOOSING AND IMPLEMENTING A CONFLICT MANAGEMENT STYLE: THE CASE OF THE SQUABBLING SUBORDINATES

The purpose of this case study is to apply the Conflict Management Styles Model and other conflict-related analyses to a more detailed real-world case involving two part-time administrative assistants who are sharing a job.

The Case

Tough Times (TT) is a small, entrepreneurial firm that provides consulting services and teaches classes to a wide variety of individuals. About 20 people are employed at TT. Half of these people are full-time employees, whereas the other half work there on a part-time basis. The president oversees the work of the consultants, while the vicepresident of operations is in charge of the administrative staff. This case concerns a conflict between two administrative staff members who are currently job-sharing the primary administrative staff position.

Sharon has been with TT since its inception some five years ago. After graduating from high school, she decided to work full-time rather than go to college. The consulting business activities interested her. Furthermore, she wanted to make some money so she could leave home and live independently, plus eventually buy a new car and clothes. She began work at TT as a combination receptionist and general "gofer." However, because she was a fast learner, she soon became involved in many other administrative aspects of the business, working closely with the president as the tiny firm slowly but surely built up a clientele. More recently, however, as the firm began to expand substantially and as Sharon widened her own horizons, she realized that she would need a college degree to be able to do what she really wanted to do. She therefore decided to go to school part-time while continuing to work part-time at TT. The new vice president of operations encouraged her to do this. The VP agreed that the firm would allow Sharon to share her job with a new part-time employee, to be hired as soon as possible.

The job search for a second part-time administrative assistant led to the hiring of a man in his mid-20s, named Dan. Dan already had one part-time job, but needed more money. Thus he was pleased to find a job-sharing situation at TT that allowed him to work 40 hours per week at two fairly different types of jobs. Dan also proved to be a fast learner. Within a couple of months, he was actually better than Sharon at several aspects of their shared job, and improving steadily on other tasks. As Dan gained knowledge and developed skills, he began to notice that Sharon had a tendency to focus on the parts of their job that she found easy, fun, or both, while letting Dan deal with the leftovers. Dan did enjoy doing some of the things that Sharon did not like to do, including several of the tasks that he was now performing very well. However, he felt it wasn't fair for Sharon to consistently dump many of the job's difficult or boring tasks on him. Dan perceived Sharon to be taking advantage of her seniority, her close relationships with the vice president and president, and her previous full-time status. Dan, a forthright individual, began to make his opinions known to other employees. Sharon quickly got the word via the grapevine.

Sharon felt both defensive and threatened by Dan and his actions. She did not feel his accusations were justified, as she had worked hard, developed quite a few new job-related skills, helped the firm grow, and so on. She was also genuinely concerned that Dan was learning many aspects of their shared job very quickly, and was performing better than her on some tasks that were undoubtedly important to the firm, if not particularly enjoyable to her (e.g., financial calculations). A further source of conflict for Sharon was that she wanted Dan to like her as a person. So Sharon attempted to resolve her conflicting feelings by trying to be nice to Dan and by continuing to do her job as she had always done. But Dan continued to feel there was a problem. Several months later, Sharon finally exploded and had long talks about the situation with both the vice president of operations and her long-term mentor, the president.

Assume you are advising the vice president of operations on how to deal with this conflict situation. The VP and the president have agreed that there is a problem, and that both employees have made some good points. The president has agreed that VP should handle the conflict, since the VP is Sharon's and Dan's direct boss.

Activity Process Outline
Form groups of 5 to 7 students.

Use the material provided in the Applications section of this chapter (plus the first page of the chapter) to determine (a) the general cause of the conflict in this case; (b) the most appropriate initial conflict management style to use to deal with this conflict; and (c) the fallback style to use if the initial conflict management style should prove to be ineffective. [Reminder: The general cause of a conflict may be a result of communication differences, structural differences, personal differences, or some combination of these.]

[Hints: Follow the implementation guidelines presented in the Application section, and take advantage of Figure 5-7 which summarizes all five conflict management styles in one place. A section that discusses fallback styles appears immediately after the implementation guidelines. The Application Example also shows how to perform the analysis needed to determine the initial conflict management style.]

Getting into more detail, exactly how would you suggest that the VP *implement* the initial conflict management style you have recommended? In other words, when, where, and how would you suggest the VP talk to Sharon and Dan about the conflict? What should the VP try to accomplish during this talk or these talks, and in what sequence? Should any other organizational members become directly involved in the effort to resolve this conflict? If so, why and how?

After all of the groups have determined the general cause, the initial style, and the fallback style for this case, along with answers to the various questions concerning implementation of the initial style, the class will compare and discuss these results.

REFERENCE NOTES

1. Robbins, S. P. *Managing Organizational Conflict: A Non-Traditional Approach.* Englewood Cliffs, NJ: Prentice-Hall, 1974.

2. See Blake & Mouton (1964); see also Thomas (1976), Ruble & Thomas (1976), Thomas (1979), Thomas (1992a), and Thomas (1992b) for a related but slightly different dichotomization. Blake, R. R., and J. S. Mouton. *The Managerial Grid.* Houston, TX: Gulf Publishing, 1964.; Thomas, K. W. Conflict and Conflict Management. In M. D. Dunnette (ed.), *Handbook of Organizational Behavior.* Chicago: Rand-McNally, 1976, pp. 889–935.; Ruble, T., and K. Thomas. Support for a Two-Dimensional Model of Conflict Behavior. *Organizational Behavior and Human Performance,* Vol. 16, 1976, pp. 143–155; Thomas, K. W. Organizational Conflict. In S. Kerr (ed.), *Organizational Behavior.* Columbus, OH: Grid Publishing, 1979, pp. 151–181; Thomas, K. W. Conflict and Conflict Management: Reflections and Update. *Journal of Organizational Behavior,* Vol. 13, 1992 (a), pp. 265–274; Thomas, K. W. Conflict and Negotiation Processes in Organizations. In M. D. Dunnette and L. M. Hough (eds.), *Handbook of Industrial and Organizational Psychology,* 2nd ed. Palo Alto, CA: Consulting Psychologists Press, Vol. 3, 1992 (b), pp. 651–717.

3. Thomas, K. W. Conflict and Conflict Management: Reflections and Update. *Journal of Organizational Behavior,* Vol. 13, 1992 (a), pp. 265–274.

4. Blake, R. R., and J. S. Mouton. *The Managerial Grid.* Houston, TX: Gulf Publishing, 1964.

5. Thomas, K. W. Organizational Conflict. In S. Kerr (ed.), *Organizational Behavior.* Columbus, OH: Grid Publishing, 1979, pp. 151–181. Thomas (1979) prefers the term "Competing" instead of "Forcing." However, while Competing applies to an individual's "Conflict-Handling Modes," Forcing is a "Related Term" that better describes the conflict *management* style that would be used by a manager who is attempting to facilitate the resolution or settlement of a conflict involving *two other* parties (e.g., two subordinates). See Table 7-1 on page 157 of Thomas (1979).

6. Blake, R. R., and J. S. Mouton. *The Managerial Grid.* Houston, TX: Gulf Publishing, 1964.

7. Blake, R. R., and J. S. Mouton. *The Managerial Grid.* Houston, TX: Gulf Publishing, 1964.

8. Thomas, K. W. Toward Multi-Dimensional Values in Teaching: The Example of Conflict Behaviors. *Academy of Management Review,* Vol. 2, 1977, pp. 484–490.

9. Thomas, K. W. Toward Multi-Dimensional Values in Teaching: The Example of Conflict Behaviors. *Academy of Management Review,* Vol. 2, 1977, pp. 484–490.

10. Ury, W. *Getting Past No: Negotiating Your Way from Confrontation to Cooperation,* rev. ed. New York: Bantam Books, 1993.

11. Baron, R. A., S. P. Fortin, R. L. Frei, L. A. Hauver, and M. L. Shack. Reducing Organizational Conflict: The Role of Socially Induced Positive Affect. *International Journal of Conflict Management,* Vol. 1, 1990, pp. 133–152.

12. Thomas, K. W. Toward Multi-Dimensional Values in Teaching: The Example of Conflict Behaviors. *Academy of Management Review,* Vol. 2, 1977, pp. 484–490.

13. Johnson, D. W., G. Maruyama, R. Johnson, D. Nelson, and L. Skon. Effects of Cooperative, Competitive, and Individualistic Goal Structures on Achievement: A Meta-Analysis. *Psychological Bulletin,* Vol. 89, 1981, pp. 47–62.

14. Vroom, V. H., and P. W. Yetton. *Leadership and Decision-Making.* Pittsburgh: University of Pittsburgh Press, 1973.

15. Thomas, K. W. Toward Multi-Dimensional Values in Teaching: The Example of Conflict Behaviors. *Academy of Management Review,* Vol. 2, 1977, pp. 484–490. The contingency factor concerning the use of Compromising as a backup has been removed from this list for Compromising because backup or "fallback" conflict management styles are covered in depth later in the chapter.

16. Thomas, K. W. Toward Multi-Dimensional Values in Teaching: The Example of Conflict Behaviors. *Academy of Management Review,* Vol. 2, 1977, pp. 484–490.

17. Vroom, V. H., and A. G. Jago. *The New Leadership: Managing Participation in Organizations.* Englewood Cliffs, NJ: Prentice-Hall, 1988; Vroom, V. H., and P. W. Yetton. *Leadership and Decision-Making.* Pittsburgh: University of Pittsburgh Press, 1973.

18. Thomas, K. W. Toward Multi-Dimensional Values in Teaching: The Example of Conflict Behaviors. *Academy of Management Review,* Vol. 2, 1977, pp. 484–490.

19. Ury, W. *Getting Past No: Negotiating Your Way from Confrontation to Cooperation,* rev. ed. New York: Bantam Books, 1993; Walton, R. E., and R. B. McKersie. *A Behavioral Theory of Labor Negotiations: An Analysis of a Social Interaction System.* New York: McGraw-Hill, 1965.

20. Ury, W. *Getting Past No: Negotiating Your Way from Confrontation to Cooperation,* rev. ed. New York, NY: Bantam Books, 1993; Walton, R. E., and R. B. McKersie. *A Behavioral Theory of Labor Negotiations: An Analysis of a Social Interaction System.* New York: McGraw-Hill, 1965.

21. This approach is substantially based on research work done at the Program on Negotiation at Harvard University. Ury, W. *Getting Past No: Negotiating Your Way from Confrontation to Cooperation,* rev. ed. New York: Bantam Books, 1993.

22. Pruitt, D. G., J. D. Carnevale, O. Ben-Yoav, T. H. Nochajski, and M. R. Van Slyck. Incentives for Cooperation in Integrative Bargaining. In R. Tietz (ed.), *Aspiration Levels in Bargaining and Economic Decision Making.* New York: Springer-Verlag, 1983, pp. 118–149.

23. This section is based on Thomas (1977) but may have been extended slightly beyond what Thomas originally intended in an effort to create a practically useful contingency theory of conflict management styles. Thomas, K. W. Toward Multi-Dimensional Values in Teaching: The Example of Conflict Behaviors. *Academy of Management Review,* Vol. 2, 1977, pp. 484–490.

24. Thomas, K. W. Toward Multi-Dimensional Values in Teaching: The Example of Conflict Behaviors. *Academy of Management Review,* Vol. 2, 1977, pp. 484–490.

25. Thomas, K. W. Toward Multi-Dimensional Values in Teaching: The Example of Conflict Behaviors. *Academy of Management Review,* Vol. 2, 1977, pp. 484–490. See also Note 15.

26. Thomas, K. W. Toward Multi-Dimensional Values in Teaching: The Example of Conflict Behaviors. *Academy of Management Review,* Vol. 2, 1977, pp. 484–490. See also Note 15.

27. Thomas, K. W. Toward Multi-Dimensional Values in Teaching: The Example of Conflict Behaviors. *Academy of Management Review,* Vol. 2, 1977, pp. 484–490.

28. Robbins, S. P. *Managing Organizational Conflict: A Non-Traditional Approach.* Englewood Cliffs, NJ: Prentice-Hall, 1974.

29. Robbins, S. P. *Training in Interpersonal Skills: TIPS for Managing People at Work.* Englewood Cliffs, NJ: Prentice-Hall, 1989.

CHAPTER 6
Analyzing Power

Power and politics appear to be inevitable at most hierarchical levels within most organizations. Thus, many organizational members have three basic options concerning power and politics: ignore them, become aware of them, or become actively involved in them.[1]

This chapter presents information that primarily supports the second of the three options noted above. Choosing the first option could lead to potentially disastrous consequences for a naive organizational member who might accidentally get in the way or unintentionally step on some powerful toes. The second option creates a level of awareness about power that helps a person survive within a work environment in which political conflicts often occur. The third option involves a shift from merely observing the power game to actually playing the power game, and frequently raises some serious ethical questions. An understanding of power (option 2) is clearly a prerequisite for becoming directly involved in exercising control or influencing important organizational decisions (option 3). Since political activity has been shown to increase at successively higher levels in an organizational hierarchy,[2] some degree of option 3 is probably necessary for *most managers*. For the record, the authors sincerely hope that readers of this chapter will use this knowledge in an ethical manner.

Some people view the terms *power* and *politics* as two alternative ways of saying essentially the same thing. However, these are two distinctly different concepts, as the following definitions will demonstrate.

A definition of **power** that effectively integrates several previously developed definitions is "the potential ability to influence behavior, to change the course of events, to overcome resistance, and to get people to do things that they would not otherwise do."[3] Note that this potential ability may never be used. Many people who have power choose to use it sparingly or not at all. A surprising number of people are not even aware of the power they have.

Politics "involves activities which lead to decisions as to what will be done in situations where an obviously correct decision does not exist."[4] In other words, in unclear or uncertain situations, people may be motivated to try to influence decisions—to achieve the results they prefer (see also Chapter 7). If such persons make use of any of the power bases available to them to enhance the effectiveness of their influence attempts, they are engaging in politics. Thus politics may be viewed as the *use of power*.

While most chapters in this book focus on a key integrated model related to the chapter's topic area, research on individual power has tended to create lists or sets of important power bases. Hence an integrated or synthesized *set* of key individual power bases is presented and explained next, followed by descriptions of several more esoteric or unusual power bases. A practical approach to assessing power then provides a framework for analyzing individual power in a real-life organization. Techniques are elucidated for determining who the most powerful people in an organization are and for estimating how much power each of these individuals has. The important issue of politics and ethics serves as the culminating concern in this chapter.

THE SYNTHESIZED SET OF KEY INDIVIDUAL POWER BASES

Organizational behavior researchers have been attempting to determine the most important bases of power since the 1950s. The original classic theory of the bases of power, plus many more recent research efforts that focus on power bases, are summarized in the supplement for Chapter 6 that appears in an appendix at the back of this book. That appendix also contains a critical analysis and synthesis—an in-depth application of those two higher-level learning categories—for all of those power bases. The results of that synthesis supply the foundation for the discussion that follows.

This section focuses on a synthesized set of the six most important *individual* power bases (see Figure 6-1). In addition to individuals having power bases, note that organizational subunits, such as functions or departments, may also have power bases. Coverage of the power bases available to organizational subunits—which, although sometimes quite similar, are frequently different than individual power bases—is beyond the scope of this book.

CONTROL OVER RESOURCES

Control Over Resources[5] has been defined by experts on power in a variety of ways, most broadly to encompass the Formal Authority, Expert Power, Referent Power, and Control Over Information power bases as well.[6] However, it has proven much more useful to consider each of these other key individual power bases separately. Therefore, Control Over Resources will refer to control over *material* resources (see also Chapter 4).

Money tends to be a very important material resource in most organizations, so managers controlling larger budgets are typically more powerful. **Equipment,** which includes such items as vehicles, computers, and machines, is another category of valued material resources. **Supplies** are different than equipment as they involve items that must be replenished periodically. Supplies include such items as raw materials, gasoline, printer toner cartridges, and paper. **Space** within the properties owned or

Figure 6-1   The Synthesized Set of Key Individual Power Bases

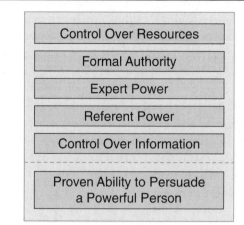

leased by the organization is another category of material resource. More powerful managers, for example, may control more total square footage of floor space.

Several factors help determine the value of each resource controlled, and thus the amount of power that results from controlling each of those resources. Control over scarce, critical, or liquid resources leads to greater overall power.[7]

Scarce resources may be defined as resources that are difficult to obtain. Note that if a substitute for a scarce resource becomes available, this would *reduce* overall power, since that resource would no longer be scarce.[8]

Critical resources are those resources that are desperately needed to accomplish some task or goal. Examples of material resources that have often attained critical resource status in a variety of organizations include monetary allocations in the form of budgets; certain kinds of equipment, such as photocopy machines; and certain kinds of supplies, such as gasoline.

Liquid resources are specifically concerned with the relative liquidity of the various forms of money.[9] The more liquid a particular form of money is, the easier it is to convince a wider variety of people to accept that money. Generally speaking, the most liquid form of money is *cash*. A storekeeper or a seller of a previously owned car might not take a personal check or even a very well-known credit card, but cash is usually acceptable to most people.

The relative liquidity of various forms of money is a fairly straightforward concept to understand, although it might be necessary to consult a financial expert to determine what major differences currently exist between the various forms of money other than cash. However, a less straightforward question is "Exactly what is scarce or critical in any particular organization?" While which resources are scarce or critical is likely to vary over time and across organizations, a helpful general answer to this question is that what is scarce or critical are the resources needed to solve the biggest problems currently facing a particular organization.[10]

For example, consider the case of a new restaurant. Establishing such a business typically requires a fair amount of money. This seems likely to be a scarce and critical resource—and perhaps a liquid one as well, depending on the kinds of funding available. Hence, a wealthy owner or partner in the business would have significant power as a result of supplying and controlling monetary resources. The restaurant general manager might gain control over the only computer in the restaurant: a scarce and critical piece of equipment. A chef responsible for ordering food supplies would control a critical resource. In fact, some types of food would be more critical than others, and possibly scarce at times as well.

One final point concerning scarce, critical, or liquid resources merits mention. Control over a resource that is *both* scarce and critical will likely lead to even greater overall power. In fact, any combination of scarce, critical, and liquid, when applied to resources, will likely lead to even greater power.[11]

APPLICATION & ANALYSIS

A Highly Scarce, Critical, and Liquid Resource

What is the only resource that can be highly scarce, critical, and liquid simultaneously, and is therefore frequently considered an extremely important resource in a wide variety of organizations?

FORMAL AUTHORITY

Most organizations give their managers **Formal Authority**[12] to control the actions of the people who work under those managers. At the lowest level of management, a manager controls his own subordinates. At higher levels of management, a manager not only controls the actions of his own subordinates, but indirectly controls the actions of his subordinates' subordinates, possibly his subordinates' subordinates' subordinates, and so forth. Thus the amount of Formal Authority held by any given manager depends on both the manager's level in the organizational hierarchy and the total number of people over whom he has the authority to exert control.

Formal Authority is generally a strong power base, and certainly one that many managers use quite frequently. Some experts on power have noted that *some* managers may also choose to make more extreme use of their Formal Authority to coerce or threaten people—particularly subordinates—into doing what these managers want.[13]

Broadly speaking, people are a form of resource—the so-called "headcount" under the direct and indirect control of any particular manager. People can be scarce, critical, or both—but not liquid. At times when people are scarce, critical, or both, managers controlling more of them will have an even greater degree of Formal Authority.

EXPERT POWER

Expert Power[14] is exactly what it sounds like: power resulting from having some level of expertise. A variety of different ways of looking at this very important power base follow. It is helpful to carefully consider all of these approaches when making an overall assessment of how much Expert Power any given individual may have.

Expert Power generally falls into one of two categories.[15] The first category, a **technical skill,** focuses on specific skills, such as operating a bulldozer or installing a computer system. In contrast, a **body of knowledge** is broader than a technical skill. Students' majors in college will provide each of them with a body of knowledge by the time they graduate. Both technical skills and bodies of knowledge can be valuable kinds of expertise.

Similarly to the case for resources, what is more valuable is likely to depend on how scarce or critical any given skill or knowledge is to an organization at any point in time. A person who has scarce, critical, or especially scarce *and* critical skills and knowledge is said to have **relative irreplaceability.**[16] A person who would be difficult to replace has relatively strong Expert Power compared to others who are more easily replaceable. Note that the concept of liquidity does not apply to this power base.

Another key perspective related to Expert Power is the use of it to cause **uncertainty reduction.**[17] While Expert Power per se is likely to be valuable, Expert Power that has been *proven* through the reduction of organizational uncertainty is arguably even more valuable. If the vice president of Finance has already managed to obtain a large loan on behalf of her company at a relatively low interest rate, it is not unreasonable for top management and the Board of Directors to anticipate that the vice president will probably be able to effectively reduce similar uncertainties in the future. This further enhances her Expert Power as perceived by those other major power players.

It is important to note that just making a decision does not create Expert Power. For example, a manager who decides which people will be laid off during a business slump merely provides an answer to an important issue about which people were uncertain. To cause uncertainty reduction and increase overall Expert Power as a result, an individual must *solve an important problem effectively*. In other words, the answer developed to cope with any particular problem must prove to be an outstanding one that provides significant benefits to the organization.

The more critical the uncertainty, the more power a particular individual will gain by effectively resolving or reducing that uncertainty. Organizational members who have reduced critical uncertainties often gain tremendous reputations for solving important problems, which lead to substantial increases in their overall Expert Power. Note that the concepts of scarcity and liquidity do not apply to uncertainty reduction.

Expert Power is a power base that *anyone* in an organization can have. In fact, everyone working in a business organization has at least some degree of it, given that a certain level of Expert Power is a requirement for virtually all jobs. Another point is that in many organizations, expertise is perceived as a legitimate basis for justifying a decision to do something in a particular way.[18] Thus, the legitimacy of expertise can sometimes be as powerful as the legitimacy of Formal Authority, if not even more so.

Expert Power in a Motorcycle Club

One of the members of a motorcycle club does not hold any formal position in the club. However, he knows just where to find the right parts and how to perform many of the repairs on the members' bikes when they break down. *Analyze* which of the various ways of looking at overall Expert Power seem likely to *apply* to this person. Consider the concepts of a technical skill, a body of knowledge, uncertainty reduction, and those important modifying factors: scarce and critical.[19]

REFERENT POWER

According to its original definition, **Referent Power** is based on identification, prestige, and attraction.[20] A reference group for a given individual might be her personal group of friends or a departmental group in which she works. Within any reference group, there are usually a number of individuals who have relatively strong appeal to other members of that group. Identification with a particular individual, the prestige of a particular individual, or attraction to a particular individual all lead to Referent Power for that individual in the context of that reference group.

Perhaps an easier, less confusing way to comprehend the concept of Referent Power is to think in terms of someone being so well liked and appealing as a person that others will often go out of their way to do what that person wants them to do.

Referent Power tends to be used frequently in many organizations. Managers who have relatively high Referent Power can use it where possible in place of Formal Authority, thus saving the latter for special cases rather than using it constantly.

As is the case for Expert Power, Referent Power is a power base that *anyone* in an organization can have. Note that Referent Power is determined almost entirely by the characteristics of the particular *person* involved, rather than the organizational *position* currently held by that person.

CONTROL OVER INFORMATION

Control Over Information[21] results when a person who is in a position to receive a large amount of useful information concerning an organization is able to decide to whom he will communicate—or not communicate—that information.

Selectively passing along only certain information to others is called **filtering**.[22] Filtering is the most common technique for controlling information, and virtually everybody does it—out of sheer necessity. In our modern world, everyone is constantly bombarded with huge amounts of information. Realistically, one could only pass along a small proportion of that information to a small number of other people. However, filtering clearly becomes a political strategy based on the Control Over Information power base when an individual *deliberately* holds back information that another person in the same organization needs to effectively perform his or her job. More commonly, people who receive a broad array of relevant information concerning a particular issue are more likely to pass along information that supports a position or approach they favor, as opposed to one they do not favor.

Information can be scarce or critical—but not liquid. As usual, controlling information that is both scarce and critical leads to even greater overall power. However, similarly to the case for resources where scarcity is concerned, the introduction of a substitute for certain information—or a substitute *source* for the *same* information—reduces overall power.

Opportunities to control information usually depend on a person's location within one or more communication networks. Two different kinds of roles within organizational communication networks have the potential to lead to an increase in power as a result of greater Control Over Information. These have been termed the *gatekeeper* and *nerve center* roles.[23]

Gatekeeping[24] occurs when information from an *outside* source flows *into* an organization through a particular individual. In other words, a **gatekeeper** basically opens an information gate by relaying some relevant outside information to one or more people inside the organization. However, exactly *where* the information will flow from the gatekeeper to other people inside the organization is often under the gatekeeper's control to a significant extent.

Note that gatekeeping is a rather common phenomenon. Anyone who talks to someone who works for another company, reads an organizationally related article, or attends a trade show may be in a position to act as a gatekeeper. What is particularly important with respect to conducting a power analysis is how valuable—i.e., how scarce, critical, or both—that external information might be to other people inside the organization. Examples might include information about a technological breakthrough, a recent survey of customer preferences, a competitor's new product, a way to successfully implement a management technique that has proven to be very effective, or the latest version of a tax law.

In contrast, a **nerve center role** occurs whenever a person occupies a position of communication centrality *within* an organization. In this scenario, information has the potential to flow from one part of the organization to another, and individuals who are in central positions within the organization's communication network are well positioned to control the internal information that flows through that network. In other words, some information manages to flow further—or more strongly or more clearly—than other information.

Managers are often in excellent positions to play nerve center roles. All of those management meetings create a large amount of information, as do managers' efforts to coordinate between departments and to communicate between levels in the organizational hierarchy. However, administrative assistants may have as much communication centrality as many managers. People occupying staff positions typically do not make decisions, but may use Control Over Information to influence decision outcomes.[25] Receptionists may also occupy central positions in at least some of the communication networks in many organizations.

PROVEN ABILITY TO PERSUADE A POWERFUL PERSON
The Proven Ability to Persuade a Powerful Person[26] power base is different compared to the five power bases covered previously in that it is *indirect* in nature. A person who has a significant degree of Control Over Resources, Formal Authority, Expert Power, Referent Power, or Control Over Information can make direct use of whichever

available power bases would best apply in any given situation. In contrast, a person who has a significant degree of the Proven Ability to Persuade a Powerful Person power base must convince the powerful person in question to use one or more of his *own* power bases in such a way that the outcome will be what the persuader wants. Thus, the persuader does not exert power directly, but through a more powerful person instead. As a result, this power base is somewhat less potent than the other five.

For example, a lower-level manager might use her Proven Ability to Persuade a Powerful Person to convince her boss—or her boss's boss—to use his Formal Authority to change a procedure or Control Over Resources to buy a new piece of equipment. This lower-level manager does not have sufficient Formal Authority or Control Over Resources of her own to create an outcome she prefers. Therefore, she creates the desired outcome indirectly, by persuading someone who *does* have enough Formal Authority or Control Over Resources to exert the necessary power instead.

Persuading a powerful person to act on a persuasive individual's suggestions or ideas or does usually require that persuasive individual to have some solid power bases of her own. In many cases, the persuasion that occurs is due to that individual having significant Referent Power or Expert Power in the eyes of the powerful person. Alternatively, it could be a result of trading favors. For example, a manager who has computer expertise might agree to consult on a computer-related problem, in exchange for the powerful person arranging to purchase a certain piece of equipment. That piece of equipment might be something that the computer expert feels is essential for her department, but the powerful person feels is a lower priority.

The more powerful the person that one has *previously displayed* an ability to persuade, and the higher the degree of influence that one has had over this person, the greater the power one obtains from the Proven Ability to Persuade a Powerful Person power base. Obviously, the previously proven ability to persuade several *different* powerful people leads to greater power than just being able to persuade only one of those powerful people.

Note that the powerful person need not necessarily work *within* the organization that is being analyzed. However, for the Proven Ability to Persuade a Powerful Person power base to be relevant, the powerful person that one has previously displayed an ability to persuade must be in a position to use his own power bases to significantly influence *key decisions within* the organization being analyzed.

APPLICATION & ANALYSIS   Your Manager's Power

It can be helpful to determine where your current (or former) manager at work stands with respect to power. *Analyze* each of the six key individual power bases presented and explained previously. How much of each power base does your current (or former) manager have? Is it a low, moderate, or high amount? For each power base, explain *why* this is so.

SOME MORE ESOTERIC POWER BASES

S ome more esoteric or unusual individual power bases exist in addition to the more potent six key individual power bases presented in the preceding section. These esoteric power bases can be significant for people holding certain kinds of positions or for certain individuals.

Occupying a position earlier in the workflow[27] focuses on one's location in the *sequencing* of the flow of the work within an organization. Occupying a Position Earlier in the Workflow creates a power base because a person working at a *position* (job) that is earlier in the sequence of work activities has a greater opportunity to change how things get done than does someone whose position is located later in the workflow. This opportunity to *control* changes to a greater extent gives such people greater power. For example, compare an architect with a house painter, a design engineer with a production manager, or a retail buyer with a member of a retail sales staff.

A classic study of the power of "lower participants" sought to determine power bases that people might have when occupying a non-management position such as production worker, sales clerk, or administrative assistant.[28] Three such power bases that have not yet been mentioned are described next.

Seniority serves as an important power base for the lower-level participants in many organizations. People who have worked at an organization for a longer time have greater security in that organization. Seniority is a particularly applicable base of power in unionized environments.

Control Over Access to Powerful People is a power base that results when an administrative support-staff member (such as an executive secretary) can control the ability of others to gain access to a powerful person (such as an executive). Which organizational members are allowed to speak to the busy executive—and which person is allowed to speak with the executive *first*—is often controlled by the administrative support staff member.

Knowledge of the Rules is especially relevant as a power base for lower-level participants working in a bureaucracy. Clerks or others within such a bureaucracy who are very knowledgeable about the organization's rules can sometimes be selective about which of several different rules to apply in a particular situation. Alternatively, such individuals may be able to either support or block a proposed action by simply reciting a particular organizational rule. It is not uncommon for students who are attending universities or colleges—especially large ones—to have experienced some effects of administrative clerks using this power base.

APPLICATION: PRACTICAL GUIDELINES FOR ASSESSING POWER IN ORGANIZATIONS

A leading expert on power named Pfeffer suggests that the assessment of power is basically a two-step process.[29] The first step is to identify the **principal political actors**. These are the individuals who appear very likely to be the most important power players within the organization being analyzed. The second step is to estimate how much power each principal political actor has.

IDENTIFYING THE PRINCIPAL POLITICAL ACTORS

Perhaps the most obvious and straightforward way to begin to identify principal political actors is to look at organizational titles.[30] Usually—but not always—those people occupying the higher-level positions within an organization will be among the most powerful people in that organization. Examples of such positions would include the chief executive officer (CEO), president, or vice president. Similarly, the department manager is usually one of the most powerful people within any given department.

However, other less obvious factors also may be helpful when analyzing which people are the organization's key power players. In many organizations, analysis of *demographic factors* can be used to reduce the number of likely possibilities. These factors include age, gender, ethnicity, educational level, and so on. Certain hobbies, such as golf, tend to be associated with power. The same is true for memberships in certain kinds of outside organizations, such as country clubs or yacht clubs.[31]

ESTIMATING THE PRINCIPAL POLITICAL ACTORS' POWER

Five possible ways to estimate a person's power have been developed.[32] The first four ways of estimating power involve determining whether that person is **exhibiting symbols of power**, **winning or losing past power battles**, **serving on one or more key committees**, or **being viewed as one of the most powerful people in the organization**. The fifth way of estimating power is to analyze that person's **power bases**.

In addition to providing ways to estimate power, the first four of these five approaches can also be used to cross-check whether a particular person is indeed a principal political actor. Such cross-checks can thereby confirm the results of the analysis conducted during the first step in assessing power. In general, applying as many of the five approaches as possible is likely to enhance the accuracy of a power analysis. This is because information related to power is often fuzzy or unclear, and frequently rather sensitive.

Exhibiting Symbols of Power

Symbols[33] are tangible items that can actually be seen and possibly touched. While not always the most accurate and reliable indicators of power, symbols of power provide a good starting point for conducting a power assessment. Note that *true symbols* of power are those given to the individual being analyzed by the organization, as opposed to being purchased by that individual. True symbols are much more accurate indicators of power. Common examples of true symbols of power include office size, location, and furnishings; reserved parking spaces; and use of a company car or a company credit card. The extent to which a computer system that has been allocated to a particular person is newer and more sophisticated may also provide a true symbol of that person's power. Indicators of relative power might include how fast the computer operates, the size of the monitor, whether a printer must be shared, and so on.

Many symbols of power mentioned in the previous paragraph are **perquisites** of the job[34]—more commonly abbreviated as "perks" by people working in industry settings. For example, a company's president and vice president may be given reserved parking spaces as perquisites simply because they are the president and vice president. However, the president's parking space may be located closer to the front door than is the vice president's parking space.

In many situations, symbols can be viewed *unobtrusively*. In other words, symbols can often be observed without making it very obvious that a power analysis is being conducted. Since power tends to be a rather sensitive issue, being unobtrusive when performing a power analysis is generally a good idea.

Winning or Losing Past Power Battles

The consequences[35] or outcomes of past power battles often provide strong indicators suggesting which people are currently powerful. The winners of prior power battles clearly become more powerful as a result, whereas the losers of those battles become less powerful. When analyzing this particular way of estimating power, focus on key decisions that involved the organization's principal political actors. For example, which actor(s) received a larger share of last year's budget, hired more people, won a battle for a promotion, and so on? Conversely, which actor(s) received a smaller share of last year's budget, had to downsize, failed to win a battle for a promotion, and so on?

The outcomes of many past power battles are *recorded* somewhere: on pieces of paper, in a book, or in a computer file. If it is possible to legitimately obtain access to such records, much can be learned without disturbing the powerful people who are being unobtrusively analyzed.

Some kinds of records are easy to obtain, some kinds may or may not be readily available, and other kinds of records are virtually impossible to acquire or view. Items such as company annual reports and university or college catalogs require little effort to obtain, and provide much relevant information. Organization charts may or may not be available, depending on such factors as the organization's culture, the turbulence of its environment, and so on. If organization charts should happen to exist and be accessible, comparisons of the current organization chart with prior charts can, among other things, indicate who is moving up and who is not. In contrast, circulation of copies of the latest budget normally tends to be extremely limited, primarily to higher-level managers and members of the budget committee.

Asking questions *may* be a viable technique for learning who has been winning or losing past power battles. It is often the case, in most organizations, that there will be at least a few people who really enjoy telling interesting stories. The challenge is to determine which people are the storytellers—and then, in particular, to figure out which of those storytellers would feel comfortable about sharing somewhat sensitive stories. It is also important to assess a given storyteller's penchant for embellishing a story to make it more interesting at the expense of accuracy. Alternatively, ask questions of people in the organization who know and *trust* you.

Direct observation of politically sensitive decisions may also be used to determine which principal political actors have been winning or losing past power battles.

Generally speaking, it is wise to check any personal observations made against observations of other knowledgeable and trusted people who are also familiar with the organization. It is possible that they may know something you do not know. Such cross-checking enhances the accuracy of a power analysis.

APPLICATION & ANALYSIS   **Winning and Losing Past Power Battles**

When *analyzing* past power battles using publicly available information during an in-class exercise a number of years ago, a group of students noted that the now former dean and former associate dean of a certain California university's College of Business had both received their doctorates in Business Administration (DBAs) from the same university in the same year.[36] What power battle had occurred? Which job candidate won? In which publicly available document would such information be found?

Serving on One or More Key Committees

Serving on one or more Key Committees within an organization provides a person with some opportunities to influence the key decisions made by one or more powerful organizational committees. Hence, powerful people will often make an effort to join such committees. As a result, another useful way to estimate power is to check whether a principal political actor is currently a member of any Key Committees.

How to identify a Key Committee is not initially obvious. There are two important criteria to evaluate to determine whether any particular committee on which a potential principal political actor might serve is in fact a Key Committee.[37]

The first criterion is making decisions concerning the **allocation of resources**. In most organizations, certain kinds of resources are relatively scarce, and hence highly valued. Therefore, any committee that is given the responsibility to decide how to allocate large amounts of money, essential pieces of equipment, and so on is arguably an extremely important—and powerful—committee.

The second criterion is making **major organizational policy decisions**. These might include, for example, decisions concerning rules, procedures, or company strategies that *must* be followed by many other people in the organization. Any committee that is in a position to make decisions regarding such major organizational policies is clearly exercising a substantial amount of power.

Being Viewed as One of the Most Powerful People

Being viewed as one of the most powerful people in the organization certainly suggests that such a person is likely to be powerful in actual fact. This kind of information must be obtained by asking a variety of other organizational members which people within that organization are among, say, the three or four most powerful overall. A major research study found a significant correlation between being viewed as one of the most powerful people in the organization (obtained by interviewing all university department chairpersons) and the proportion of the university budget received.[38]

Obtaining honest and accurate responses from interviews with a large number of managers, as was accomplished in the above-noted research study, is an impressive accomplishment. Unlike the three approaches to assessing power described earlier, which may be relatively *un*obtrusive or not so easily noticed, this approach is a great deal more obtrusive. This is because organizational members must be asked direct questions about who has power in the organization. It is advisable to try to obtain such information from friends or friends of friends, and to clearly indicate that the information obtained will be kept *confidential*. Generally speaking, it is not a good idea to use this approach when speaking with any of the principal political actors—or any of their close friends or work colleagues—unless a high degree of trust exists. The people who exhibit the most sensitivity related to power tend to be those who indeed *have* a lot of power.

Power Bases

Power bases, also known as the determinants[39] of power, constitute the fifth and final approach to estimating power. The most accurate way to estimate a particular individual's overall power involves analyzing that individual's power bases. This requires a three-stage assessment. First, analyze which power bases each particular principal political actor possesses. Second, estimate just how much power is associated with each of those power bases. Third, estimate the sum of all of the previously determined amounts of power.

It is very important to recognize that a political actor's overall power depends largely on *how much* of each of the *key* individual power bases a person has—as opposed to the total number of *different* power bases that person has. To illustrate this point, consider a simplified example in which a higher-level manager controls a 10 million dollar budget, while a first-level manager controls a budget of only 10,000 dollars. Both managers in this example have Control Over Resources and Formal Authority power bases. If the first-level manager happens to have some Referent Power, while the higher-level manager does not, the first-level manager will have more different power bases than the higher-level manager (three versus two). However, the higher-level manager has one thousand times as much Control Over Resources plus far greater Formal Authority, and therefore clearly has greater overall power.

To take the preceding example a step further, further assume that both managers have equal Expert Power and Control Over Information, but the first-level manager also has some degree of Proven Ability to Persuade a Powerful Person with respect to his immediate boss. The first-level manager would then have six different power bases, compared to the higher-level manager's four. Nonetheless, the higher-level manager would continue to have the most overall power, based on the "how much" aspect of this power base analysis.

Note that a person's overall power is said to depend largely on how much of each of the *key* individual power bases that person has. This is a reference to the six power bases included in the Synthesized Set of Key Individual Power Bases shown in Figure 6-1. However, if any of the more esoteric power bases covered in this chapter are also strong power bases for a particular person, they can add a bit more to that person's overall power.

APPLICATION EXAMPLE

Power in Company X

To illustrate the essentials of conducting a power analysis[40] of a real-life situation, the following is an example involving a small advertising company. Three managers appear likely to be this organization's primary candidates for principal political actor status. The owner, a male in his fifties with an MBA degree, often plays golf with current and potential clients, and belongs to the local country club. The ad manager, who is a 42-year-old male with a B.S. in Business, plays a very important role in creating ads for the firm's clients. The graphics manager, a 35-year-old woman with a degree in Art (specializing in graphic arts), plays a major role in creating the layout and the artistic effects that go with the advertising text.

Figure 6-2 presents a partial Power Analysis Matrix for these three principal political actors that covers all of the five ways of assessing power discussed earlier in this Application section. Only the six key individual power bases, plus a few highlights from the first four ways of assessing power, have been analyzed for this particular example. Note that much more detail could have been included in the Power Analysis Matrix if it had been created on a much larger sheet of paper (which is highly recommended when one is conducting an in-depth power analysis).

Which of these principal political actors has the most overall power?

Many people might immediately point to the first four ways of estimating power, which along with the title appear to favor the owner as being the most powerful actor in Company X. However, a more in-depth analysis of the actual power bases suggests a very close race between the owner and the ad manager.

The first five of the six power bases in the Synthesized Set of Key Individual Power Bases (in Figure 6-1) are the most important power bases overall, for reasons explained earlier in this chapter. Comparing the owner and the ad manager across these five power bases, note that each person has one "very high" and one "moderately high" power base. In addition, the owner has two "high" power bases, whereas the ad manager has only one. However, the ad manager has two "moderate" power bases, whereas the owner has one "very low" power base. Thus, the difference in power between these two people hinges on comparing the second "high" plus the one "very low" power base with the two "moderates." Note that if the average of the "high" and the "very low" is viewed as being "moderate," these two actors are virtually tied for most overall power. In fact, if the sixth key power base (Proven Ability to Persuade a Powerful Person) is considered, the ad manager might even have a slight edge on the owner.

continues

Figure 6-2   An Example of a Power Analysis Matrix

FIRST FOUR WAYS OF ESTIMATING POWER	PRINCIPAL POLITICAL ACTORS		
	Owner	**Ad Manager**	**Graphics Manager**
Exhibiting Symbols of Power	Large office w/view, BMW company car, reserved parking, etc.	Small corner office, wooden desk, firm pays for cell phone	State-of-the-art computer, metal desk
Winning or Losing Past Power Battles	Won cost-cutting battle with members of the budget committee	Received a larger share of the budget last year	Lost battle with owner over new software
Serving on One or More Key Committees	Chairs the budget committee, which allocates financial resources	Serves on the budget committee	Not applicable (N/A)
Being Viewed as One of the Most Powerful People	All five employees surveyed say that he is most powerful	Four employees say he is the second most powerful; all five say he in the top 3	One employee says she ranks second; four of five say she is in the top 3
POWER BASES			
Control Over Resources	Very high: controls $—scarce, critical (+liquid?)	Moderately high: big budget, eqpt.	Low: some eqpt., some supplies
Formal Authority	High: he's the overall boss	Moderate: 12 people	Low: 1 person
Expert Power	Fairly high: MBA plus 32 years of experience, finds some new clients	Very high: strong regarding developing ads, scarce + critical	High: scarce + critical technical skill in graphics
Referent Power	Very low, not well liked	High w/everyone	High w/many
Control Over Information	High: strong gatekeeper, filters a lot	Moderate: some gatekeeping and nerve center roles	Moderate: more specialized
Proven Ability to Persuade a Power Person	N/A with respect to affecting this firm	High influence over owner	Moderate: sometimes sways ad manager regarding graphics

continues

So what does this virtual tie with respect to overall power imply for who might win any particular power battle that might occur between these two actors at some point in the relatively near future? Could the ad manager win the future power battle if expertise is the key issue? Probably so. On the other hand, what if the owner should happen to strongly *disagree* with the ad manager on a question involving expertise? Suddenly, the ad manager's Proven Ability to Persuade a Powerful Person—the owner—would no longer apply. And what if the issue concerned the allocation of resources? The owner has the edge with respect to this key power base, and thus would probably win that kind of future power battle.

POLITICS AND ETHICS

Power and politics appear to be inevitable in most organizations, and politics in particular seems to inevitably raise concerns about ethics. Stories chronicling the *abuse* of power—as opposed to merely the *use* of power—are legion. Once again, for the record, the authors sincerely hope that all readers of this chapter will use the knowledge acquired from it in an ethical manner.

Unfortunately, a major problem facing ethical managers is that most of them will probably be forced to become involved in their company's politics to at least some extent, whether they like it or not. Again, this will be particularly true as they are promoted to successively higher levels in their organization. Fortunately, methods of countering unethical political behavior do exist.

ANALYSIS & EVALUATION   **The Ethics of Politics**

Despite the advances in technology that have swept us into the new millennium at a frantic and exciting pace, ethical questions related to the use of power are often unresolved issues in many organizations. *Analyze* and *evaluate* the following questions. What is ethical versus unethical political behavior in organizations? In other words, where should a line be drawn? What could ethical managers do to counter the efforts of serious abusers of power?

CONCLUSION

This chapter has provided theoretical knowledge and practical techniques that enable readers to analyze power within most kinds of formal organizations.

The methods presented in this chapter for identifying the likely principal political actors in an organization can be followed up by examining the first four ways for assessing power: exhibiting symbols of power, winning or losing past power battles, serving on one or more key committees; and being viewed as one of the most powerful people in the organization. These four ways of conducting a preliminary power assessment allow the analyzer to narrow the focus of a power analysis to the three or four most powerful people within the initial group of *potential* principal political actors. How these three or four high-impact political actors rank in overall power can then be determined through careful analysis of the Synthesized Set of Key Individual Power Bases covered at the beginning of this chapter, plus any esoteric power bases that may also apply particularly strongly. Analysis of the power bases themselves leads to a more accurate determination of how much of which kinds of power each principal political actor has.

The results of such a power analysis could then be used as a basis for predicting which of the principal political actors will probably win any particular political battles that seem likely to occur in the relatively near future. Performing such a power analysis can also help to prevent the analyzer from unwittingly getting caught in the middle of these kinds of political battles—with potentially disastrous career consequences.

EXERCISES AND OTHER ACTIVITIES
■ *Experiential Exercise: In-Class 6-1*

ANALYZING POWER IN A NEARBY ORGANIZATION
The purpose of this exercise is to begin to apply concepts from the Application section on analyzing power to a nearby organization about which at least *some* relevant data can be fairly readily obtained.

Exercise Process Outline
Form groups of 5 to 7 students.

Using the material provided at the beginning of the Application section of this chapter, determine the names and titles of a number of the most powerful people in a nearby organization. Your instructor will specify the name of the organization and the number of most powerful people to identify. Your instructor will also indicate a maximum time limit for collecting this information. During that time frame, some or all members of each group may choose to leave the classroom to obtain access to various sources of nearby information.

When all of the groups have compiled a list of names and titles—or when the time limit expires—items from these lists will be presented, one principal political actor at a time. The class will then discuss the groups' findings.

Your instructor may provide additional information concerning this organization and how some of the ways of estimating power appear to apply to it.

■ *Experiential Exercise: In-Class 6-2*

ANALYZING A WAY OF ASSESSING POWER: SYMBOLS
The purpose of this exercise is to analyze actual data from actual organizations that is related to a way of assessing power covered in the Application section.

Exercise Process Outline
Form groups of 5 to 7 students.

Use the information that has been collected by the individual members of your group during Experiential Exercise: Field 6-1 (page 163) as a basis for discussing several questions related to symbols of power.

What are the most commonplace types of symbols observed by members of your group? Which two of the symbols observed appear to be the most unusual? Which of the powerful people whose symbols of power were observed by members of your group appears to be the most powerful person overall, based on symbols alone? Would that person probably be the most powerful overall if the analysis was based on all five ways of estimating power rather than just symbols? Why or why not?

When all of the groups have completed their analyses, the class will discuss the groups' findings.

■ *Experiential Exercise: In-Class 6-3*

ANALYZING A WAY OF ASSESSING POWER: KEY COMMITTEES
The purpose of this exercise is to analyze actual data from actual organizations that is related to a way of assessing power covered in the Application section.

Exercise Process Outline
Form groups of 5 to 7 students.

Use the information that has been collected by the individual members of your group during Experiential Exercise: Field 6-2 (page 164) as a basis for discussing several questions related to key committees.

What are the most commonplace types of key committees observed by members of your group? Do such key committees typically allocate resources, make important policy decisions, or both? Which of the key committees studied appears to be the most unusual? Which of the powerful people who are members of these key committees appear(s) to be the most powerful overall, based on key committees alone? Would that person (or those people) probably be the most powerful overall if the analysis was based on all five ways of estimating power rather than just key committees? Why or why not?

When all of the groups have completed their analyses, the class will discuss the groups' findings.

■ *Experiential Exercise: In-Class 6-4*

CRITIQUING THE CRITICAL ANALYSIS AND SYNTHESIS IN THE
APPENDIX: SUPPLEMENT FOR CHAPTER 6
The purpose of this exercise is to further develop critical thinking skills by reviewing
the material underlying the Synthesized Set of Key Individual Power Bases.

Exercise Process Outline
[Carefully read Chapter 6—and especially the Appendix: Supplement for Chapter 6,
Analyzing Power—in advance.]

Form groups of 5 to 7 students.

Critique the series of decisions in the Critical Analysis and Synthesis section of the
Appendix: Supplement for Chapter 6. Is this the best possible synthesis of the various
lists of power bases that are covered in the preceding sections of the chapter supplement? If so, explain why. If not, justify your own synthesis.

When all of the groups have completed their analyses, the class as a whole will discuss
this issue and attempt to create a thoroughly justified overall synthesis of the most
important individual power bases.

■ *Experiential Exercise: Field 6-1*

ASSESSING POWER: SYMBOLS
The purpose of this exercise is to practice assessing power by observing the symbols
of power that exist in the office of a manager in a real-world organization.

Arrange to visit the office of a manager that you, a friend, or relative knows. As is
recommended in the Application section, try to make your assessment of symbols
within the office as **unobtrusive** or non-obvious as possible. It would be best to visit
the office when the manager is not in it. It would also be advisable to merely look at
the office and then leave, as opposed to studying it intently while taking notes on a pad
of paper. Writing notes in plain sight is **not** unobtrusive, and can create problems.
Instead, write your notes somewhere else, preferably as soon as possible after you
leave the office so as to minimize the amount of information you forget. Talking to people about the symbols you observe is also more obtrusive, so avoid doing this.

After obtaining information concerning the symbols of power in the office of this
particular manager, write a brief description and analysis of what you noted (1 page
maximum). In this short paper, be sure to include:

1. A brief description of the manager's organization (but not its name)

2. The manager's title (but not his or her name)

3. A description of the kinds of symbols observed in the manager's office

4. Your preliminary assessment of this manager's overall power in this organization
   based on the symbols observed.

■ *Experiential Exercise: Field 6-2*

ASSESSING POWER: KEY COMMITTEES

The purpose of this exercise is to practice assessing power by discovering and then analyzing a key committee that exists within a real-world organization.

Choose an organization in which you or a friend or relative works. Talk to one or two people that you or your friend or relative know personally within the organization, and ask the person or people how important decisions are made in this organization. Examples of important decisions might include budget decisions, company policies, and overall company strategies. Try to determine whether such important decisions are made by individuals or groups. Note that groups are involved in making these kinds of decisions, chances are reasonably good that at least some of these groups will be key committees.

Talking to people directly about power is obtrusive, so avoid doing this. Instead, try to be as **unobtrusive** or non-obvious as possible by focusing on the decision-making process, which is a key factor affecting an organization's ability to achieve its goals effectively.

Taking notes in plain sight is **not** unobtrusive, and can create problems. Instead, write your notes immediately after you leave the organization, preferably as soon as possible to minimize the amount of information you forget.

After obtaining information concerning a likely key committee, write a brief description and analysis of what you noted (1 page maximum). In this short paper, be sure to include:

1. A brief description of the organization (but not its name)

2. A brief description of the committee and what it does

3. An analysis indicating why you believe this committee is a key committee

[Tip: See the Application section for criteria concerning what constitutes a key committee.]

■ *Experiential Exercise: Field 6-3*

POWER PAPER GUIDELINES

Focus of the Paper

This paper should focus on power within a formal, real-world organization of your choice. You may focus on an entire organization or an organizational subunit, such as a department, function, or division, within that organization.

The total number of people within whichever organizational entity you choose to study is less important than the *number of principal political actors* operating within it. If there is only one dominant political actor, you will not have much scope for demonstrating your understanding of power. Therefore, be sure to choose an organization in which some *distribution of power* exists. However, an organization containing more than three or four principal political actors will be difficult to analyze in the space available unless some of these actors are clearly less powerful than others. Thus your paper should focus on the *three to four **most powerful people** within* whichever organizational entity you choose to study.

Should you be so fortunate as to discover an organizational entity in which power has little or no impact, seriously consider applying for a job there—it might well be a great place to work! However, it is recommended that you *not* conduct a power analysis in such an organizational entity, as doing so will not provide you with much opportunity to display your understanding of power and your ability to analyze power in a real-world setting.

Many different kinds of formal organizations have proven to be appropriate choices for analysis. Examples include business organizations, university organizations, student organizations, churches, hobby clubs, and volunteer organizations. If you do not have direct connections to any such organizations yourself, some of your friends, relatives, or neighbors surely do.

Your paper should provide answers to the following key questions.

1. Who are the principal political actors in this organizational entity?

2. How much of which kinds of power bases do the three to four most powerful actors have?

3. Based on how power is distributed among the principal political actors in this organizational entity, who is likely to win a specific major power battle that seems likely to occur in the relatively near future?

4. How ethically have these principal political actors used their power in the past?

Required Format

Your paper should begin with a title page and contain eight sections.

Title Page

1. Introduction

2. The Organization To Be Analyzed

3. Preliminary Power Assessment

4. Power Base Analysis

5. Overall Power Summary

6. Future Predictions

7. Ethical Implications

8. Bibliography

The **Title Page** should contain a descriptive title, your name, your affiliation, and the date. A descriptive title provides some indication of the type of organization you are analyzing and should include the word "power." In this course, your affiliation is the course number and the name of your university or college.

The **Introduction** tells the reader what the paper will be about. It tells what you are trying to accomplish by writing this paper, *not* what you found. In other words, briefly state the purpose of the paper, not the results or conclusions.

The Organization To Be Analyzed section presents a fairly brief description of the *organizational entity* (i.e., the department, functional area, division, or entire organization) that you have studied. Talk about its products, services, or purpose; indicate how large it is; and so on. If you are analyzing a subunit—a department, function, division, or other entity within a larger organization—briefly describe the larger organization and then explain how the smaller entity fits into the larger one. Note that the highest- level principal political actor within a subunit is almost always the manager of that subunit—and *only* that subunit. Including a principal political actor in an analysis of a single subunit who in fact manages several such subunits will invalidate your analysis. For example, a department manager is the highest level manager *within* a particular department, and a store manager is the highest level manager *within* one particular store. However, a district manager is likely to be in charge of several stores, and hence cannot be considered a principal political actor within just a single store. Instead, he or she would be a principal political actor within that *district*.

The **Preliminary Power Assessment** section applies the first four of the five ways of estimating power to help determine which three or four people within in your organizational entity are its principal political actors. The four ways are exhibiting symbols of power, winning or losing past power battles, serving on one or more key committees, and being viewed as one of the most powerful people in the organization. A discussion of titles, demographic factors, and the like may also be incorporated into this preliminary assessment. *Be sure to use titles rather than names or numbers* to identify any political actors you analyzed. This section answers the first key question presented near the beginning of these guidelines.

The **Power Base Analysis** section discusses which of the power bases explained in this chapter actually apply to each of those principal political actors, and to what extent. While it is an excellent idea to create a Power Analysis Matrix to provide an outline for writing this section (see the Application example), this section should explain the contents of that matrix in paragraph form and in greater detail, as opposed to leaving it up to the reader to figure out what the matrix information means. This section answers the second key question presented near the beginning of these guidelines: How much of which kinds of power bases does each of the principal political actors have?

The **Overall Power Summary** section briefly reviews the power bases for each principal political actor and how much of each of these power bases each actor has. It then develops an overall power ranking for each actor, indicating which actor is the most powerful, which actor is the second most powerful, and so on.

The **Future Predictions** section uses the results from the last two sections to predict the winner(s) of a specific major future power battle involving any two or more of the principal political actors you analyzed. First, clearly state what you think the major future power battle is likely to concern. For example, who will get promoted to a higher-level job or who will receive a larger share of the budget next time? Second, clearly state which principal political actor(s) you think will win the future power battle. Finally, be sure to provide some justification for your predictions based on the results of the preceding sections. This section answers the third key question presented near the beginning of these guidelines.

The **Ethical Implications** section discusses how ethically the three or four principal political actors have used their power in this organizational entity in the past. It answers the fourth and last key question presented near the beginning of these guidelines.

The **Bibliography**—or the List of References or simply References—is a list of the sources you have drawn upon to write your paper. These sources should be presented in alphabetical order, by the first authors' last names. To save you from having to expend a great deal of time and effort doing research in the library, *for this class only* you should *base your paper on the same original sources that were used to write this chapter.* In other words, *for this class only*, use the content of this chapter as if it was a set of notes that you had taken in the library about material in these original sources (but don't go overboard and quote the chapter directly). Then, reference whichever of those original sources you actually use when writing your paper. In addition, *for this class only*, it is not necessary to reference *Organizational Behavior*, even though that would be technically correct.

Keep in mind that your Bibliography should include *only* those books and articles that you actually cite in your paper. If you did not credit a source within the body of your paper, do not include that source in your Bibliography.

Additional Comments on Format

The format for this paper is similar to what is found in academic journals that discuss organizational behavior topics such as power. It differs in that this paper analyzes real-life cases of people with power bases in organizations as opposed to testing research hypotheses that support new theories or models concerning power. This paper is also different in that you do *not* have to include a Literature Review, which reviews and explains prior research so the reader can better understand what the rest of the paper is about. Such a Literature Review has been done for you already, in this chapter plus its Appendix. Your task, in your paper, is to *apply* the material reviewed in this chapter to a real organization, *analyze* the key power players, and *synthesize* your results in a way that allows you to make a logical and practical future prediction. Along the way, you will undoubtedly *evaluate* the usefulness of this material as well.

Even though you do not have to write a Literature Review, you should be sure to **give the *original authors* credit for their ideas when you use these ideas in your paper**. This must be done **even when you are not quoting other writers directly**, since you are still making use of these writers' good ideas. Copying other writers' work is permissible only if you use quotation marks, give proper credit, and do not quote extensively. Otherwise, copying other writers' work is plagiarism, which is both unethical and illegal, so be sure to do your own writing as well as give credit to other authors for any ideas you choose to include in your paper. [Again, technically speaking, you could give credit simply by citing the course textbook, *Organizational Behavior*. For purposes of this paper, however, please cite the *original sources*.]

You can give credit within the body of your paper by citing the author(s) and the year of publication. For example, you might give credit to Pfeffer for an idea taken from his 1992 book by inserting Pfeffer (1992) or (Pfeffer, 1992) as appropriate. Virtually all U.S. organizational behavior journals use this technique rather than footnotes or endnotes. The only reason that textbooks such as *Organizational Behavior* do not also use this citation technique is because they typically contain so many citations that confusion would be created for the reader. The following examples illustrate how the citation technique works:

> The Synthesized Set of Key Individual Power Bases includes Pfeffer's (1978) control over information power base and that uniquely labeled power base known as referent power (French and Raven, 1959).

These examples illustrate two ways to cite a source. The first method, in which only the year of publication appears in parentheses, can be used anywhere within a sentence as long as the wording makes sense grammatically. The second method, in which both the name(s) of the author(s) and the year of publication appear in parentheses, can be used anywhere within a sentence *except* at its beginning. Either method correctly gives credit where credit is due.

Notice that all citations—such as Pfeffer (1978) and (French and Raven, 1959)— are included **within** the normal sentence structure. It is *not* correct to place citations after the period at the end of a sentence or paragraph. A citation is most commonly placed in the first sentence that discusses the ideas obtained from a particular author or set of authors, and is presumed to apply until the writer switches to using a different set of ideas, which then triggers the inclusion of a different citation.

Please note that beginning a section with a paragraph containing all of the citations you plan to use in that section is poor writing technique. Citing a subtitle is also poor writing technique; instead, insert that citation somewhere in the first sentence in which the ideas of a particular author or set of authors are used.

For similar ideas that come from more than one source, separate these sources by a semicolon, and list them in order by earlier date of publication, as follows:

> Control over resources (Pfeffer, 1978; Mintzberg, 1983) is often a strong base of power for higher-level managers, who typically control larger amounts of resources than do their lower-level counterparts.

The full reference, which includes the title, publisher, and so on, should appear *only* in the Bibliography (List of References) that you place at the end of your paper. As was indicated earlier, the easiest way to create a bibliography for your paper—*for this class only*—is to copy from the References section of *Organizational Behavior* **only** those sources that you actually cited in your paper.

Writing Tips

In longer sections, using additional *subtitles* can be helpful in keeping the reader organized and on track.

When writing a paper of this kind, be sure to *avoid an outline format* in your writing style. In other words, *write complete sentences*, put the sentences in standard paragraph form, and so on.

Avoid using bullets or numbered lists. They are appropriate for advertisements, and possibly for executive summaries, but not for a paper of this kind.

Proofreading your paper after it has been completed is highly recommended. If possible, put the paper aside for a day or two (or at least a few hours) before reviewing it. This should greatly increase your proofreading effectiveness.

Finally, before you print your paper, *use a spell-checking program.* It probably will not catch all of your mistakes, but it will spot many of the worst errors. Such errors are eady tp makr (easy to make), but difficult to understand. [Additional Tip: A common misspelling is "manger" instead of "manager." Since "manger" is a correctly spelled word, catch it by doing a search-and-replace.]

Paper Length Limits

The length of your paper should be **8 to 10 pages, double-spaced**, using a 12-point font with 1-inch margins. Be sure to number each page. This paper length limit does not include the Title Page, Bibliography, Abstract, or any Appendices.

[Tip: It is helpful to print the Title Page separately from the body of the paper, so that it does not get numbered as page 1.]

Grading Criteria

These are the criteria (standards) that will be used to evaluate your paper. Read them before beginning to write or proofread. If your paper has addressed all of the questions asked in the criteria, it is likely to get a higher grade than a paper for which this kind of checking has not been done.

1. **Overall Grasp of Material.** Based on the information supplied in this paper, does its writer really understand power, particularly individual power bases and how to apply them?

2. **Effectiveness of Preliminary Power Assessment.** Did the writer accurately apply Pfeffer's first four ways of estimating power to preliminarily determine who appear to be the three or four most powerful people within the organizational entity being analyzed? Again, those first four ways of estimating power include exhibiting symbols of power, winning or losing past power battles, serving on one or more key committees, and being viewed as one of the most powerful people in the organization.

3. **Effectiveness of Analysis.** Did the writer accurately apply Pfeffer's fifth way of estimating power—analyzing actual power bases—to those three or four principal political actors? In other words, did the writer convincingly explain how much of which kinds of power bases each of the three or four principal political actors has, and supply appropriate examples to support those explanations? Were the "how much" aspects of the analysis covered clearly?

4. **Effectiveness of Concluding Sections.** Did the writer effectively summarize the overall power of each of the three or four principal political actors by briefly reviewing his/her power bases, the extent of power obtained from each power base ("how much"), and then determining an overall power ranking for that actor that makes logical sense? Did the writer make—and then effectively support—a prediction about the likely winner(s) of a *specific* major *future* power battle involving two or more of the principal political actors? Did the writer clearly indicate how ethically the three or four principal political actors have used their power in the past, supplying brief examples to support these contentions?

5. **Overall Effectiveness of Communication.** In the paper as a whole, is the content organized according to the required format, including required and optional subtitles? Have citations for all of the original sources used been provided where appropriate within the body of the paper, using the modern citation technique? Is the paper presented in a writing style that is clear, flowing, and easy for the reader to follow? Is the paper written in a more objective third-person format, rather than a more subjective first-person format using "I" or "we"? Is the paper free from typographical errors? Do the sources listed in the Bibliography match the sources that are cited in the body of the paper? Are the Bibliography sources listed in alphabetical order by first author's last name? Are the pages numbered properly?

REFERENCE NOTES

1. Mintzberg, H. *Power in and Around Organizations.* Englewood Cliffs, NJ: Prentice-Hall, 1983.

2. Gandz, J., and V. V. Murray. The Experience of Workplace Politics. *Academy of Management Journal,* Vol. 23, 1980, pp. 237–251.

3. Pfeffer, J. *Managing with Power.* Boston, MA: Harvard Business School Press, 1992.

4. Pfeffer, J. *Power in Organizations.* Marshfield, MA: Pitman Publishing Company, 1981.

5. Pfeffer, J. *Organizational Design.* Arlington Heights, IL: AHM Publishing Company, 1978; Mintzberg, H. *Power in and Around Organizations.* Englewood Cliffs, NJ: Prentice-Hall, 1983.

6. Pfeffer (1981, p. 101) indicates that resources "include money, prestige, legitimacy, rewards and sanctions, and expertise, or the ability to deal with uncertainty." Pfeffer (1978, p. 18) notes that "one special resource is information." Pfeffer, J. *Power in Organizations.* Marshfield, MA: Pitman Publishing Company, 1981; Pfeffer, J. *Organizational Design.* Arlington Heights, IL: AHM Publishing Company, 1978.

7. Pfeffer, J. *Power in Organizations.* Marshfield, MA: Pitman Publishing Company, 1981; see also Mintzberg, H. *Power in and Around Organizations.* Englewood Cliffs, NJ: Prentice-Hall, 1983.

8. Mintzberg, H. *Power in and Around Organizations.* Englewood Cliffs, NJ: Prentice-Hall, 1983; see also Hickson, D. J., C. R. Hinings, C. A. Lee, R. E. Schneck, and J. M. Pennings. A Strategic Contingency Theory of Intra-organizational Power. *Administrative Science Quarterly,* Vol. 16, 1971, pp. 216–229.

9. Pfeffer, J. *Power in Organizations.* Marshfield, MA: Pitman Publishing Company, 1981.

10. Mintzberg, H. *Power in and Around Organizations.* Englewood Cliffs, NJ: Prentice-Hall, 1983.

11. Pfeffer, J. *Power in Organizations.* Marshfield, MA: Pitman Publishing Company, 1981.

12. Pfeffer, J. *Organizational Design.* Arlington Heights, IL: AHM Publishing Company, 1978; see also French, J. R. P., Jr., and B. Raven. The Bases of Social Power. In D. Cartwright (ed.), *Studies in Social Power.* Ann Arbor, MI: University of Michigan Institute of Social

Research, 1959, pp. 150–167.; Mintzberg, H. *Power in and Around Organizations*. Englewood Cliffs, NJ: Prentice-Hall, 1983.

13. French & Raven label one of their power bases "Coercive Power." French, J. R. P., Jr., and B. Raven. The Bases of Social Power. In D. Cartwright (ed.), *Studies in Social Power*. Ann Arbor, MI: University of Michigan Institute of Social Research, 1959, pp. 150–167.

14. French, J. R. P., Jr., and B. Raven. The Bases of Social Power. In D. Cartwright (ed.), *Studies in Social Power*. Ann Arbor, MI: University of Michigan Institute of Social Research, 1959, pp. 150–167; see also Mechanic, D. Sources of Power in Lower Participants in Complex Organizations. *Administrative Science Quarterly*, Vol. 7, 1962, pp. 349–364.

15. Mintzberg, H. *Power in and Around Organizations*. Englewood Cliffs, NJ: Prentice-Hall, 1983.

16. Mechanic, D. Sources of Power in Lower Participants in Complex Organizations. *Administrative Science Quarterly*, Vol. 7, 1962, pp. 349–364.

17. Pfeffer, J. *Organizational Design*. Arlington Heights, IL: AHM Publishing Company, 1978; Hickson, D. J., C. R. Hinings, C. A. Lee, R. E. Schneck, and J. M. Pennings. A Strategic Contingency Theory of Intra-organizational Power. *Administrative Science Quarterly*, Vol. 16, 1971, pp. 216–229.

18. Podsakoff, P. M., and C. A. Schriesheim. Field Studies of French and Raven's Bases of Power: Critique, Re-Analysis, and Suggestions for Future Research. *Psychological Bulletin*, Vol. 97, 1985, pp. 387–411.

19. This is based on a composite case example developed from several anonymous student term papers analyzing power in real-life organizations.

20. French, J. R. P., Jr., and B. Raven. The Bases of Social Power. In D. Cartwright (ed.), *Studies in Social Power*. Ann Arbor, MI: University of Michigan Institute of Social Research, 1959, pp. 150–167.

21. Pfeffer, J. *Organizational Design*. Arlington Heights, IL: AHM Publishing Company, 1978.

22. Pfeffer, J. *Organizational Design*. Arlington Heights, IL: AHM Publishing Company, 1978.

23. Mintzberg, H. *Power in and Around Organizations*. Englewood Cliffs, NJ: Prentice-Hall, 1983.

24. Allen, T. S., and S. I. Cohen. Information Flow in Research and Development Laboratories. *Administrative Science Quarterly*, Vol. 14, 1969, pp. 12–19.

25. Pfeffer, J. *Organizational Design*. Arlington Heights, IL: AHM Publishing Company, 1978.

26. See Mintzberg, who labels this power base "Access to Powerful People." Mintzberg, H. *Power in and Around Organizations*. Englewood Cliffs, NJ: Prentice-Hall, 1983.

27. Sayles, L. R. *Leadership: What Effective Managers Really Do . . . and How They Do It*. New York, NY: McGraw-Hill, 1979.

28. Mechanic, D. Sources of Power in Lower Participants in Complex Organizations. *Administrative Science Quarterly*, Vol. 7, 1962, pp. 349–364.

29. Pfeffer, J. *Power in Organizations*. Marshfield, MA: Pitman Publishing Company, 1981.

30. Pfeffer, J. *Power in Organizations*. Marshfield, MA: Pitman Publishing Company, 1981.

31. Pfeffer, J. *Power in Organizations*. Marshfield, MA: Pitman Publishing Company, 1981.

32. Pfeffer's (1981) original labels for his five ways of assessing power are symbols, consequences, representational indicators, reputational indicators, and determinants of power. These labels have been altered for use in this text due to frequent student misinterpretation of all of the five ways of assessing power except symbols. The new labels appear to be better understood, as they typically have been much more accurately applied in assessments of power in real-life organizations. Pfeffer, J. *Power in Organizations*. Marshfield, MA: Pitman Publishing Company, 1981.

33. Pfeffer, J. *Power in Organizations*. Marshfield, MA: Pitman Publishing Company, 1981; Pfeffer, J. *Managing with Power*. Boston, MA: Harvard Business School Press, 1992.

34. Pfeffer, J. *Power in Organizations*. Marshfield, MA: Pitman Publishing Company, 1981.

35. Pfeffer, J. *Power in Organizations*. Marshfield, MA: Pitman Publishing Company, 1981; Pfeffer, J. *Managing with Power*. Boston, MA: Harvard Business School Press, 1992.

36. Anonymous former students, San Jose State University.

37. Pfeffer, J., and G. Salancik. Organizational Decision Making as a Political Process: The Case of a University Budget. *Administrative Science Quarterly*, Vol. 19, 1974, pp. 135–151; Pfeffer, J. *Power in Organizations*. Marshfield, MA: Pitman Publishing Company, 1981.

38. Pfeffer, J., and G. Salancik. Organizational Decision Making as a Political Process: The Case of a University Budget. *Administrative Science Quarterly*, Vol. 19, 1974, pp. 135–151; Pfeffer, J. *Power in Organizations*. Marshfield, MA: Pitman Publishing Company, 1981.

39. Pfeffer, J. *Power in Organizations*. Marshfield, MA: Pitman Publishing Company, 1981.

40. This is a composite case example that has been developed from a variety of anonymous student term papers that focused on analyzing power in real-life organizations.

CHAPTER 7
Decision Making

Decision making is something that everyone does every day. Some decisions revolve around minor issues, such as what to wear, where to have lunch, or which movie to see. Other decisions are more significant, such as which college to attend, which job offer to accept, which employee to hire to fill a key position, or what action to take to support the long-term growth of one's company. Obviously, these decisions have a much greater impact on the direction people's lives take and on their career success.

Some people demonstrate a propensity to make good decisions, whereas others seem to consistently make the "wrong call" and pay the price for it. Decision making within an organizational context is similar in many ways. Managers must make decisions that affect others (e.g., employees, the company, customers) each day. These decisions often have a direct and long-term effect on the effectiveness of the organization. Managers who are able to demonstrate good judgment and decision-making skills often perform at a higher level and are better able to achieve the objectives of their organizations.

However, many of the real-world problems that managers face are complex, ambiguous, and dynamic. This makes the decision-making process even more challenging for managers. For example, suppose that you are a manager in a company that needs to dramatically reduce its costs and increase its efficiency in order to survive in a highly competitive industry (such as computers, automobiles, or wireless phones). What decisions must you make in order to reduce costs while at the same time increase efficiency? What are some alternative courses of action for addressing these issues? What are the strengths and weaknesses of each alternative? Which alternative is the best overall? How do you then implement that choice once you have made it? These are some of the fundamental challenges that underlie the decision-making process managers go through in real-world organizations.

This chapter explores a decision-making model that helps managers analyze a situation using a variety of diagnostic questions in order to determine the most appropriate decision-making style for handling that situation. As demonstrated throughout this book, the answer to the question, "What is the best way to handle a situation?" is "It depends." The model discussed in this chapter specifies the factors that managers must consider in determining the most appropriate style for making a specific decision.

This chapter also examines a group decision-making phenomenon called "groupthink," which tends to be associated with the norming stage of group development discussed in Chapter 4. Groupthink can contribute to a group making poor decisions that can sometimes have disastrous consequences. This chapter describes the symptoms of groupthink, its consequences, and some strategies for preventing or overcoming it.

ANALYSIS & APPLICATION

Examples of Good and Bad Decisions Made by Managers in Real-World Organizations

Use a standard Internet browser (such as Internet Explorer or Netscape) to research business-oriented web sites (such as http://www.fortune.com and http://www.businessweek.com) in order to identify three examples of good decisions and three examples of bad decisions made by a manager in a real-world organization. Explain why you think that each of these decisions is a good or bad one.

A NORMATIVE THEORY OF LEADERSHIP: DECISION-MAKING OPTIONS

Decision making can be defined as the process through which a choice is made among a set of alternatives. Based on this definition, some people have the impression that decision making is easy or just a matter of common sense. However, nothing could be further from the truth. There are two key reasons why decision making is so difficult. The first is that decision makers are human and, therefore, imperfect. They possess limitations in terms of being able to analyze information, to generate alternatives, and to evaluate alternatives in order to make a final decision.

The second reason why decision making is difficult is that the context in which decision makers exist presents a variety of barriers to making the right choices. Business problems are often extremely complex, hard to define, and constantly changing. For example, it may sound straightforward to say that a decision maker needs to "define the problem," but this can be a very challenging part of the decision-making process. There may also be serious problems with the quality (i.e., reliability and validity) of the information that is used to support the decision-making process. In fact, a significant amount of the information that is used to make decisions in the real world is far from perfect. Finally, organizations themselves can make decision making more difficult. Political dynamics, pressure to achieve "bottom-line results," and time constraints (i.e., the need to be decisive) can all "short-circuit" the decision-making process.

In order to make good decisions, it is important for managers to understand how decisions *can* be made. The **Normative Theory of Leadership,** developed by Vroom and Jago,[1] is an extremely valuable theory that helps leaders analyze a problem and then identify the most appropriate of five decision-making styles to use to solve that problem. These five decision-making styles are defined in terms of the amount of participation that a leader should use in making a decision. The five decision-making styles are as follows:

- **AI:** Using the AI decision-making style, the leader solves the problem himself using information available at that time. This decision-making style does not involve any participation from a leader's subordinates and is therefore faster than the other four decision-making styles. As discussed later in the chapter, this is a very appropriate decision-making style for some situations.

- **AII:** Using the AII decision-making style, the leader obtains the necessary information from her subordinates and then decides on the solution to the problem by herself. The leader may or may not tell her subordinates what the problem is when she obtains information from them. The role played by subordinates in making the decision is clearly one of providing necessary information to the leader rather than generating or evaluating alternative solutions.

- **CI:** Using the CI decision-making style, the leader shares the problem with relevant subordinates individually, getting their ideas and suggestions without bringing them together.

- **CII:** Using the CII decision-making style, the leader shares the problem with his subordinates as a group, collectively obtaining their ideas and suggestions. The leader then makes the decision that may or may not reflect his subordinates' influence.

- **GII:** Using the GII decision-making style, the leader shares the problem with her subordinates as a group. Together, the group generates and evaluates alternatives and attempts to reach agreement (consensus) on a solution. The leader's role is much like that of chairperson. The leader does not try to influence the group to adopt a certain preferred solution and is willing to accept and implement any solution that has the support of the entire group.

The decision-making styles that begin with an "A" stand for "autocratic." These styles primarily involve the leader making the decision by himself and then informing the group of that decision. The decision-making styles that begin with a "C" stand for "consultative." These styles emphasize the leader consulting with his subordinates before making a final decision. This may involve asking subordinates for ideas or suggestions regarding the handling of a specific problem. The decision-making style that starts with a "G" stands for "group." This style involves all members of the group and attempts to build consensus regarding the solution to a problem.

It should be noted that the decision-making styles described above are similar to the five styles for handling conflict described in Chapter 5. For example, the autocratic decision-making styles (AI, AII) are similar to the Forcing (Competing) conflict-handling style (discussed in Chapter 5). In addition, the group decision-making style (G) is similar to the Collaborating conflict-handling style.

DIAGNOSTIC QUESTIONS: USING THE VROOM-JAGO MODEL OF DECISION MAKING

Now that we have defined the five decision-making styles in the Normative Theory of Leadership, a natural question is, "Which one is the best?" Again, there is no one decision-making style that is universally superior to the others; it all depends on the situation. In determining the most appropriate decision-making style for any given situation, Vroom and Jago's theory states that leaders must ask themselves the following diagnostic questions:

1. **Quality Requirement (QR): How important is the technical quality of the decision?** "Technical quality" refers to whether one alternative is clearly superior to other alternatives based on objective criteria (e.g., sales, costs, profits). For example, if a manager is trying to decide which of two suppliers to use for a key service that the company needs, and both suppliers are comparable in terms of quality and cost, then the quality requirement in this situation would be "low." However, if there is a difference between the two suppliers, then the quality requirement would be "high."

2. **Commitment Requirement (CR): How important is subordinate commitment to the decision?** This refers to the degree to which a leader will need the "buy-in" or support of subordinates in achieving the successful implementation of a decision. Generally, if subordinates will be the implementers of a decision once it is made, then the answer to this question will be "high." The key thing to remember is that people generally need to feel some ownership and involvement in things that they create or implement. If the involvement of subordinates is in more of an advisory role and they will not be directly or indirectly involved in the implementation of the decision, then the answer to this question would be "low."

3. **Leader's Information (LI): Does the leader have sufficient information to make a high-quality decision?** This is the extent to which a leader possesses the information needed to make a quality decision in a given situation. For example, in some situations, a manager may be very knowledgeable and experienced in dealing with the problem at hand so that she possesses sufficient information to make a good decision (i.e., the answer is "yes" to the question). However, in other situations, a manager might be dealing with a problem that she has never encountered or knows almost nothing about. In this case, the manager does not have sufficient information to make a good decision (i.e., the answer is "no").

4. **Problem Structure (ST): Is the problem well structured?** This refers to the degree to which the problem in a given situation is clearly defined in terms of procedures for handling it and knowledge of where to obtain the information needed to make a decision. For example, a manager may have a problem with an employee who is performing below expectations for his job. The company has clear policies and procedures in place regarding what a manager should do to handle this situation. This would be an example of a well-structured problem

(i.e., the answer to the question is "yes"). However, if the problem is new and very complex, such as how to enhance the long-term creativity of an organization's product development process, then this would most likely be an unstructured problem (i.e., the answer to the question is "no").

5. **Commitment Probability (CP): If the leader made the decision by herself, is it reasonably certain that her subordinates will be committed to the decision?** Basically, this is the degree to which a leader's subordinates will go along with or support the decision of the leader. Commitment probability refers to the likelihood of employees being committed to a course of action if a leader makes the decision by herself while commitment requirement refers to the importance of obtaining employee commitment to a solution to a problem.

6. **Goal Congruence (GC): Do subordinates share the organizational goals to be attained in solving this problem?** This refers to whether there is alignment between the goals of subordinates and those of the organization as a whole. For example, if one of the key goals of the organization is to be more quality-focused and its employees possess a quality-oriented attitude, then the answer to this question would be "yes." However, if the organization's goal is to be more customer service focused but its employees do not acknowledge that they even have customers, then the answer to the question would be "no."

7. **Subordinate Conflict (CO): Is conflict among subordinates over preferred solutions likely?** This refers to the degree to which a leader expects to experience conflict between subordinates in terms of selecting the best alternative. For example, if a manager is considering various solutions for a product quality problem and the employees in the work unit all share a common value system and philosophy about quality and how to achieve it, then the answer to this question would be "no." However, if a manager knows that the issue is a sensitive one that employees have been divided over in the past, then it is likely that the answer to the question would be "yes."

8. **Subordinate Information (SI): Do subordinates have sufficient information to make a high-quality decision?** For example, if the problem involves a strategic issue that subordinates have had no involvement with and, thus, possess little knowledge of, then the answer to this question would be "no." On the other hand, if the problem deals with an operational problem that subordinates encounter every day, then the answer would be "yes."

Figure 7-1 shows the **Vroom-Jago Model of Decision Making.** Managers can use this tree to evaluate a situation in order to identify the most appropriate decision-making style. To do so, managers answer each of the questions listed on the right-hand side of the figure and then follow the corresponding branches of the decision tree until they reach an endpoint, or the most appropriate decision-making style for the given problem. To make this clearer, let's look at a few examples of how a real-world manager can use this model, or decision tree, to determine the most appropriate decision making style to use in a situation.

Figure 7-1   The Vroom-Jago Time-Driven Model of Decision Making

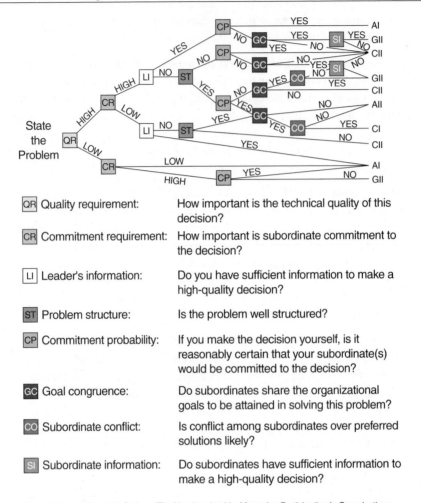

QR	Quality requirement:	How important is the technical quality of this decision?
CR	Commitment requirement:	How important is subordinate commitment to the decision?
LI	Leader's information:	Do you have sufficient information to make a high-quality decision?
ST	Problem structure:	Is the problem well structured?
CP	Commitment probability:	If you make the decision yourself, is it reasonably certain that your subordinate(s) would be committed to the decision?
GC	Goal congruence:	Do subordinates share the organizational goals to be attained in solving this problem?
CO	Subordinate conflict:	Is conflict among subordinates over preferred solutions likely?
SI	Subordinate information:	Do subordinates have sufficient information to make a high-quality decision?

Source: Vroom V.H. and A.G. Jago, *The New Leadership: Managing Participation in Organizations*. Englewood Cliffs. NJ: Prentice Hall (1988), p. 184. © 1987 V.H. Vroom and A. G. Jago. Used with permission of the authors.

VROOM-JAGO MODEL OF DECISION MAKING EXAMPLE 1

The project manager at a consumer products company needs to make a decision about which job candidate to hire for a position vacancy on her team. She has narrowed the pool of applicants to three finalists, all whom are very comparable to one another in terms of educational background, experience, and quality of work references. She knows that it will be critical to hire a person who will fit in with the rest of the team. The manager feels that she has enough information from each of the candidate's resumes and the interviews to make an informed decision. In addition, the manager believes that due to her strong working relationships with her team, they trust her to hire the best person for the job and that they will support her decision.

Which decision-making style should the manager use in this situation?

Application of the Vroom-Jago Model

1. **Quality Requirement (QR): Low.** All three of the job candidates are viewed as being of comparable quality.

2. **Commitment Requirement (CR): High.** Subordinates feel that the person who is hired must be someone who can fit in with the team so they must approve of the new hire as well.

3. **Leader Information (LI): Yes.** The leader feels that she has enough information from a variety of sources to make an informed decision.

Solution

Use decision-making style A1. (The manager should make the decision herself based on available information.)

VROOM-JAGO MODEL OF DECISION MAKING EXAMPLE 2

The production manager at a consumer electronics company has just received the results of the most recent employee attitude survey of his 300 employees. The purpose of the survey was to assess his employees' perceptions of their jobs, work environment, managers, and the organization as a whole. Based on the production manager's review of the key findings from the survey, he has identified a set of six action items that he would like to potentially implement in his work unit. The action steps vary in their focus on small changes (e.g., change rules regarding work breaks) and large changes (e.g., redesigning production jobs to provide more autonomy) and short-term and long-term benefits. The success of some of the action steps appears to be far more certain than others that are riskier.

One challenge for the production manager is that he is relatively new to the job so he does not fully understand the organization or the work unit very well. The support of the production workers will be critical to the long-term success of any of the action steps since they will be the individuals implementing the changes. Although the action steps are fairly clear, they do not paint a clear picture of the nature of the problems facing the production unit. For the most part, the production workers are very experienced and committed to the organization. Their work philosophy about the importance of quality, teamwork, managing costs, and so on are very much in alignment with the culture of the organization. Overall, the production workers are very knowledgeable about their jobs and how the production unit needs to function to get the job done.

Which decision-making style should the manager use in this situation?

Application of the Vroom-Jago Model

1. **Quality Requirement (QR): High.** There is a significant difference in the quality of the various action steps under consideration.

2. **Commitment Requirement (CR): High.** Subordinates must support the action steps that are selected since they will be the ones to implement them.

3. **Leader Information (LI): No.** The leader does not have all of the information he needs to select the best course of action since he is new to the job.

4. **Problem Structure (ST): No.** The underlying problems facing the production unit are complex and not clear in this situation.

5. **Commitment Probability (CP): No.** If the production manager made the decision by himself, it is not likely that the subordinates would be committed to the decision.

6. **Goal Congruence (GC): Yes.** The goals of employees appear to be in alignment with those of the organization as a whole.

7. **Subordinate Information (SI): Yes.** Subordinates appear to have all of the information they need to make the right decision about which action items from the survey would be most effective in relation to their jobs and the production unit.

Solution

Use decision-making style GII. (The manager should share the problem with his subordinates as a group. Together the group generates and evaluates alternatives and attempts to reach agreement, or consensus, on a solution.) The leader's role is much like that of chairperson. He does not try to influence the group to adopt his solution and he is willing to accept and implement any solution that has the support of the entire group.

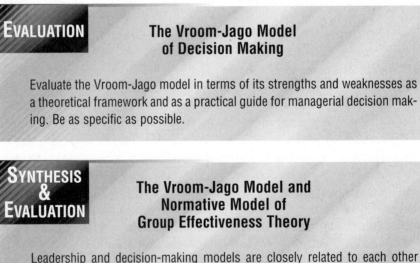

EVALUATION

The Vroom-Jago Model of Decision Making

Evaluate the Vroom-Jago model in terms of its strengths and weaknesses as a theoretical framework and as a practical guide for managerial decision making. Be as specific as possible.

SYNTHESIS & EVALUATION

The Vroom-Jago Model and Normative Model of Group Effectiveness Theory

Leadership and decision-making models are closely related to each other given that a critical aspect of a leader's job is to make decisions in order to achieve the goals of the organization. Based on this, discuss how the Normative Model of Leadership could be synthesized with the Normative Model of Group Effectiveness Theory. Next, evaluate the synthesized model in terms of its value as a theoretical framework and its usefulness to management practitioners.

ANALYSIS & APPLICATION — Applying the Vroom-Jago Model

The new director of game development at a video game design firm oversees the work of 50 video game programming professionals. These individuals are responsible for helping to develop concepts for new video games and then working collaboratively in teams of 7 to 10 people to develop the content and features for the actual games. Most of the programmers are young, highly creative, fiercely independent, and experts at what they do. Some of the programmers exhibit rather large egos and are unwilling to compromise in terms of getting their ideas and features integrated into the games they are developing. This can result in a high degree of conflict in the project team.

The director started with the firm about three years ago as a game programmer himself. He excelled in this area and was recently promoted to his current position. This new position poses many challenges for the director as it is critical to develop the "right kinds of games" (i.e., those that will be passionately embraced by video gamers). The cost of failure in this industry is extremely high, and it can be very difficult to actually predict which games will be a hit with customers. Since the director just started in his new position, he has a lot to learn about how to manage the video game development process and about managing a team of programmers as opposed to being one himself. He has some new ideas for potentially "breakthrough" video games and he needs to decide which ones to move forward with, if any. How should he proceed?

Based on this situation, use the Vroom-Jago model to determine the most appropriate decision-making style(s) to use in this situation.

APPLICATION & EVALUATION — A Training Program for Using the Normative Theory of Leadership

Suppose that you were asked by your boss to develop a one-day workshop for managers on using the Normative Theory of Leadership. How would you design and present your training program in order for other managers in your company to learn how to use the theory to improve their decision-making skills?

ANALYSIS &
APPLICATION
ANALYSIS & APPLICATION   Using the Normative Theory of Leadership in a Real-World Organization

Use a standard Internet browser (such as Internet Explorer or Netscape) to research business-oriented web sites (such as http://www.fortune.com or http://www.businessweek.com) to identify an article about a leader of an organization and a problem that he or she must solve in some way. Apply the Normative Theory of Leadership to assess the problem and to identify the most appropriate decision-making style for the leader to use in this situation. Support your assessment using specific information from the article.

GROUPTHINK

Because more and more organizations are using group-based approaches at the workplace, more and more decisions are being made by groups as well. As we have already noted, the decision-making process can be quite challenging when implemented on an individual basis. The use of groups to make business decisions adds a new layer of complexity to the process. Clearly, there can be some significant advantages to group decisions. Having "more than one head" provides additional information, ideas, and perspectives than any one individual is likely to possess. However, group decision making can be problematic for a variety of reasons. First, one person may attempt to exert a disproportionate influence over the group's process. Second, some members of the group may be hesitant to participate in the group's discussion because they feel inhibited by the presence of others. Third, groups are often less efficient than individuals when making decisions.

One decision-making phenomenon that can have a very negative impact on the quality of a group's decision-making process as well as its outcomes is "groupthink." Basically, **groupthink** is defined as the tendency for highly cohesive groups to value consensus at the expense of decision quality.[2] This can be linked to the norming stage of the stages of group development model discussed in Chapter 4. Some of the most dramatic events in history have identified groupthink as a factor that contributed to a decision made by a group that ended in disaster. For example, the decision by NASA officials to "green light" the launch of the space shuttle *Challenger* in 1986 despite concerns that were raised by insiders about a defective part on the space shuttle. The infamous Japanese attack of Pearl Harbor that resulted in the United States entering World War II in 1941 is another example of groupthink. U.S. military officials were blamed for making a series of faulty decisions that left Pearl Harbor completely vulnerable to attack, despite concerns raised by others in the military and the government about a real threat of an air raid.

THE JANIS GROUPTHINK MODEL

Figure 7-2 shows one groupthink model called the **Janis Groupthink Model.** Let's examine each of the major components of the model in greater depth.

Figure 7-2   The Janis Groupthink Model

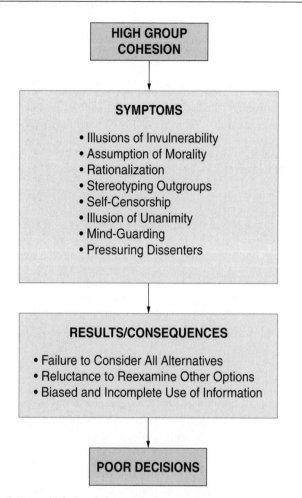

Source: Janis, I. *Groupthink: Psychological Studies of Policy Decisions and Fiascoes*, 2nd Ed. Boston: Houghton Mifflin, 1982.

A major factor that makes a group vulnerable to groupthink is a high level of cohesiveness. The strong positive feelings that permeate a group can undermine its ability to make decisions in a constructive and systematic manner. One of the key features associated with a high level of group cohesiveness is pressure to go along with the group in the decisions that it makes. In highly cohesive groups, it can be taboo for any member to "rock the boat" or to express dissent.

Symptoms

The major symptoms or "warning signs" of groupthink include the following:

- **Illusions of Invulnerability**—The group erroneously perceives that it cannot fail no matter what it does.

- **Assumption of Morality**—The group believes that what it is doing is the right thing to do. The group does not feel the need to question or critically evaluate its actions.

- **Rationalization**—The group justifies to itself that what it is doing is the right decision to make.

- **Stereotyping Outgroups**—The group tends to develop a "we versus them (the outsiders)" mentality that views all individuals outside the group as not understanding the group or as threats tot he group's welfare and success.

- **Self-Censorship**—The group dismisses any concerns or doubts expressed by group members about a decision that has been made.

- **Illusion of Unanimity**—The group members mistakenly perceive that everyone is in agreement about a decision that has been made by the group.

- **Mind-Guarding**—The group takes actions to protect its decisions by ignoring or dismissing information or positions that are not consistent with the group's thinking or decisions.

- **Pressuring Dissenters**—The group actively pressures anyone who disagrees with a decision to change their minds and to do what is best for the team. Group members who go against a group decision may be accused of being disloyal or of not being a team player.

Results/Consequences

The major impact of groupthink is that it damages the effectiveness of the group's decision-making process in a variety of ways. First, the group **Fails to Consider Alternative** solutions before selecting a course of action. This in itself makes it less likely that the group will identify the best solution to a problem. Second, the group is **Reluctant to Reexamine Other Options.** This means that the evaluation of alternatives is not thorough and effective and that the group is not in a position to make an informed decision once it finally decides on a course of action. Third, the group's use of information is **biased** and **incomplete.** This may result in the group only considering information that supports its position and dismissing other information.

In the end, the defects that occur in the decision-making process of a group in groupthink result in **Poor Decisions** that often have terrible consequences for the groups themselves as well as for their organizations.

STRATEGIES FOR PREVENTING OR OVERCOMING GROUPTHINK

Although groupthink can certainly produce disastrous results, there are strategies available to group leaders to deal with this phenomenon. For example, group leaders should focus on prevention. It is much easier to actively monitor and manage a group to prevent it from falling into groupthink than it is to be reactive in trying to break a group that is in groupthink out of that condition. The following are some of the key guidelines for preventing or overcoming groupthink:

1. **Do a critical evaluation of group ideas "openly."** This requires the group leader (and group members as well) to create a work environment in which everyone feels comfortable sharing their ideas and concerns with each other. Some leaders do this by setting a basic ground rule for the group stating that every idea or proposed course of action must be evaluated openly and thoroughly by the group before a final decision is made.

2. **Have key group members take a neutral stance on solutions.** This strategy is particularly important when there is a higher-ranking manager or executive who is a member of a group, as other group members may feel pressured to agree with any position that this individual may take. In practice, this would involve having the higher-ranking manager or executive refrain from voting on a given decision being considered by the group.

3. **Hold discussions with outsiders to obtain reactions.** This enables a group to get an objective perspective on a given issue and proposed course of action. An outsider will be much less likely to be influenced by any of the internal group dynamics in evaluating a group's decision.

4. **Assign the role of the devil's advocate to a group member.** The role of the devil's advocate is to identify potential problems or weaknesses with a proposed solution to a problem in order to facilitate the evaluation of the solution. In the end, this can enhance the likelihood of the group making the best decision.

5. **Form subgroups to develop alternative solutions.** Subgroups are formed by simply dividing the group up into smaller units and assigning the same task to each group. After each subgroup meets independently, the group may reconvene. The subgroups can each present their evaluation of a problem and a recommended solution. The value of this strategy is that the creation of subgroups diminishes the impact of groupthink on the decision-making processes of group members.

6. **Hold "second chance" meetings to reconsider major decisions**. The purpose of these meetings is to provide a group with a second opportunity to evaluate a decision before it moves forward with implementation. This is especially helpful when a major decision that requires a significant investment of time, financial resources, and staff is being considered.

SYNTHESIS & EVALUATION
The Janis Groupthink Model and the Stages of Group Development

Decision making and group process models are closely related to each other given that much of a leader's job involves making decisions within the context of a group. Based on this, discuss how the Janis Groupthink Model could be *synthesized* with the Stages of Group Development Model discussed in Chapter 4. Next *evaluate* the synthesized model in terms of its value as a theoretical framework and its usefulness to management practitioners.

SYNTHESIS & EVALUATION

Linking the Janis Groupthink Model with Path-Goal Theory

Leadership and decision-making models are closely related to each other given that a critical aspect of a leader's job is to make decisions in order to achieve the goals of the organization. Based on this, discuss how the Janis Groupthink Model could be *synthesized* with House's Path-Goal Theory (see Chapter 8). Next, *evaluate* the synthesized (i.e., combined) model in terms of its value as a theoretical framework and its usefulness to management practitioners.

ANALYSIS & APPLICATION

Identifying Groupthink in a Real-World Organization

Use a standard Internet browser (such as Internet Explorer or Netscape) to research business-oriented web sites (such as http://www.fortune.com or http://www.businessweek.com) in order to identify an example of groupthink taking place in an organization. Justify why you believe that the group you selected was participating in groupthink.

COMPREHENSION & APPLICATION

You Be the Consultant on Group Decision Making

Suppose that senior management at a large financial services firm has hired you as a management consultant to advise them on how to enhance the effectiveness of group decision making at all levels of the organization. Apparently, some poor decisions have been made by various groups because they either failed to consider critical information in making their decisions and/or they did not involve the right people in their decision-making processes and ended up making the wrong call. Based on the material covered in this chapter, develop a basic explanation (i.e., using "lay terms") of the Vroom-Jago Model for Decision-Making and the Janis Groupthink Model and prepare a presentation for senior management that discusses how these models can be applied in their organization to enhance group decision making.

APPLICATION: PRACTICAL GUIDELINES FOR APPLYING THE VROOM-JAGO DECISION TREE MODEL

The first step in applying the Vroom-Jago Model is for the leader to *analyze the current situation and attempt to identify the problem.* It is the leader's conceptualization of the problem that provides the basis for determining how to make a decision. Second, the leader should assess the situation further by *answering the diagnostic questions in the Vroom-Jago Model.* This will enable the leader to identify the decision-making style that is most appropriate for the situation. Third, the leader should *formulate an action plan for implementing the decision-making style in terms of specific behaviors.* This will enable the leader to see the link between the decision-making style to be used and concrete action. Fourth, the leader should now implement his action plan and then follow-up to assess the effectiveness of the decision.

By following these guidelines, managers build a more general and complete decision-making process around the Vroom-Jago Model and they link decision making to implementation.

APPLICATION EXAMPLE

Applying the Vroom-Jago Model

Use the Vroom-Jago decision tree in Figure 7-1 to analyze each of the scenarios that follow and to determine the most appropriate decision-making style to use. Be sure to develop an action plan for implementing each of your final decisions. After you have completed your analysis of the scenarios, answer the discussion questions.

Scenario 1: The Case of the Accounting Software Programs

You are the financial manager at a small, family-owned manufacturing firm. You supervise the work of five financial analysts and accountants. In the past, the company has been slow to embrace new technology. This has even been true in terms of its financial management systems. The company has been using an antiquated accounting software program to track its cash flow. You are now in the process of evaluating three accounting software programs that are all vastly superior to the current system you are using. Basically, all three programs are pretty much the same in terms of their capabilities, user-friendliness, and cost. You know that your employees will be ecstatic about getting any of these programs since they have been asking you to replace the current system for over a year now. In addition, you feel that you have all of the information you need to make an informed decision in this situation.

continues

Using the Vroom-Jago Model, identify the most appropriate decision-making style that should be used in this situation.

Scenario 2: The Case of the Project Assignment Dilemma

You are a senior consultant at a management consulting firm. You have just received a new assignment from a major client. The project involves a comprehensive evaluation of information technology systems and processes at the client firm. One of your key challenges going into this process is to determine the composition of the consulting team that will be working on this project. Clearly, there is a lot of variation in the quality, experience, expertise, and work styles of the consultants that you have to choose from in the firm. Many of the team members have worked together for many years, so it is important that they support whoever is ultimately selected to be on the team. One complicating factor is that your information technology background is not particularly strong, so you will need to compensate for this deficiency in staffing the team. Finally, the issue of selecting the composition of a team is something that occurs with every project that the firm works on but there are no formal guidelines and procedures in place to support the handling of this issue. The members of your team have said that they trust you to make the decision and that they will support it.

Using the Vroom-Jago Model, identify the most appropriate decision-making style that should be used in this situation.

Scenario 3: The Case of the Strategic Planning Process

You are the president of an automobile manufacturing company. You have scheduled a meeting to conduct the company's annual strategic planning process. The purpose of this activity is for the top executives in the company to meet with you to evaluate the current mission and strategies of the company in relation to the external environment (industry, market) and to possibly make modifications in the strategy.

The auto industry is very complex and global. Fortunately, you have an excellent team of executive vice-presidents in charge of marketing, product development, finance, and design. They are all excellent managers, but they demand to be given appropriate direction, support, and autonomy in executing their strategic plans. These individuals exhibit values and beliefs that are consistent with yours and those of the organization. When it comes to discussing issues relating to their areas of responsibility, these executives are far more knowledgeable than you are. You know that it will be critical to obtain their support for whatever you choose to do in the end.

In the past, the company has not used a very formal strategic planning process. However, given the need for companies to stay focused and lean in order to remain competitive, you feel that it is important to start using a formal process. The key problem is that you have no established mechanism in place to guide you through the strategic planning process.

continues

Clearly, there are many new directions in which you could guide the organization. This makes the strategic planning process even more daunting.

Using the Vroom-Jago Model, identify the most appropriate decision-making style that should be used in this situation.

Discussion Questions

1. To what extent was the Vroom-Jago Model helpful to you in determining the most appropriate decision-making style(s) in each of the scenarios? Do you agree with the recommendations generated from the theory? Why do you feel this way?

2. What are the key practical implications of the Vroom-Jago Model for you as a future leader and manager?

CONCLUSION

This chapter has explored two major decision-making models that have a variety of practical implications for managers. One important point is that the decision-making style that should be used depends on the characteristics of a situation. In addition, managers must be cautious about groups that are highly cohesive as they are especially vulnerable to the groupthink phenomenon. Group leaders must remember that they need to monitor the group dynamics associated with decision-making processes and to take appropriate action to ensure that solutions to problems are carefully discussed and evaluated by all members of the group before a final decision is made.

REFERENCE NOTES

1. Vroom, V. H., and A. G. Jago. *The New Leadership: Managing Participation in Organizations.* Englewood Cliffs, NJ: Prentice Hall, 1987.

2. Janis, I. *Groupthink: Psychological Studies of Policy Decisions and Fiascoes*, 2nd Ed. Boston: Houghton Mifflin, 1982.

CHAPTER 8
Leadership

Who comes to mind when you think of the greatest business practitioners in recent years? What do these individuals have in common with each other? Intelligence? Analytical skills? Political savvy? While these traits are certainly important, it is leadership skills that are arguably the most important skills shared by all of these individuals. In fact, leadership is one of the most critical skills any individual needs for his or her long-term effectiveness and success as a manager. The higher an individual moves up the management hierarchy, the more important leadership skills become as a determinant of managerial effectiveness.

In addition, many employers use leadership skills and potential as major selection criteria when hiring college graduates. However, many employers express concern that they cannot find enough job candidates with leadership qualities to fill some positions as management trainees, team leaders, and supervisors.

In short, **leadership** is defined as the process of influencing others in order to achieve organizational objectives. Leadership is about taking action to influence the behavior of other members of an organization. This involves articulating a vision for the organization and then inspiring organizational members to behave in ways to support the achievement of this vision. This is not the same thing as **management,** which deals more with the process of developing plans and goals and implementing them. Some people are good managers but not good leaders, and vice versa. While effective managers are skilled in the execution of plans, effective leaders must be able to find ways to "paint a picture" of a desired goal and to persuade other members of the organization to work together to realize this goal.

This chapter will explore two major conceptual frameworks of leadership. It will begin with a review of **House's Path-Goal Theory**, which is an example of the contingency approach to organizational behavior that is a major theme throughout this book. The Path-Goal Theory helps managers determine which type of behavioral leadership style they should use in any given situation. Next, Goleman's concept of **Emotional Intelligence** is discussed. This type of "intelligence" is considered by many to be more important for leadership effectiveness than traditional measures of IQ and other individual differences.

THE PATH-GOAL MODEL

One of the most challenging aspects of leadership in real-world organizations is determining the most appropriate approach to leadership for any given situation. Organizational leaders face many complex, ambiguous, and dynamic problems. One thing we do know is that there is no one best way to lead. In some situations it makes sense for a leader to focus on clarifying the tasks that need to be performed, whereas in other situations a leader may need to focus on being supportive in order to enhance the self-confidence of the members of a work unit. Likewise, it is sometimes appropriate for leaders to involve followers in a decision-making process whereas in other situations leaders should make the decision on their own.

The one thing that is common across all leadership situations is the objective of achieving and maintaining a good match between the style of a leader and the demands of a situation. But how does one establish a good leader-situation match? House's Path-Goal Theory is one of the best theories of leadership for this purpose. The strengths of this theory are that it is user-friendly and widely supported by empirical research. Figure 8-1[1] presents the Path-Goal Theory.

LEADER BEHAVIORS

The first component in Path-Goal Theory is **Leader Behaviors.** House argues that a leader, much like a baseball pitcher, has a repertoire she can use to handle any given situation. In baseball, a pitcher may be able to throw a fastball, a slider, knuckleball, or a forkball. Similarly, in Path-Goal Theory, a leader can use **Directive** behavior, **Supportive** behavior, **Participative** behavior, or **Achievement-oriented** behavior.

Directive behavior refers to the degree to which a leader provides direction or structure to his followers. Think of this as the things a leader does to clarify what followers need to do to complete a task. For example, when a leader takes the time to

Figure 8-1   House's Path-Goal Theory

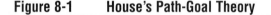

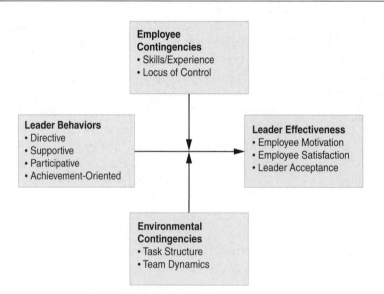

Source: Based on House, R. J. A Path-Goal Theory of Leader Effectiveness. *Administrative Science Leadership Review,* Vol. 16, 1991.

define the role of each team member so that the team member knows what to do and how it relates to the activities of other team members, the leader is exhibiting a high level of Directive behavior. When a leader does not clarify what a team member needs to do to perform his job effectively, the leader is exhibiting a low level of Directive behavior.

Supportive behavior refers to the degree to which a leader shows concern for the satisfaction and well-being of his followers. For example, a leader who touches base regularly with his employees to make sure that they are doing okay is exhibiting a high level of Supportive behavior. A leader who spends time getting to know his employees and tries to make them feel like part of the team is also exhibiting a high level of Supportive behavior. A leader who does not offer encouragement or show concern for his followers is exhibiting a low level of Supportive behavior.

Participative behavior refers to the actions a leader takes to involve followers in decisions that the leader needs to make. If a leader makes decisions with no employee involvement, the leader is exhibiting a low level of Participative behavior. If the leader involves employees in the decision-making process and uses consensus building, the leader is exhibiting a high level of Participative behavior.

Achievement-oriented behavior refers to the actions a leader takes to clarify goals for employees and to enhance their commitment and motivation to achieve these goals. For example, a leader who takes the time to educate his employees about what their goals are and why they are important for the success of the organization is exhibiting a high level of Achievement-oriented behavior. A leader who spends little or no time emphasizing goals and their importance is exhibiting a low level of Achievement-oriented behavior.

EMPLOYEE CONTINGENCIES

The second component in Path-Goal Theory is **Employee Contingencies.** Basically, these are characteristics of a leader's followers that the leader needs to assess before he can identify the most appropriate behavior(s) to use in a given situation.

Skills/Experience include the abilities and competencies of employees and the nature and amount of relevant Experience they possess. In some cases, employees may possess high levels of all of the necessary Skills and Experience required for a given project or task. However, in other situations, a leader may have a group of employees who have little or no relevant work Experience and some Skill deficiencies as well. A leader could easily encounter either of these situations.

Locus of Control refers to the degree to which an employee believes that she controls the outcome associated with a situation. An individual with an internal Locus of Control believes that she can control or strongly influence the outcome of a situation. On the other hand, an individual with an external Locus of Control believes that some outside force or factor determines the outcome of situation. Some people view this as a fatalistic viewpoint. For example, if someone says, "If it was meant to be, it will happen," this reflects an external Locus of Control.

Locus of Control can be a very important consideration since employees who have an external Locus of Control may not see how their actions can influence their job performance or their success. This can certainly make a leader's job more difficult.

ENVIRONMENTAL CONTINGENCIES

The third component in Path-Goal Theory is **Environmental Contingencies.** Environmental Contingencies include contextual factors that surround the leader and her employees within a team or work unit. There are two main environmental contingencies.

Task Structure refers to the degree to which a task is clearly defined. A task that is complex and oftentimes ambiguous (e.g., determining how to improve the quality of a product) tends to possess low Task Structure. A task that specifies exactly what an employee needs to do (e.g., following a step-by-step procedure for performing maintenance of a piece of equipment) possesses high Task Structure.

Team Dynamics refer to the characteristics of the process through which members of a team interact with each other. This includes patterns of communication, conflict resolution, decision-making styles, and the culture of the team (i.e., its collective personality). To the extent that a team exhibits dysfunctional ways of thinking and acting, there will be a stronger need for the leader to engage in behavior that effectively addresses these problem areas.

LEADER EFFECTIVENESS

The final component in Path-Goal Theory is **Leader Effectiveness.** The primary reason it is important to be concerned with leadership behaviors, employee contingencies, and environmental contingencies is that a leader seeks to achieve desired employee outcomes that will enhance their job effectiveness and success. Leader Effectiveness is based on three main elements.

Employee Motivation is defined as the desire an employee possesses to expend effort toward achieving one or more goals. Motivation is a critical employee outcome since it has a strong impact on the job performance of the employee. That is, employees with a high level of motivation tend to perform significantly better than employees with moderate or low levels of motivation.

Employee Satisfaction refers to an employee's beliefs, feelings, and behavioral tendencies toward various aspects of her job (e.g., the work itself, supervision, compensation and benefits, opportunities for advancement, and so on). Employee Satisfaction is one of the most widely studied aspects in the field of organizational behavior. One of the major reasons for this attention is that Employee Satisfaction has been shown to be correlated with employee behaviors that are of concern to leaders, such as retention and attendance. Specifically, high Employee Satisfaction is associated with high employee retention and attendance behavior.

Leader Acceptance refers to the degree to which employees view an individual as having credibility and legitimacy as the leader of their work unit. This is important since it is difficult for a person to be an effective leader if her employees do not perceive her as having the right and ability to lead them. This is sometimes referred to as a leader having "legitimate power."

THE LEADER-SITUATION MATCH

According to Path-Goal Theory, the ultimate objective of a leader is to establish and sustain a strong "leader-situation match." This means that the behavior of a leader satisfies the needs of the situation. When there is a strong leader-situation match, the leader will be effective. There are many different types of potential leader-situation matches. The following are a few examples of strong leader-situation matches:

- If Employee Satisfaction is low, the leader needs to exhibit a high degree of Supportive behavior. This may involve the leader taking actions to improve his working relationship with followers or offering encouragement to increase follower motivation. By exhibiting Supportive behavior, the leader may increase Employee Satisfaction regarding their job, work environment, supervisor, and the organization as a whole.

- If Task Structure for employees is low, the leader needs to exhibit a high degree of Directive behavior. If a task is very complex and not clearly defined, the leader needs to provide direction and guidance to clarify what needs to be done and how it should be done.

- If Employee Motivation is low or if employee commitment to meeting performance objectives is low, the leader needs to exhibit a high degree of Achievement-oriented behavior. In this case, the leader focuses on trying to obtain the "buy-in" of his followers by articulating a vision desired goal in a way that convinces followers that the vision or goal is meaningful and important to them so that they are committed to support it.

- If Leader Acceptance is low, the leader should exhibit a high degree of Participative behavior. By doing this, the leader acknowledges the value of his followers in addressing an issue. This can help to break down barriers between the leader and followers and open up the communication process.

POOR LEADER-SITUATION MATCHES
When there is a weak match between the leader and the situation, one of three options is available:

- **Option 1: Modify the behavior of the leader to match the situation.** This can be accomplished through training that enhances a leader's ability to assess a situation and to apply the appropriate leadership behavior(s) for that situation. Coaching can also be used. In coaching, a leader's boss works with him to identify and implement behavioral strategies that will enhance his effectiveness.

- **Option 2: Change the nature of the situation.** Within the context of Path-Goal Theory, there are a number of factors that leaders can influence to change a situation. One is to redesign the jobs of followers so that there is more structure and clarity built into the basic definitions of the jobs. Another strategy involves a leader changing her hiring practices so that more experienced individuals with higher levels of knowledge and skills are integrated in a work unit. These are examples of steps leaders can take to make a situation more favorable.

- **Option 3: Replace the leader.** In some cases, the leader may need to be replaced with another individual whose style better matches the situation. Although this should not be the first option in most situations, in some cases it may become evident that a given leader is simply the wrong type of leader for the situation or is not capable of changing his style to a degree that would make it a good match to the situation.

APPLICATION: PRACTICAL GUIDELINES FOR APPLYING PATH-GOAL THEORY

This section provides some practical suggestions regarding the implementation of House's Path-Goal Theory. These guidelines can be used by leaders of work groups and real-world organizations. (Figure 8-2 shows the steps involved in applying Path-Goal Theory).

The first step in applying the Path-Goal Theory of leadership is for the leader to **assess the situation.** The leader accomplishes this by examining the Employee and Environmental Contingency factors identified by Path-Goal Theory. The leader may collect relevant data (e.g., quarterly financial data, administering surveys, or interviewing employees) as part of this step. It is critical that this diagnosis take place first as it ultimately provides the foundation for determining the most appropriate leadership style to use in a situation.

The second step is to **identify the needs of the situation** based on the assessment of the situation in the first step. Specifically, a leader must now pinpoint the key needs of the situation. These needs may revolve around issues such as employees who do not understand what their objectives are, employees who lack the self-confidence to be able to take on a challenging project, or employees who are not committed to their job objectives.

The third step is for the leader to **select the leadership behavior that best satisfies the needs of the situation and to apply it.** Based on the availability of the four key leadership behaviors (Directive, Supportive, Participative, and Achievement-oriented), the leader must decide which behavior is needed for the situation and then demonstrate a high level of this behavior.

The fourth step is to **evaluate the quality of the leader-situation fit.** If the leader has correctly assessed the situation and implemented the appropriate leadership behavior for the situation, the leader should be effective. A leader in this situation would need to work to maintain the leader-situation match. If there is a poor match between the leader and situation, there are three options:

- Train the current leader to behave in ways that are more compatible with the needs of the situation.

- Modify contingency factors in the theory to make the situation more compatible with the leader's style. This requires a leader to address relevant environmental and employee contingency factors.

- Replace the leader with another leader whose style is more compatible with the situation.

Figure 8-2   Steps in Applying House's Path-Goal Theory

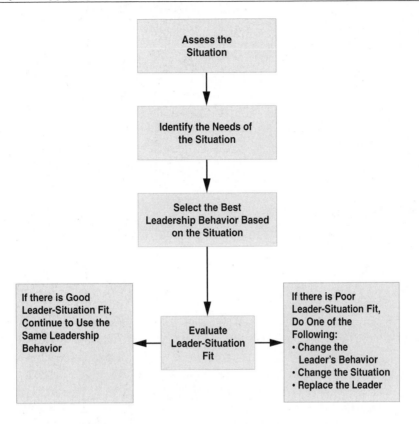

Assess the
Situation

↓

Identify the Needs of
the Situation

↓

Select the Best
Leadership Behavior Based
on the Situation

↓

If there is Good
Leader-Situation Fit,
Continue to Use the
Same Leadership
Behavior

← Evaluate
Leader-Situation
Fit →

If there is Poor
Leader-Situation Fit,
Do One of the
Following:
• Change the
  Leader's Behavior
• Change the Situation
• Replace the Leader

APPLICATION & EVALUATION

Designing a Leadership Training Program

Suppose that you work as a production supervisor for a manufacturing company that specializes in making wireless phones. Senior management recently met to evaluate the current performance of the company and to identify new initiatives that will support the long-term competitiveness and success of the organization. Your boss has asked you to be involved in a new "leadership task force" created in order to identify and develop future leaders of the company. One of the key elements of this initiative is to develop a formal leadership training program for new supervisors and managers. *Apply* House's Path-Goal Theory to develop the new leadership training program and *evaluate* it in terms of the degree to which you feel it would be effective.

SYNTHESIS & EVALUATION

Creating an Elaboration of the Basic Path-Goal Theory

A central issue in Path-Goal Theory is establishing and maintaining a good match between the leader's behavioral style and characteristics of the situation in order to enhance leader effectiveness. While Path-Goal Theory identifies a number of Employee and Environmental Contingencies, what are some other relevant contingency factors that could be included in the model? In addition, what are some additional measures of leader effectiveness that would be appropriate to include in the theory?

SYNTHESIS & EVALUATION

Linking Path-Goal Theory with the Expanded Expectancy-Theory of Motivation

Leadership and work motivation are closed related topics since the actions of leaders can have a significant impact on the motivation of their followers. The close relationship between these two topics offers an opportunity to link the major theoretical frameworks from these respective areas into a more comprehensive and powerful model. Given this, how can the Expanded Expectancy-Theory Model discussed in Chapter 3 be *synthesized* with the Path-Goal Model of leadership discussed in this chapter? Now *evaluate* this new model in terms of its value to management practitioners.

SYNTHESIS & EVALUATION

Linking Path-Goal Theory with the Bases of Power

Leadership can be defined as the process through which an individual influences the actions of followers in order to achieve organizational objectives. It is important to note that *influence* is a key element of leadership whereas *power* can be viewed as the capacity of an individual to influence others. Based on the close relationship between leadership and power, how can the Path-Goal Model of leadership be *synthesized* with the bases of power discussed in Chapter 6? *Evaluate* this new model in terms of its value to management practitioners.

ANALYSIS & APPLICATION

Using Path-Goal Theory to Assess Leader-Situation Fit in a Real-World Organization

Use a standard web browser (such as Internet Explorer or Netscape) to research business-oriented web sites (e.g., http://www.fortune.com or http://www.businessweek.com) in order to identify an article about a leader of an organization and the situation in which this leader exists. Use House's Path-Goal Theory to assess the quality of the leader-situation fit described in the article. Support your assessment using specific information from the article. If there was a poor leader-situation fit, make specific recommendations regarding what could be done to enhance the fit.

GOLEMAN'S CONCEPT OF EMOTIONAL INTELLIGENCE[2]

Many people assume that individuals who have high levels of intelligence (i.e., a high IQ) necessarily perform better in their jobs and become more "successful" in the real world. However, research has found that our traditional concept of intelligence may not be the best predictor of job and career success. Specifically, empirical research conducted by Goleman has indicated that something called "Emotional Intelligence" may be a more appropriate and valid predictor of future success, and in particular, the success of a leader.

What is Emotional Intelligence? In short, Goleman defines **Emotional Intelligence** as the degree to which an individual is able to understand and manage his own feelings as well as those of others. Figure 8-3 presents a model of Emotional Intelligence. In relation to House's Path-Goal Theory, Emotional Intelligence is most closely linked to the Supportive leadership behavior.

THE DIMENSIONS OF EMOTIONAL INTELLIGENCE
Emotional Intelligence is composed of five dimensions:

- **Self-awareness** refers to an individual's ability to recognize and understand his moods, emotions, and drives as well as their effect on others. Individuals with high Emotional Intelligence are very conscious of their emotional state in a given situation and how it might be influencing the reactions of others involved in a meeting, discussion, or business presentation.

- **Self-regulation** is defined as the ability of a person to control or redirect disruptive impulses and moods and the propensity to suspend judgment (i.e., to think before acting). Individuals with high Emotional Intelligence are able to maintain their composure and to cope with negative situations and emotions in a more constructive manner. This is an absolutely critical trait for leaders. No matter what a leader does, something can go wrong that may diminish his performance. When this happens, it is the way in which a person responds to and handles the situation that may very well determine his success in that organization. People who "freak out," "blow their tops," or have a "mental meltdown" usually do not fare well in these situations. These individuals are low on Self-regulation.

Another aspect of Self-regulation is a person's ability to defer rewards and gratification and to persevere in pursuing long-term goals. In short, people who are high on this trait are better able to achieve their goals despite adversity or setbacks they may experience.

- **Self-motivation** is an individual's passion for work for reasons that go beyond money or status and her propensity to pursue goals with energy and persistence. This dimension is partially related to the delay of gratification trait inherent in the Self-regulation component of Emotional Intelligence discussed above. A person who is high on Emotional Intelligence is motivated by the task itself (i.e., the person focuses on intrinsic factors as opposed to extrinsic factors such as recognition or pay). It is the challenge, satisfaction, meaning, and sense of accomplishment derived from performing the task that motivates individuals with high Emotional Intelligence.

- **Empathy** is an individual's ability to understand the emotional makeup of other people and to treat them according to their emotional reactions. Individuals who are empathetic are able to read the emotional reactions of others and to respond appropriately. They can identify what a person is really communicating based on their words, tone of voice, body posture, and degree of eye contact. In short, Empathy is about being able to walk in someone else's shoes.

Figure 8-3   Goleman's Emotional Intelligence (EQ) Framework

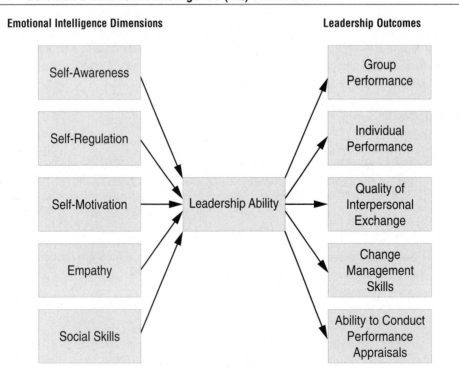

Source: Based on Goleman, D. *Working With Emotional Intelligence.* New York: Bantam, 1998.

- **Social Skills** refer to a person's proficiency in managing relationships and building networks as well as the ability to find common ground and build rapport with others. Individuals who have high Emotional Intelligence are excellent team players. They also excel as customer service representatives and in other jobs that require the ability to work with people.

As noted earlier, Goleman's research has found that there is a strong relationship between the Emotional Intelligence of a leader and her effectiveness. Thus, Emotional Intelligence is extremely important.

APPLICATION: PRACTICAL GUIDELINES FOR APPLYING EMOTIONAL INTELLIGENCE

The basic process for applying Goleman's Theory of Emotional Intelligence involves the following five steps:

- **Step 1: Conduct an assessment.** The first step in applying Goleman's Theory of Emotional Intelligence is to conduct an assessment of an individual's Emotional Intelligence. Ideally, the individual's manager or a trusted colleague is involved in this process to ensure accuracy and accountability for the assessment and action plan. This can be done formally using various surveys or more informally using the feedback and observations of the individual's manager and co-workers. The key is to have an empirical basis for assessing whether an individual is low, moderate, or high on each of the five dimensions of Emotional Intelligence (Self-awareness, Self-regulation, Self-motivation, Empathy, and Social Skills).

- **Step 2: Identify strengths and opportunities for improvement.** The next step involves evaluating the results of the assessment conducted in Step 1. An individual who is highly emotional intelligent would score high on each of the five dimensions, so the focus of this step is to identify on which dimensions an individual is high and low. The dimensions on which an individual scores high are considered strengths. Dimensions on which the individual scores low are considered opportunities for improvement. The individual and his manager (or colleague) should talk about the assessment of each dimension and identify examples of how the individual demonstrates each of the five dimensions of Emotional Intelligence at his job.

- **Step 3: Formulate an action plan.** The individual and his manager (or colleague) should now develop an action plan based on the identification of strengths and opportunities for improvement. This action plan should specify specific and measurable goals for the individual and specific action steps that will support the achievement of each improvement goal. Specific target dates for achieving each of the goals should also be included in the plan. This action plan should be formally documented and signed by both the individual and his manager (or colleague). Figure 8-4 presents a sample template for documenting an action plan for enhancing an individual's Emotional Intelligence.

Figure 8-4   Template for Enhancing An Individual's Emotional Intelligence

Name:

Name of Manager (or Colleague):

Dimension	Improvement Goals	Action Steps	Target Completion Date

- **Step 4: Implement the plan.** Next, the individual must start working toward achieving the improvement goals by implementing the action steps in the plan. The individual's manager (or colleague) should support the implementation of the plan by observing the individual's behavior and providing feedback.

- **Step 5: Evaluate the plan.** Finally, the individual and his manager (or colleague) need to schedule regular meetings to formally discuss the individual's progress on implementing the plan and achieving his goals. Some elements of the plan (e.g., target dates) may need to be adjusted as a result of these meetings. Ultimately, the individual and his manager (or colleague) should discuss how to integrate further Emotional Intelligence improvements into a broader focus on performance improvement for the individual. These would focus on any other aspect of the individual's performance that may need improvement, regardless of whether it is directly related to Emotional Intelligence.

APPLICATION & EVALUATION
Enhancing the Emotional Intelligence of Management

Suppose that the CEO of your company just read Goleman's book about Emotional Intelligence and she wants to create a committee to develop a set of strategies for enhancing the Emotional Intelligence of all managers in the company. You have been asked to serve on this new committee. The focus of the Emotional Intelligence initiative will be on all supervisors, managers, and executives. Based on Goleman's Emotional Intelligence Theory, develop a set of strategies for enhancing the Emotional Intelligence of the managers in the organization. In addition, *evaluate* the strategies you developed in terms of justifying why you would expect them to be effective.

SYNTHESIS & EVALUATION
Viewing Emotional Intelligence as a Contingency Theory

Goleman proposes that Emotional Intelligence be viewed as a set of qualities that are related to leadership effectiveness and career success. However, a major theme in this book revolves around a Contingency Theory approach to organizational behavior. Given this, develop a set of contingency factors that you believe would be appropriate for Emotional Intelligence. That is, what kinds of situational considerations (e.g., employee, task, or contextual) would determine whether a leader should apply the various dimensions of Emotional Intelligence to a given situation?

ANALYSIS & APPLICATION
Assessing the Emotional Intelligence of Real-World Leaders

Use a standard web browser (such as Internet Explorer or Netscape) to research business-oriented web sites (http://www.fortune.com or http://www.businessweek.com) in order to identify two leaders of organizations who you feel have a high level of Emotional Intelligence and two leaders who you feel have a low level of Emotional Intelligence. On what basis would you make this assessment? What is the relationship between these individuals' Emotional Intelligence and their effectiveness as leaders?

CONCLUSION

This chapter has discussed one of the most established and valid models of leadership (Path-Goal Theory) as well as Emotional Intelligence, an area of great focus in recent leadership research. Together, these two models provide a balanced emphasis between what leaders do (behaviors) as well as the qualities that they possess (traits) that contribute to their effectiveness.

In the end, there simply is no one best way to lead people. Each leadership situation is unique in terms of employee and environmental contingencies, and an effective leader must recognize this reality. Effective leadership in a complex, ambiguous, and constantly changing environment demands a flexible approach in which a leader must continuously monitor a situation and adapt her actions to meet the needs of any given situation.

Another critical point is that it is possible to develop the leadership skills of individuals through formal training, mentoring and coaching, and challenging work assignments. A focus on leadership behaviors facilitates the development of leadership skills, as these are things that can be observed, trained, rewarded, and reinforced in the performance of a leader's job.

Although Emotional Intelligence is a leadership trait or attribute, it has been shown to be one of the most important qualities needed for leadership effectiveness. In addition, each of the various dimensions of emotional intelligence is linked with behaviors that can enhance leadership effectiveness.

EXERCISES AND OTHER ACTIVITIES
■ *Experiential Exercise: In-Class 8-1*

APPLYING THE PATH-GOAL LEADERSHIP MODEL TO AN APPLIANCES DEPARTMENT

Background Information

The sales manager of an appliances department at a department store is asking you for advice once again. This time, the issue is leadership style. He vaguely recalls learning several years ago that a leader should choose a style that fits the situation, but he no longer has a clear idea of which style should be used when.

The sales manager has 12 employees working for him: eight full-time and four part-time. Information about half of these employees is provided below.

Your task is to analyze this information and make a recommendation about the most appropriate *leadership style* to use with each employee, based on the Path-Goal Model of Leadership. Be prepared to *explain why* you made your choices for each of these employees.

Employee Information

Nadine Johnson is a new part-time employee. She has no prior sales experience and is thus not sure what to expect from her new job.

Bjorn Stevenson, a full-time employee with six years of experience in the appliances department, has performed exceptionally well during the past two years in particular. He has a strong desire for autonomy.

Arnold Levin has had a good track record with the men's wear department within the same department store. After spending three years in men's wear, he requested a transfer to the appliances department so that he could "try something different." His transfer has just come through, and he is now a full-time employee in appliances.

Maria Perez is a senior at a local university, majoring in industrial/organizational psychology and getting good grades. She started working part-time for the appliances department a couple of weeks ago, and plans to graduate next semester. Maria is outgoing and personable, and has a strong work ethic.

Sam Littman is a veteran salesperson who has been an effective performer for many years. However, he is currently going through a difficult divorce that is beginning to affect his work significantly.

Miriam Bradford is a full-time employee who has worked in the appliances department for eight years. She is a steady but not spectacular performer. She is aware that she is not one of the department's top salespeople despite her many years of experience, and this makes her feel uncomfortable.

APPLYING THE PATH-GOAL LEADERSHIP MODEL: PART II

A New Challenge

After reviewing the revised recommendations for which leadership styles to use with half of his employees, the sales manager of the appliances department was very pleased with your recommendations. Since this information was so helpful to him, he has provided you with some information about his other six employees in hopes of receiving some additional feedback. In his opinion, the most appropriate style for each of these six employees is a little harder to figure out—but he could be wrong about that.

Once again, analyze this information and make a recommendation about the most appropriate leadership style(s) to use with each employee, based on the Path-Goal Theory of Leadership. As usual, be prepared to *explain why* you made your choices for each of these employees.

A New Group of Employees

Lan Tran, a full-time employee for about a year now, has improved significantly over that time. While she has become comfortable dealing with the general sales routine, unusual situations tend to create problems for her. She still asks a lot of questions about how to handle various situations and customer concerns.

Charlene Williams, a full-time employee, has worked in the appliances department for four years. She has been one of the better performers in the department for the past three months. She is very vocal about any concerns she has about how the department is being run. Sometimes she demonstrates a "whatever" attitude about her work, and she attempts to just do the minimum needed to get the job done.

Chien Lu has signed up to work in the appliances department only on weekends to make some extra money. During the regular work week, he sells industrial machine tools for another firm, which he has been doing for a number of years. He began working for the department last weekend. He is highly motivated by a strong desire to excel in all of his jobs and work activities.

Robert Stanford has worked full-time in the appliances department for six months. Robert's performance had improved slowly but steadily until three weeks ago, when it leveled off briefly and then dropped slightly during the past 10 days. (Note that the new sales manager took over the department 10 days ago.) Robert's job has not changed at any point.

Mitra Kazai worked in the appliances department as a full-timer 10 years ago, before she and her husband decided to begin a family. She performed reasonably well at that time. Now that her two children have gotten older, she has rejoined the appliances department this week on a part-time basis to supplement the family income while still having time for her children. The plan is for her to flexibly "fill in" as needed for about 10 hours a week while her children are at school. She is looking forward to going back to work again, although she is a bit apprehensive about selling the more technically sophisticated appliances that are now available.

Jose Ortega has been an enthusiastic and popular full-time employee for several years. A month after the new sales manager began his job, however, Jose became more moody.

EXERCISE EXTENSION: PATH-GOAL MODEL OF LEADERSHIP
Although you have analyzed the appliances department sales manager's 12 employees using the Path-Goal Model of Leadership and have made recommendations as to which leadership style appears to be the most appropriate for each employee, the sales manager's leadership job is not yet finished. The next issue, which the Path-Goal Model does **not** explicitly address is what a leader must do to apply a given leadership style. For each of the employees that you analyzed, develop an action plan that includes the specific actions that a leader would need to take in order to apply the leadership style that you recommended for that particular employee.

REFERENCE NOTES

1. House, R. J. A Path-Goal Theory of Leader Effectiveness. *Administrative Science Leadership Review*, Vol. 16, 1991, pp. 321–339.

2. Goleman, D. *Working With Emotional Intelligence*. New York: Bantam, 1998.

CHAPTER 9
Performance Management

A central aspect of any manager's job is "getting things done through people."[1] A frequent theme in many of the chapters in this book has been that employee performance is a critical concern for most managers.

This chapter focuses on three important elements that can strongly affect employee performance. **Goal-setting** sets the stage for good performance and acts as an important motivator for good performance. **Informal Feedback** ensures that the performance efforts triggered by the goal-setting activity are likely to stay on track. Finally, formal **Performance Evaluation** provides the basis for giving contingent rewards for recent good performance, as well as suggesting some ideas for future performance improvement. Note that a high-quality performance evaluation would most effectively conclude by initiating further goal-setting activities that will apply to the next Goal-setting→Feedback→Performance Evaluation cycle.

This chapter commences by describing a highly integrated model that emphasizes Goal-setting, Feedback, and Performance Evaluation, and includes a number of other relevant factors. Next, some additional useful results from organizational behavior research concerning these three important elements are discussed. The chapter concludes with some practical guidelines for implementing each of these three key elements in actual work situations.

THE HIGH-PERFORMANCE CYCLE MODEL

The **High-Performance Cycle Model**, created as a result of a thorough synthesis conducted by Locke and Latham,[2] is displayed in Figure 9-1. This model has a great deal in common with the Expanded Expectancy-Theory Model discussed in Chapter 3.

While the High-Performance Cycle Model focuses more on the *individual* level of analysis (covered in Chapters 2 and 3), evidence suggests that it can also apply to the *group* level of analysis (covered in Chapters 4–9). In fact, some substantial similarities are readily apparent between the High-Performance Cycle Model and the Normative Model of Group Effectiveness presented in Chapter 4.

The various factors included in the High-Performance Cycle Model diagram in Figure 9-1 will be described next.

DEMANDS

Initially, some kinds of **Demands** or **Challenges** from a customer, one's manager, or the job itself trigger a response on the part of the manager or employee who is going through the High-Performance Cycle. The primary approach to dealing with such Demands or Challenges, according to the model, is in the form of goal-setting. Goal-setting theory contends that **Goals** are the *direct* causes of performance, while factors such as needs, motives, and values are less direct. It is plausible, however, that needs, motives, and values affect the choices of goals, which then affect Performance.

Goals that are specific and challenging (High) lead to better task Performance than do Goals that are general, easy, or moderate. This is a very strong research finding and one that applies to groups as well as individuals.

Meaningful, Growth-facilitating Tasks or **Series of Tasks** can be created by applying the Job Characteristics Model (e.g., skill variety, task identification, and so forth, per Chapter 3).

Figure 9-1   The High-Performance Cycle Model

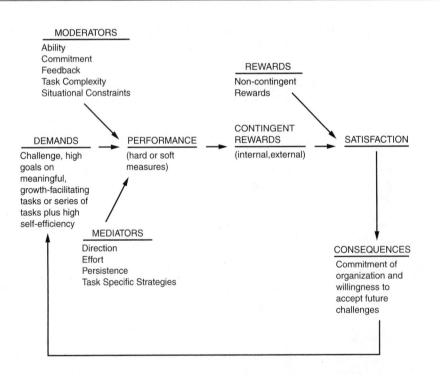

Source: Locke, E. A., and G. P. Latham. *A Theory of Goal Setting and Task Performance.* Englewood Cliffs, NJ: Prentice-Hall, 1990.

ANALYSIS   **Inclusion of the Job Characteristics Model Within the High-Performance Cycle Model**

Analyze why the Job Characteristics Model would be an excellent choice for creating meaningful, growth-facilitating tasks or series of tasks.

Self-efficacy is the degree to which an individual is generally confident about being able to do whatever is necessary to deal with a future situation. The concept of Self-efficacy is based on a broad variety of factors, including Ability, Effort, Situational Constraints, adaptability, and so forth. Research indicates that higher Self-efficacy is related to higher Performance. Self-efficacy also leads to high goal Commitment, and to High Goals when the Goals are self-chosen.

MODERATOR FACTORS

As was true in the case of the Job Characteristics Model in Chapter 3, moderators are contingency factors (see Chapter 1). In the High-Performance Cycle Model, these factors moderate how Demands made—or more accurately, Goals set—actually lead to effective task Performance.

Ability is an obvious Moderator that will eventually limit an individual's capacity to perform at a higher level (see also Chapter 3). Research shows that Performance eventually levels off when an individual's Ability level is reached, even if that individual's Goals happen to be set at still higher levels of Performance.

Commitment is essential if High Goals are to be achieved. A very common cause of high Commitment is Formal Authority (see Chapter 6). Many people commit to doing what authority figures tell them to do. Of course, authority figures also tend to control the Rewards that (hopefully) follow Performance, so that is also a strong motivator to commit. Another factor affecting the degree of goal Commitment, in addition to authority and Rewards, is Self-efficacy. Peer pressure and group Norms (see Chapter 4) likewise affect the amount of goal Commitment, as do peers who serve as role models for their co-workers. Additional factors that have an impact on goal Commitment include how public the goal is—in other words, how many people know about it—and the degree to which a person's ego is involved in achieving the goal.

Feedback is a crucial Moderator. Goal-setting *without* Feedback is not nearly as effective as Goal-setting *with* Feedback. Most people appreciate knowing if what they are doing is appropriate and effective. Feedback also aids in the development of Task-Specific Strategies for accomplishing a particular task. Feedback about an employee's Performance, in many instances, is significantly under the control of that employee's manager. Some techniques managers can use to provide effective Feedback appear later in this chapter.

Task Complexity has a significant effect on task Performance independent of Goals set. For relatively simple tasks, greater Effort is required to perform more-complex simple tasks than less-complex simple tasks. For example, working with another person to set 20 tables at a restaurant requires greater Effort than bolting wheels onto new cars.

Genuinely complex tasks, however, can reduce task Performance even when High Goals are set and a great deal of Effort is made. This is because Performance on such complex tasks also depends strongly on having a good Task Specific Strategy. Good Task-Specific Strategies are seldom easy to determine for a very complex task, such as designing an effective organizational quality system. In contrast, some strategies for performing even relatively complex simple tasks are generally well known or fairly obvious to those who perform such tasks.

Situational Constraints are aspects of a situation that impede Goal attainment. A shortage of money is an example of a common Situational Constraint. Bad weather might be another. Clearly, Performance will be better without such roadblocks. It should be noted, however, that a person with High Goals and High Self-efficacy may be challenged by existing Situational Constraints to perform even better to overcome them.

In general, then, challenging and specific Goals are especially likely to lead to high Performance when a person has high Ability and high Commitment, receives helpful Feedback in a timely manner, is faced with a relatively simple task, and faces no Situational Constraints. On the other hand, a lower level of Ability, a lower level of Commitment, very little or no Feedback, a relatively complex task, or any significant Situational Constraints contribute to reduced Performance. This will take place no matter how challenging and specific the Goals happen to be.

MEDIATOR FACTORS

While the Moderators discussed in the preceding section determine how likely it is that Goals will be effective, Mediators are ways in which Goals actually affect Performance. Think of Moderators as either setting limits on Performance (in the case of Ability, Commitment, Task Complexity, or Situational Constraints) or expanding limits on Performance (in the case of helpful Feedback). In contrast, the four Mediators in the High-Performance Cycle Model determine either the quality of the path taken from the Goals to Performance (i.e., Direction and Task-Specific Strategies), or how hard a person tries to follow that path (i.e., Effort and Persistence). Thus, Mediators are a different form of contingency factor than Moderators.

Direction means to pay attention or to focus. If a person focuses hard on doing something, he is more likely to achieve it. Research shows that having very specific Goals make it easier for a person to focus.

Effort as a key factor affecting Performance has already appeared in the Expanded Expectancy-Theory Model in Chapter 3 and the Normative Model of Group Effectiveness in Chapter 4. Research shows that challenging Goals, if accepted, lead to more intense Effort by the individual who has been challenged.

Persistence essentially refers to *directed* Effort repeated over and over again. Research shows that harder Goals will lead to more extended Effort over time than will easier Goals—if reasonably strong goal Commitment exists and if there are no time limits on completing those harder Goals.

Task-Specific Strategies have a direct effect on the quality of task Performance *regardless* of the quality of the Performance Goals. However, some research on the relationship between Goals and strategies does indicate that specific and challenging Goals generally stimulate strategy development and often lead to high-quality strategic plans. Furthermore, specific and challenging Goals increase the chances that Task-Specific Strategies recommended during training sessions on how to perform a task effectively will actually be applied later by the person undergoing that training.

On the other hand, specific and challenging Goals can lead to poor Task-Specific Strategies under three conditions:

1. When the task is complex, which will make creating a good strategy much more difficult

2. When the people involved do not have previous experience on which to base a possible strategy

3. When the people involved are under high pressure to perform well immediately, and hence will begin under a high degree of stress

ANALYSIS   Is It a Moderator or a Mediator?

Moderator and Mediator factors in the High-Performance Cycle Model have just been discussed and explained. Now *analyze* the factor from the Job Characteristics Model in Chapter 3 labeled "Growth Need Strength." Is it a Moderator or a Mediator? Why? Is the Locus of Control factor in the Path-Goal Theory in Chapter 8 a Moderator or a Mediator? Why?

PERFORMANCE

Performance is a key factor appearing in many of the models described in this book (see also Chapters 3, 4, and 8). The High-Performance Cycle Model adds a little to the accrued information about Performance by noting that either Hard or Soft Measures of Performance can be used.

Hard Measures deal directly with job *outcomes*, or outputs that can be measured numerically. Hard Measures are objective in nature. Some common Hard Measures include units produced, profitability, defect rates, and revenues.

Unfortunately, appropriate Hard Measures are not necessarily available for use in evaluating Performance in many types of jobs, including many management jobs. When Hard Measures cannot be applied, Soft Measures must be used instead.

Soft Measures deal with job *behaviors* rather than job outcomes, and are thus more indirect measures of Performance than are Hard Measures. Soft Measures can also be considered subjective if the frequency of such behaviors is estimated rather than accurately tallied (the latter is typically difficult to accomplish). The primary rationale for the viability of Soft Measures is that a manager or employee who frequently exhibits certain desirable behaviors *should* be performing better than one who seldom or never exhibits such behaviors. Examples of desirable behaviors include helping an employee to set specific and challenging Goals, providing useful Feedback to an employee on job Performance, or smiling at customers.

Determining which measures are feasible for a given job, choosing which of the available measures would be most appropriate for a given individual performer, and then evaluating how well that individual is actually performing are all challenging managerial tasks. Additional information on Performance Evaluation methods and how to conduct a Performance Evaluation is supplied later in this chapter.

REWARDS

Similar to the case for the Expanded Expectancy-Theory Model in Chapter 3, the High-Performance Cycle Model stresses the importance of giving deserved Rewards following good Performance. It also notes that Rewards can be **Internal** (similar to Intrinsic) or **External** (similar to Extrinsic). Another contribution of the High-Performance Cycle Model is to incorporate the concept that Rewards can be Contingent or Non-contingent on good performance. A bonus for a project well done is an example of a **Contingent Reward**, whereas one type of **Non-contingent Reward** is medical insurance. The model indicates that Performance leads only to Contingent Rewards, but both Contingent and Non-contingent Rewards lead to job Satisfaction. Although Non-contingent Rewards are not linked to Performance, they can play an important role in motivating an employee to choose to *stay* with an organization rather than leaving it.

SATISFACTION

Satisfaction has also appeared in several of the models presented in prior chapters (see Chapters 3, 4, and 8). In particular, the Performance→Rewards→Satisfaction linkages in the High-Performance Cycle Model are quite similar to those in the Expanded Expectancy-Theory Model of Chapter 3. The creators of the High-Performance Cycle Model note that job Satisfaction is fundamentally a result of a person's values and how well that person's job fulfills, or facilitates attainment of, those values.

For example, an individual who values a high level of achievement might feel Satisfaction with a job providing difficult Challenges that lead to high achievement when those Challenges are overcome. Or, if a person values money, a challenging job that is well rewarded for high Performance would facilitate the attainment of a larger bank account, which would then lead to feelings of Satisfaction.

CONSEQUENCES

Consequences refer to the outcomes of an individual's assessment of her current job Satisfaction. Research shows that Satisfaction is moderately strongly correlated to Commitment to the organization. If the assessment is positive, Commitment is likely to continue. On the other hand, dissatisfaction with the job can eventually lead to the *intention to quit*.[3] Research indicates that this is frequently followed by quitting.

Hopefully, from a manager's or the organization's point of view, an individual will experience job Satisfaction. Based on the research findings indicated above, the High-Performance Cycle Model suggests that such Satisfaction leads to **Commitment to the Organization and Willingness to Accept Future Challenges**. The latter factors in turn lead—via the feedback loop shown in Figure 9-1—back to the beginning of the High-Performance Cycle.

Most people performing jobs in work organizations repeat many aspects of the High-Performance Cycle Model daily. Some aspects involve a longer time cycle, such as the effects of new training on Task-Specific Strategies. Rewards—especially External Contingent Rewards as well as many of the most popular Non-contingent Rewards—are typically received much less often than daily. If the level of job Satisfaction becomes negative, weeks or possibly even months may go by before the dissatisfied person actually quits. Unfortunately, Commitment to the Organization and Willingness to Accept Future Challenges is likely to drop much sooner.

APPLICATION, ANALYSIS, SYNTHESIS & EVALUATION

The High-Performance Cycle Model and the Expanded Expectancy-Theory Model

How are the High-Performance Cycle Model and the Expanded Expectancy-Theory Model similar? How do they differ? Which of these models appears to be the most practically useful? Could a practicing manager benefit from using either one or the other of these models, depending on the situation?

ADDITIONAL USEFUL RESULTS FROM ORGANIZATIONAL BEHAVIOR RESEARCH

A simultaneous statistical analysis of a substantial number of different organizational behavior research studies—called a **meta-analysis**—was undertaken to determine which managerial techniques have the greatest impact on Performance.[4] According to this meta-analysis, *training* and *Goal-setting* have the strongest overall effects on Performance. *Financial incentives* (monetary rewards in the form of raises, bonuses, and so on) have a fairly strong effect. *Work redesign* (see the Job Characteristics Model in Chapter 3), *Feedback*, and *Performance Evaluation* have somewhat less impact than the three other techniques but still appear to play important roles. Thus, all of the three major topics on which this chapter is focused are important determinants of Performance, although Goal-setting appears to have a greater impact than either Feedback or Performance Evaluation.

GOALS

While setting difficult (challenging) Goals generally motivates people to perform at a higher level, this may not apply when the person being motivated has yet to acquire the knowledge needed to perform effectively. In such cases, it appears to be better to set a difficult *learning* Goal.[5]

The powerful effect of training has been linked to several factors appearing in the High-Performance Cycle Model that are related to Goals. Research has shown that training helps to increase Self-efficacy, and therefore goal Commitment.[6]

A review of many previous studies convincingly confirms that setting *group* Goals clearly leads to much better group Performance, just as setting *individual* Goals clearly leads to much better individual Performance.[7] However, while group Goals definitely lead to much better group Performance, individual Goals may or may not lead to better group Performance. One research study found that group performance is highest when both group Goals and "group-centric" individual Goals are used.[8]

Group cohesiveness leads to the setting of group Goals that are strongly supported by the group. Such Goals then positively affect group Performance[9] *if* the Goals of the group match the Goals of the organization[10] (see also Chapter 4).

A controversial topic that has arisen in organizational behavior research on Goals is whether **participation** in Goal-setting leads to better Performance. Many studies suggest that individual participation in Goal-setting does not appear to motivate better individual Performance than simply assigning the Goals.[11] However, individual participation in Goal-setting may provide a way to ensure that individual expectations are clear,[12] which might well have a positive effect on individual Performance. Such expectations have much in common with Role Perceptions (see the Expanded Expectancy-Theory Model in Chapter 3). Likewise, group participation in Goal-setting may result in Reduced Process Losses[13] (see the Normative Model of Group Effectiveness in Chapter 4), which could have a similar positive impact on group Performance. Finally, a more recent study of individual participation in Goal-setting indicates that participation does appear to increase Self-efficacy.[14] Since higher Self-efficacy is related to higher Performance,[15] participation would appear to be beneficial overall, even if not directly correlated with Performance.

FEEDBACK

Feedback, like Performance Evaluation, tends to be more positive than it should be if the Feedback is given directly to the Feedback recipient, as opposed to indirectly.[16] This is due to such concerns as fear of conflict (see Chapter 5) that may result from the negative Feedback. Interestingly, there is some evidence that Feedback may be more effective when delivered by computer rather than directly in person.[17]

One research study suggests that while Feedback is considered to be one of the most effective motivational tools available, leaders often do a poor job of providing it. Prior research has indicated that when faced with a poor-performing employee, leaders have a general tendency to avoid providing Feedback, delay providing Feedback, and distort the Feedback to make it less negative. However, this particular study's results suggest that if evaluations of the leader's *own* Performance will be strongly affected by the Performance Evaluations of his or her subordinates, the Feedback the manager provides is likely to be more frequent, more immediate, and more directive. In particular, if the poor Performance is perceived as being a result of low employee Ability, the Feedback will be more directive (as in the Directive Behavior described in the Path-Goal Theory in Chapter 8). However, if the poor Performance is perceived as being a result of low employee Effort, the Feedback provided will be more frequent, more immediate, and more punitive (punishing).[18]

Integrating the Findings on Feedback with Key Sections of the Expanded Expectancy-Theory Model

The research study just described determined that the feedback a leader supplies is likely to be different in nature if a subordinate's poor Performance is perceived as being caused by low employee Ability versus low employee Effort. *Analyze* how these findings might be *synthesized* with the Expanded Expectancy-Theory Model. What seems likely to be the nature of a leader's Feedback if a subordinate's poor Performance is perceived as being caused by low employee Role Perceptions?

Rather surprisingly, one revealing organizational behavior research study found evidence that giving Feedback on *very* complex tasks can actually *hurt* Performance. Hence, Feedback on such tasks is best given infrequently and with careful thought prior to giving the Feedback.[19]

Feedback on Very Complex Tasks

Common sense would suggest that Feedback about Performance is likely to enhance future Performance. However, the research study just described suggests that Feedback can actually *hurt* Performance for very complex tasks. *Analyze* how this surprising finding might be explained.

PERFORMANCE EVALUATIONS

Accuracy of Performance Evaluations is greater when using **comparative** rather than **absolute evaluation methods.**[20] In other words, it is usually easier for people to say, "This is a little better than that" than it is for them to accurately determine that "This rates as a 7 on a 10-point scale."

Methods for Evaluating Performance

Recall that the High-Performance Cycle Model described in this chapter contains a Performance factor that is assessed through Hard or Soft Measures. Consider these two forms of measures in light of the research finding that accuracy of Performance Evaluations is greater when *using* comparative rather than absolute evaluation methods. *Analyze* whether Hard Measures are typically comparative or absolute forms of measurement. Likewise, are Soft Measures typically comparative or absolute forms of measurement? Now, *synthesize* these ideas to determine if research finding makes sense. Why or why not? [Hint: Would a contingency approach be helpful here?]

When a series of Performance Evaluations is being conducted one after another, Performance ratings are significantly affected by the rating given to the prior individual. For example, an average performer who follows a low performer will receive a much higher rating than she would have had when that average performer followed a high performer. The least biased ratings will be given when employees are evaluated separately and independently.[21]

The **360-degree feedback technique** for Performance Evaluation covers the "full circle" (360 degrees) by obtaining manager, self, peer (co-worker), and consultant evaluations. This approach may also be called a **multi-source, multi-rater feedback technique.**[22] Research on the application of this technique has found that all of these different sources of ratings tend to produce fairly similar results except for self-ratings, which tended to be self-serving and thus higher than the others.[23] In addition, as noted in many prior research studies, ratings based on *observable behaviors* appear to be the most accurate in terms of agreement between Performance raters.[24] One study notes that people who receive 360-degree feedback that is negative tend to perceive it as being less accurate and less useful, even though it is fairly consistent and coming from a wide variety of sources.[25]

The extent to which employees will participate during a Performance Evaluation depends significantly on the manager who is conducting the evaluation. A serious problem is the limited extent to which many managers alter their own behavior during Performance Evaluations, regardless of the characteristics of the employee being evaluated.[26] Managers capable of effectively following a contingency approach (see Chapter 1) will elicit greater participation (see also Chapter 8).

APPLICATION: PRACTICAL GUIDELINES FOR SETTING GOALS, PROVIDING FEEDBACK, AND CONDUCTING PERFORMANCE EVALUATIONS

As indicated in the introduction to this chapter, these three topics (setting Goals, providing Feedback, and conducting Performance Evaluations) form a natural Goal-setting→Feedback→Performance Evaluation cycle in the ongoing process of Performance Management. Therefore, they are highly interdependent, and have a substantial amount in common. However, each of these topics is also a bit different from the other two. The practical guidelines that follow place primary emphasis on the differences in an effort to reduce redundancy, but also note key points of commonality where appropriate.

SETTING GOALS
Probably the most logical starting point when setting Goals for a new employee is to identify the important tasks in that employee's job.[27] Once this first step has been accomplished, it should not be necessary to repeat it during later goal-setting sessions unless the employee's job changes in significant ways.

The key to effective Goal-setting is to make sure that Goals are challenging and specific.[28] However, it is very important to consider each individual's Ability level when setting Goals.[29] A Goal that is challenging for one employee may be impossible for another. In addition to the individual goals for an employee, be sure to remind the employee of any group goals that may apply.[30]

Per the High-Performance Cycle Model, discuss the Contingent Rewards that will be given if the Performance Goals being set are eventually met.[31] Keep in mind that while Performance is the major outcome concern of the manager during a Goal-setting session, the major outcome concern of most employees is the Rewards they can receive.

Since training enhances Self-efficacy, and therefore goal Commitment,[32] consider building in some training as appropriate. A managerial commitment that such training is planned can show support (see Chapter 8), and can help to boost an employee's Perceived Effort→Reward Probability (discussed in Chapter 3) and increase goal Commitment.

Set deadlines for meeting Goals. Otherwise, progress is likely to proceed at a much slower pace.[33] If multiple Goals are set during a Goal-setting session—as seems quite likely—it is important to ensure that the employee clearly understands which of these Goals are of higher priority.[34] Otherwise, the employee will tend to focus on the easier, more fun, or more interesting Goals and pay less attention to the more difficult, less fun, or less interesting Goals.

Research findings presented in the prior section suggest that while participation in Goal-setting does not appear to motivate better Performance than simply assigning the goals,[35] it may have a variety of beneficial effects that can eventually affect Performance. These include clarifying individual expectations[36] (Role Perceptions), Reducing Process Losses within a group setting,[37] and increasing Self-efficacy (the degree to which an individual is generally confident about being able to do whatever is necessary to deal with a situation).[38] As noted earlier, higher Self-efficacy is directly correlated to higher Performance.

PROVIDING FEEDBACK

Experience shows that providing Feedback is likely to be more comfortable if the Feedback session begins and ends with *positive* Feedback. Keep in mind that most employees do at least some things reasonably well (or they should not have been hired in the first place!). Providing *informal* Feedback well in advance of a formal Performance Evaluation creates a situation in which Feedback can be spread out over time, if appropriate, to ensure the maximum possible benefit.

In general, use a contingency approach (see Chapter 1) to provide more or less Feedback depending on the knowledge, skills, experience, and personality (see Chapter 2) of the Feedback recipient.[39]

As is the case with Goals, it is important to be specific when providing Feedback.[40] Some research suggests doing Goal-setting in conjunction with giving Feedback.[41]

Focus on the job task and the Performance of that task, not the person.[42] For example, telling an employee, "You are really slow" will cause the employee to become defensive and hence will most likely *not* improve Performance. Instead, focus attention on job behaviors *observed* and job behaviors *required*. It may be helpful to point out that *any* employee engaging in such behaviors would receive the same kind of negative Feedback.

Negative Feedback is more likely to be accepted when it comes from a highly respected, credible source.[43] Another way to increase the probability that negative Feedback will be accepted is to present objective reasons supported by hard facts—numbers can be helpful—as well as specific examples.[44] Generally speaking, it helps to focus on only one or two key areas of criticism so as not to overwhelm the person receiving the negative Feedback.[45]

Timing is important for Feedback in general, and negative Feedback in particular. Giving immediate Feedback is often best;[46] otherwise the so-called "forgetting curve" may create recall problems. However, if either the Feedback provider or the Feedback recipient is currently angry or upset, it is more effective—and also more fair—to give that person some time to calm down before providing the negative Feedback.[47]

When giving Feedback, include information about how the employee can improve his or her Performance.[48] While focusing on information related to improving Performance, try to avoid talking about the relative Performance of others.[49] (This will be easier to do when Performance is evaluated using absolute rather than comparative methods.) Be sure to provide specific ideas for improving future Performance[50] as opposed to very general suggestions such as "Get motivated" or "Make an effort."

To conclude a Feedback session, it is helpful to obtain Feedback on the Feedback provided to make sure that the employee clearly understood it.[51] This might be accomplished by asking the person receiving the Feedback to summarize the key points just covered. Note that very astute employees may choose to initiate such Feedback on their own, to confirm that their revised Role Perceptions are accurate and thus likely to lead to higher future Performance (see Chapter 3).

CONDUCTING PERFORMANCE EVALUATIONS

Most of the guidelines concerning how to provide Feedback also apply to conducting Performance Evaluations, which are a *formal* form of Feedback. The major exception is the timing of the evaluation, which will usually be significantly delayed rather than relatively immediate. This is because formal Performance Evaluations are typically conducted either every six months or once a year.[52] To compensate for this delay, it is helpful to provide *informal* Feedback more frequently. That way, the formal Performance Evaluation is unlikely to provide any major surprises for the employee. As a result, the evaluation becomes more of a formality, which reduces stress for both the employee and the manager.

Performance Evaluations will also be much easier to conduct if specific Goals have been clearly set. Then, the evaluation can simply focus on comparing those Goals with actual Performance. Routinely collecting Performance data, in the form of some output numbers or specific examples of desired job-related behaviors, will likewise make Performance Evaluations go more smoothly.

Other elements of the Goal-setting process that are especially relevant when conducting a Performance Evaluation include a discussion of overall Goal Performance with respect to the Goal *priorities* established earlier and the giving of Contingent Rewards for meeting the Performance Goals set previously. The latter will be much easier to do if the Contingent Rewards have been linked to the Goal priorities in the preceding Goal-setting session.

If possible, a worthwhile way to conclude a Performance Evaluation is to engage in Goal-setting for the next Performance Evaluation. However, if the employee is upset or distracted by the results of the current evaluation, it may be better to conclude the Performance Evaluation by simply setting a time to meet and renew the Goal-setting process. This approach may be especially appropriate if the evaluator chooses to have the employee participate in the Goal-setting process. The new Goal-setting meeting should be scheduled to take place in the reasonably near future, after the employee has had an opportunity to calm down and hopefully begin to consider how to constructively cope with the issues that arose during the Performance Evaluation (see also temporary Avoiding in Chapter 5).

APPLICATION EXAMPLE

Setting Goals, Providing Feedback, and Conducting Performance Evaluations in a Very Small Backpack Manufacturing Company

To illustrate the essentials of *applying* these three important managerial skills to a real-life situation, the following is an example involving an employee who works for a small company that makes backpacks for students. Student Backpacks, Inc., was started by two business majors shortly after they graduated, based on a business plan that they had developed as a team project in a course on entrepreneurship.

The new backpacks include several unique features. One is a specially padded pocket for protecting small wireless communication devices. Another is an organizer pocket with a clear plastic front panel that allows the pack owner to easily see its contents (whenever it isn't covered by its optional protective cloth flap). Specially reinforced strips of ultra-heavy-duty cloth in the main compartment, in areas where textbook corners tend to dig into the pack sides, is a third special feature. And last but not least, each backpack has a very distinctive logo that comes in six different colors, ranging from forest green to hot pink. The packs were initially sold only at the university from which the two founders graduated, but now orders are pouring in from colleges all over the state.

Student Backpacks, Inc., currently consists of six employees: two full-time and two part-time employees whose jobs are to make the packs, and the two founders, who make some packs as well as do everything else. This example focuses on how the Goal-setting→Feedback→Performance Evaluation cycle for a full-time employee is managed by the company co-founder who did the major design work on the pack.

When this full-time employee was initially hired, one of the first things the co-founder did was to train her to make the backpacks. That process involves cutting pieces of material based on patterns, doing a great deal of hard work on an industrial-strength sewing machine, and so on. The employee struggled a bit at first, but after several weeks had improved tremendously with respect to both the quality and quantity of her work. The co-founder then decided to sit down with this employee and set goals.

continues

Since the co-founder had already identified the important tasks in the employee's job while doing the initial training, it was not necessary to repeat that information during this goal-setting session. Instead, the co-founder began by talking about how the employee had been performing recently. She had been producing 10 packs a day, with very few major errors and only a small number of minor ones. The co-founder felt that she could increase her output by 20%, to 12 packs a day, with a similar high level of quality. The employee agreed that this would be possible, but felt that a raise in pay should accompany this improvement in output. The co-founder agreed, and promised a 10% pay raise if this key goal was met without a sacrifice in quality. Both agreed that the employee would have a month to figure out how to increase her output to 12 packs per day, and then would have to maintain that level for the next five months to qualify for the raise. Both also agreed that the company could not afford to damage its growing reputation by producing packs with quality problems, so quality was given priority over quantity (i.e., the goal of 12 backpacks per day). Thus, specific and challenging goals were set that were within the capabilities of the full-time employee, with training plus contingent rewards being provided. Deadlines were set, as were clear goal priorities. The employee was encouraged to participate in the goal-setting process.

During the next several weeks in particular, but also during the next several months, the co-founder took time out of an extremely hectic schedule to monitor the employee's work quality as well as the quantity of backpacks she produced, and to give her informal feedback on how she was doing. Since her quality had improved to a very high standard, that was what the co-founder often focused on first when giving her feedback. The feedback on the quantity she produced was very specific, involving actual numbers. The numbers were slow to improve until the employee experimented with different ways of preparing the materials in batches, which increased her efficiency. The co-founder also suggested some techniques that reduced problems with broken thread, which wasted a lot of time and thus slowed production. Sometimes the employee had a bad day or was under stress due to a family illness, and the numbers dropped. After one of these incidents, the co-founder just said "Hi" and left, but then came back the next day for a longer talk. Therefore, the co-founder made a point to provide informal feedback, matching it to the needs of the employee and being very specific with numbers where possible. He focused on job behaviors (and outcomes), not the employee as a person. Sometimes he was too busy to give feedback in a timely manner, but he tried to do this, and gave information about how to improve performance (as well as giving the employee autonomy to develop good techniques on her own). Within a short period of time, the employee had recognized the value of giving feedback on any feedback she got to make sure she got it right, and hence could perform better.

Six months after the goal-setting meeting took place, the co-founder conducted a formal performance evaluation of the employee. In this case, the performance evaluation was straightforward because the goals had been clearly set, both parties were already aware

continues

of the output numbers (no surprises), and the top priority of high quality had consistently been met. The co-founder gave the employee the contingent reward of a 10% raise, along with praise for a job well done. This was followed by a discussion of how the demand for the student backpacks was increasing, and the need to figure out how to produce more of them. Both the employee and the co-founder made suggestions about how this might be accomplished, and agreed that when these new methods were applied, it would be possible to produce 14 packs a day. Thus, the foundation provided by the goal-setting and informal feedback allowed the co-founder to focus the formal evaluation on goals and goal priorities met, and the contingent rewards based on them. Since the formal performance evaluation was concluded by doing some goal-setting for the future, the initial Goal-setting→Feedback→Performance Evaluation cycle blended smoothly into the next cycle.

CONCLUSION

This chapter is built around a solid, well-established integrated model that emphasizes goal-setting and includes feedback and performance as well. The High-Performance Cycle Model also provides a somewhat different approach to motivation that includes many of the same factors as the Expanded Expectancy-Theory Model (see Chapter 3). In addition, it emphasizes the motivational value and the effectiveness of goals in particular, and suggests a number of other useful factors to consider. For the industry practitioner who feels comfortable with a more complex model, this can be a valuable alternative to include in a collection of managerial tools.

More recent organizational behavior research has been strongly supportive of many aspects of the High-Performance Cycle Model, and also contributes some interesting refinements and extensions that lead to an in-depth understanding of goals, feedback, and performance evaluations. Performance management through the recurrent cycle of setting a goal, providing informal feedback, and conducting a formal performance evaluation should be a central focus for managers because a manager cannot succeed if his employees do not perform effectively. Developing strong behavioral skills in these key areas is essential!

EXERCISES AND OTHER ACTIVITIES
■ *Experiential Exercise: In-Class 9-1*

ANALYZING SIMILARITIES AND DIFFERENCES BETWEEN THE HIGH-PERFORMANCE CYCLE MODEL AND THE EXPANDED EXPECTANCY-THEORY MODEL

The purpose of this exercise is to analyze similarities and differences between the High-Performance Cycle Model and the Expanded Expectancy-Theory Model. This analysis can then be used as a basis for evaluating the two theories and determining when they might be the most useful to a practicing manager.

In this exercise, these two models are being analyzed at the *individual level* of analysis. In other words, the focus is on applying these two models to one person—most commonly a particular subordinate of a practicing manager.

Exercise Process Outline
Form groups of 5 to 7 students.

Carefully review the material concerning these two models in Chapters 9 and 3.

Develop answers to the following questions: How are the High-Performance Cycle Model and the Expanded Expectancy-Theory Model similar? How do they differ? Which of these models appears to be the most practically useful? Could a practicing manager benefit from using either one or the other of these models, depending on the situation?

When all of the groups have prepared their answers to the preceding questions, they will present them and discuss them with the class as a whole.

■ *Experiential Exercise: In-Class 9-2*

ANALYZING SIMILARITIES AND DIFFERENCES BETWEEN THE HIGH-PERFORMANCE CYCLE MODEL AND THE NORMATIVE MODEL OF GROUP EFFECTIVENESS

The purpose of this exercise is to analyze similarities and differences between the High-Performance Cycle Model and the Normative Model of Group Effectiveness. This analysis can then provide a basis for evaluating the two theories and determining when they might be the most useful to a practicing manager.

In this exercise, these two integrated models are being analyzed at the *group level* of analysis. As was noted at the beginning of the chapter, evidence suggests that the High-Performance Cycle Model can be applied to groups as well as individuals.

Exercise Process Outline
Form groups of 5 to 7 students.

Carefully review the material concerning these two models in Chapters 9 and 4.

Develop answers to the following questions: How are the High-Performance Cycle Model and the Normative Model of Group Effectiveness similar? How do they differ? Which of these models appears to be the most practically useful? Could a practicing manager benefit from using either one or the other of these models, depending on the situation?

When all of the groups have prepared their answers to the preceding questions, they will present them and discuss them with the class as a whole.

■ *Experiential Exercise: In-Class 9-3*

CONDUCTING A PERFORMANCE EVALUATION

The purpose of this exercise is to role-play the process of conducting a performance evaluation.

Exercise Process Outline

Form pairs of students.

Carefully review the material provided in the Applications section of Chapter 9 that deals with providing feedback and conducting performance evaluations.

Each pair should decide who will play the supervisor's role and who will play the employee's role during the *first* role play. [Hint: In most cases, both of you will eventually play both roles.] Once you have made that decision, your instructor will provide you with a role-related information sheet concerning the situation you should role-play. Be sure to read *only* your own role, or the role-play will be less effective. Then perform the role-play as realistically as possible. Try not to laugh, as that kind of behavior would be considered "unprofessional" in a real-world context. (Imagine how you would react in a situation where your real boss laughed while evaluating your recent performance.)

After finishing the first role-play, look around for another group that has also finished. Switch people to role-play with as well as switch roles to play. In other words, for the second role-play, be the employee if you were previously the supervisor, or vice-versa, and work with someone from another group. In addition, each new supervisor should attempt to deal with a situation that he or she did not experience in the first role-play. Then perform the role-play as realistically as possible, again trying your best to "be professional" by not laughing. [Tip: This may require making a special effort, even in the real world.]

When both pairs of students have finished the second role-play, they should get together as a group of four to discuss how these performance evaluations could have been handled most effectively.

After all of the four-person groups have decided how to best cope with their particular situations, the class as a whole will discuss the results as a whole.

■ *Experiential Exercise: In-Class 9-4*

CONDUCTING A MORE SOPHISTICATED PERFORMANCE EVALUATION

The purpose of this exercise is to role-play setting goals for an employee, and then later to role-play conducting a performance evaluation of that employee.

Exercise Process Outline

Form pairs of students. Form a pair with someone you have not been in a group with recently.

Carefully review the material provided in the Applications section of this chapter that deals with setting goals, providing feedback, and conducting performance evaluations.

Each pair should decide who will play the manager's role and who will play the employee's role.

In the manager's role, you may:

a. choose a management position that is based on your current position at work (be yourself if you are already a manager; otherwise, be your boss); or

b. act as sales manager for a salesperson or a retail-store clerk; or

c. act as manager of a sports coach (e.g., act as the athletic director or the general manager).

Before setting goals as a manager, it is important to be realistic about the kinds of resources available to support any extrinsic (external) rewards (see the control over resources power base in Chapter 6 and the integrated models in Chapters 3 and 9). Since the person who typically has this information is the manager's boss, your instructor will give you a goals information sheet indicating which kinds of extrinsic rewards your boss is willing to support. This information will apply regardless of the goals you and your subordinate choose to set during your role-play. Notice that each goals information sheet assumes that the three most important goals have been *prioritized* and that you will set *numerical* goals for any *extrinsic* rewards promised.

Once the person playing the manager's role has studied the goals information sheet, the first role-play can begin. The purpose of this role-play is to set some goals for the person who is playing the employee's role. Follow the guidelines presented in the Applications section on setting goals. To keep the role-play simpler, it is acceptable to discuss *only* the employee's three most important goals ("most important" as defined by the manager).

After the goal-setting role-play, assume that a full "year" has passed. Your instructor will supply the manager with a performance results information sheet to use as a basis for conducting the performance evaluation. [Tip: The manager may find it useful to briefly review the Applications section again.] Now the second role-play can begin, during which the employee's performance over the past "year" will be evaluated by the manager.

After all of the various two-person groups have finished both role-plays, the class will discuss the outcomes and strategies of these role-plays.

■ *Experiential Exercise: In-Class 9-5*

CONDUCTING A MORE SOPHISTICATED PERFORMANCE EVALUATION: EXTENDING THE EXERCISE

The purpose of this exercise is to role-play setting goals for an employee, and then later to role-play conducting a performance evaluation of that employee.

Exercise Process Outline

The process for this exercise extension is essentially the same as it was for the prior exercise (Experiential Exercise 9-4). The difference is that each pair of students will get together with another pair of students that has finished the first two role-plays (goal-setting plus performance evaluation), and switch roles as well as role-playing partners. Thus, each person will be playing a different role with a different person than in the first set of two role plays.

While the goals information sheet will be common to role-plays for this exercise, your instructor will provide a different Performance Results Information Sheet that each new manager should use as a basis for conducting the performance evaluation in the second set of goal-setting and performance evaluation role-plays.

When both pairs have finished the second set of role-plays, they should get together as a group of four to discuss how the goal-setting and performance evaluation could have been handled more effectively.

After all of the four-person groups have shared ideas about what happened and what other approaches they might have tried instead, the class will discuss the outcomes and strategies of the various role-plays.

■ *Experiential Exercise: In-Class 9-6*

PROVIDING FEEDBACK
The purpose of this exercise is to role-play the process of providing feedback to an employee.

Exercise Process Outline
Form pairs of students.

Carefully review the material provided in the Applications section of this chapter that deals with providing feedback.

Each pair should decide who will play the manager's role and who will play the employee's role.

Turn to Case Study 5-4 and read the section entitled "The Case." The "manager" will play the role of the vice president of Operations, while the "employee" may play the role of either Sharon or Bob.

After the "employee" has informed the VP about his or her choice to play the role of either Sharon or Bob, the VP should think carefully about how to handle the feedback for this particular individual before initiating the role-play.

Perform the role-play as realistically as possible, trying your best to "be professional" by not laughing. Doing a good job of giving feedback is actually not easy in situations like the one you are role-playing.

After all of the two-person groups have finished the role-play, the class will discuss the results of the role-play. What aspects of providing feedback are especially difficult to perform?

REFERENCE NOTES

1. Barnard, C. *The Functions of the Executive*. Cambridge, MA: Harvard University Press, 1938.

2. Locke, E. A., and G. P. Latham. *A Theory of Goal Setting and Task Performance*. Englewood Cliffs, NJ: Prentice-Hall, 1990.

3. Mobley, W. H., R. W. Griffeth, H. H. Hand, and B. M. Meglino. Review and Conceptual Analysis of the Employee Turnover Process. *Psychological Bulletin*, Vol. 86, 1979, pp. 493–522.

4. Guzzo, R. A., R. D. Jette, and R. A. Katzell. The Effects of Psychologically Based Intervention Programs on Worker Productivity: A Meta-Analysis. *Personnel Psychology*, Vol. 38, 1985, pp. 275–291; Pritchard, R. D., S. D. Jones, P. L. Roth, K. K. Stuebing, and S. E. Ekberg. Effects of Group Feedback, Goal Setting and Incentives on Organizational Productivity. *Journal of Applied Psychology*, Vol. 73, 1988, pp. 337–358.

5. Seijts, G. H., and G. P. Latham. The Effect of Distal Learning, Outcome, and Proximal Goals in a Moderately Complex Task. *Journal of Organizational Behavior*, Vol. 22, 2001, pp. 291–307.

6. Locke, E. A., and G. P. Latham. *A Theory of Goal Setting and Task Performance*. Englewood Cliffs, NJ: Prentice-Hall, 1990.

7. O'Leary-Kelly, A. M., J. J. Martocchio, and D. D. Frink. A Review of the Influence of Group Goals on Group Performance. *Academy of Management Journal*, Vol. 37, 1994, pp. 1285–1301.

8. Crown, D. F., and J. G. Rosse. Yours, Mine, and Ours: Facilitating Group Productivity Through the Integration of Individual and Group Goals. *Organizational Behavior and Human Decision Processes*, Vol. 64, 1995, pp. 138–150.

9. Klein, H. J., and P. W. Mulvey. Two Investigations of the Relationships Among Group Goals, Goal Commitment, Cohesion, and Performance. *Organizational Behavior and Human Decision Processes*, Vol. 61, 1995, pp. 44–53.

10. Seashore, S. *Group Cohesiveness in the Industrial Work Group*. Ann Arbor, MI: Institute for Social Research, 1954.

11. Wagner, J. A., and R. Z. Gooding. Shared Influence and Organizational Behavior: A Meta-Analysis of Situational Variables Expected to Moderate Participation-Outcome Relationships. *Academy of Management Journal*, Vol. 30, 1987, pp. 524–541; Locke, E. A., and G. P. Latham. *A Theory of Goal Setting and Task Performance*. Englewood Cliffs, NJ: Prentice-Hall, 1990.

12. O'Leary-Kelly, A. M., J. J. Martocchio, and D. D. Frink. A Review of the Influence of Group Goals on Group Performance. *Academy of Management Journal*, Vol. 37, 1994, pp. 1285–1301.

13. O'Leary-Kelly, A. M., J. J. Martocchio, and D. D. Frink. A Review of the Influence of Group Goals on Group Performance. *Academy of Management Journal*, Vol. 37, 1994, pp. 1285–1301.

14. Latham, G. P., D. C. Winters, and E. A. Locke. Cognitive and Motivational Effects of Participation: A Mediator Study. *Journal of Organizational Behavior*, Vol. 15, 1994, pp. 49–63.

15. Locke, E. A., and G. P. Latham. *A Theory of Goal Setting and Task Performance*. Englewood Cliffs, NJ: Prentice-Hall, 1990.

16. Waung, M., and S. Highhouse. Fear of Conflict and Empathic Buffering: Two Explanations for the Inflation of Performance Feedback. *Organizational Behavior and Human Decision Processes*, Vol. 71, 1997, pp. 37–54.

17. DeNisi, A. S., and A. N. Kluger. Feedback Effectiveness: Can 360-Degree Appraisals Be Improved? *Academy of Management Executive*, Vol. 14, 2000, pp. 129–139.

18. Moss, S. E., and M. J. Martinko. The Effects of Performance Attributions and Outcome Dependence on Leader Behavior Feedback Following Poor Subordinate Performance. *Journal of Organizational Behavior*, Vol. 19, 1998, pp. 259–274.

19. DeNisi, A. S., and A. N. Kluger. Feedback Effectiveness: Can 360-Degree Appraisals Be Improved? *Academy of Management Executive*, Vol. 14, 2000, pp. 129–139.

20. Wagner, S. H., and R. D. Goffin. Differences in Accuracy of Absolute and Comparative Performance Appraisal Methods. *Organizational Behavior and Human Decision Processes*, Vol. 70, 1997, pp. 95–104.

21. Woehr, D. J., and S. G. Roch. Context Effects in Performance Evaluation: The Impact of Ratee Sex and Performance Level on Performance Ratings and Behavioral Recall. *Organizational Behavior and Human Decision Processes*, Vol. 66, 1996, pp. 31–41.

22. Bailey, C., and C. Fletcher. The Impact of Multiple Source Feedback on Management Development: Findings from a Longitudinal Study. *Journal of Organizational Behavior*, Vol. 23, 2002, pp. 853–867.

23. Furnham, A., and P. Stringfield. Congruence in Job-Performance Ratings: A Study of 360-Degree Feedback Examining Self, Manager, Peer, and Consultant Ratings. *Human Relations*, Vol. 51, 1998, pp. 517–530; Beehr, T. A., L. Ivanitskaya, C. P. Hansen, D. Erofeev, and D. M. Gudanowski. Explanation of 360 Degree Feedback Ratings: Relationship with Each Other and with Performance and Selection Predictors. *Journal of Organizational Behavior*, Vol. 22, 2001, pp. 775–788.

24. Furnham, A., and P. Stringfield. Congruence in Job-Performance Ratings: A Study of 360-Degree Feedback Examining Self, Manager, Peer, and Consultant Ratings. *Human Relations*, Vol. 51, 1998, pp. 517–530.

25. Brett, J. F., and L. E. Atwater. 360 Degree Feedback: Accuracy, Reactions, and Perceptions of Usefulness. *Journal of Applied Psychology*, Vol. 86, 2001, pp. 930–942.

26. Greller, M. M. Participation in the Performance Appraisal Review: Inflexible Manager Behavior and Variable Worker Needs. *Human Relations*, Vol. 51, 1998, pp. 1061–1083.

27. Robbins, S. P. Training in Interpersonal Skills: *TIPS for Managing People at Work*. Englewood Cliffs, NJ: Prentice-Hall, 1989.

28. Mento, A. J., R. P. Steel, and R. J. Kasser. A Meta-Analytic Study of the Effects of Goal Setting on Task Performance: 1966-1984. *Organizational Behavior and Human Decision Processes*, Vol. 39, 1987, pp. 52–83; Locke, E. A., and G. P. Latham. A Theory of Goal Setting and Task Performance. Englewood Cliffs, NJ: Prentice-Hall, 1990; Klein, H. J., and P. W. Mulvey. Two Investigations of the Relationships Among Group Goals, Goal Commitment, Cohesion, and Performance. *Organizational Behavior and Human Decision Processes*, Vol. 61, 1995, pp. 44–53.

29. Locke, E. A., E. Frederick, E. Buckner, and P. Bobko. Effect of Previously Assigned Goals on Self-Set Goals and Performance. *Journal of Applied Psychology*, Vol. 69, 1984, pp. 694–699.

30. O'Leary-Kelly, A. M., J. J. Martocchio, and D. D. Frink. A Review of the Influence of Group Goals on Group Performance. *Academy of Management Journal*, Vol. 37, 1994, pp. 1285–1301.

31. Locke, E. A., and G. P. Latham. *A Theory of Goal Setting and Task Performance*. Englewood Cliffs, NJ: Prentice-Hall, 1990.

32. Locke, E. A., and G. P. Latham. *A Theory of Goal Setting and Task Performance*. Englewood Cliffs, NJ: Prentice-Hall, 1990.

33. Latham, G. P., and E. A. Locke. Goal Setting: A Motivational Technique That Works. *Organizational Dynamics*, Vol. 8, 1979, pp. 68–80.

34. Robbins, S. P. *Training in Interpersonal Skills: TIPS for Managing People at Work*. Englewood Cliffs, NJ: Prentice-Hall, 1989.

35. Wagner, J. A., and R. Z. Gooding. Shared Influence and Organizational Behavior: A Meta-Analysis of Situational Variables Expected to Moderate Participation-Outcome Relationships. *Academy of Management Journal*, Vol. 30, 1987, pp. 524–541; Locke, E. A., and G. P. Latham. *A Theory of Goal Setting and Task Performance*. Englewood Cliffs, NJ: Prentice-Hall, 1990.

36. O'Leary-Kelly, A. M., J. J. Martocchio, and D. D. Frink. A Review of the Influence of Group Goals on Group Performance. *Academy of Management Journal*, Vol. 37, 1994, pp. 1285–1301.

37. O'Leary-Kelly, A. M., J. J. Martocchio, and D. D. Frink. A Review of the Influence of Group Goals on Group Performance. *Academy of Management Journal*, Vol. 37, 1994, pp. 1285–1301.

38. Latham, G. P., D. C. Winters, and E. A. Locke. Cognitive and Motivational Effects of Participation: A Mediator Study. *Journal of Organizational Behavior*, Vol. 15, 1994, pp. 49–63.

39. Robbins, S. P. *Training in Interpersonal Skills: TIPS for Managing People at Work*. Englewood Cliffs, NJ: Prentice-Hall, 1989.

40. Mill, C. R. Feedback: The Art of Giving and Receiving Help. In L. Porter and C. R. Mill (eds.), *The Reading Book for Human Relations Training*. Bethel, ME: NTL Institute for Applied Behavioral Science, 1976, pp. 18–19; Baron, R. A. Countering the Effects of Destructive Criticism: The Relative Efficacy of Four Potential Interventions. *Journal of Applied Psychology*, Vol. 75, 1990, pp. 235–245.

41. DeNisi, A. S., and A. N. Kluger. Feedback Effectiveness: Can 360-Degree Appraisals Be Improved? *Academy of Management Executive*, Vol. 14, 2000, pp. 129–139.

42. Mill, C. R. Feedback: The Art of Giving and Receiving Help. In L. Porter and C. R. Mill (eds.), *The Reading Book for Human Relations Training*. Bethel, ME: NTL Institute for Applied Behavioral Science, 1976, pp. 18–19; Robbins, S. P. *Training in Interpersonal Skills: TIPS for Managing People at Work*. Englewood Cliffs, NJ: Prentice-Hall, 1989; Baron, R. A. Countering the Effects of Destructive Criticism: The Relative Efficacy of Four Potential Interventions. *Journal of Applied Psychology*, Vol. 75, 1990, pp. 235–245; DeNisi, A. S., and A. N. Kluger. Feedback Effectiveness: Can 360-Degree Appraisals Be Improved? *Academy of Management Executive*, Vol. 14, 2000, pp. 129–139.

43. Ilgen, D. R., C. D. Fisher, and M. S. Taylor. Consequences of Individual Feedback on Behavior in Organizations. *Journal of Applied Psychology*, Vol. 64, 1979, pp. 349–371.

44. Burke, R. J., W. Weitzel, and T. Weir. Characteristics of Effective Employment Performance Review and Development Interviews: Replication and Extension. *Personnel Psychology*, Vol. 31, 1978, pp. 903–919.

45. Burke, R. J., W. Weitzel, and T. Weir. Characteristics of Effective Employment Performance Review and Development Interviews: Replication and Extension. *Personnel Psychology*, Vol. 31, 1978, pp. 903–919.

46. Mill, C. R. Feedback: The Art of Giving and Receiving Help. In L. Porter and C. R. Mill (eds.), *The Reading Book for Human Relations Training*. Bethel, ME: NTL Institute for Applied Behavioral Science, 1976, pp. 18–19.

47. Robbins, S. P. *Training in Interpersonal Skills: TIPS for Managing People at Work*. Englewood Cliffs, NJ: Prentice-Hall, 1989.

48. DeNisi, A. S., and A. N. Kluger. Feedback Effectiveness: Can 360-Degree Appraisals Be Improved? *Academy of Management Executive*, Vol. 14, 2000, pp. 129–139.

49. DeNisi, A. S., and A. N. Kluger. Feedback Effectiveness: Can 360-Degree Appraisals Be Improved? *Academy of Management Executive*, Vol. 14, 2000, pp. 129–139.

50. Baron, R. A. Countering the Effects of Destructive Criticism: The Relative Efficacy of Four Potential Interventions. *Journal of Applied Psychology*, Vol. 75, 1990, pp. 235–245.

51. Mill, C. R. Feedback: The Art of Giving and Receiving Help. In L. Porter and C. R. Mill (eds.), *The Reading Book for Human Relations Training*. Bethel, ME: NTL Institute for Applied Behavioral Science, 1976, pp. 18–19.

52. Burke, R. J., W. Weitzel, and T. Weir. Characteristics of Effective Employment Performance Review and Development Interviews: Replication and Extension. *Personnel Psychology*, Vol. 31, 1978, pp. 903–919.

PART IV
The Organizational Level

Chapter List

CHAPTER 10
Organizational Change and Culture

Organizations today face a variety of opportunities and threats in their external environments. A look at the newspapers finds many companies struggling to redefine themselves in the midst of great change and business pressures. For example, in recent years, Motorola has been attempting to re-establish itself as the number one wireless phone manufacturer after losing this position to the Finnish phone company Nokia in the 1990s. Now it must also compete against strong new competitors such as Samsung and Sony Ericsson, which are gaining global market share in the cellular phone marketplace. Similarly, General Motors is attempting to transform itself into the number one auto-maker in the world based on quality and design leadership. Although the company has achieved some remarkable gains in terms of product quality and design, it must overcome strong challenges from a host of foreign auto-makers, including Toyota, Honda, BMW, Volkswagen, Kia, and Hyundai. Other companies facing significant pressures to change include Eastman Kodak, Kmart, Ford, McDonalds, and United Airlines. These are just a few examples of organizations attempting to implement significant changes to survive in today's tough external environment.

What is the "external environment" exactly? The external environment is composed of a number of forces (discussed below) that affect the organization's management and that organizational leaders need to understand in order to plan and implement appropriate changes. The challenge for any organization is to determine which forces in its external environment are most significant and to implement appropriate strategies to enable it to respond appropriately to these challenges. Ultimately, the objective of managing organizational change is to enable the organization to establish a good fit or alignment with its external environment in terms of the elements of the organization's system (i.e., its strategy, structure, systems, and so on).

Specifically, the external environment is composed of the following factors:

- **Customers.** Customers are an important part of an organization's external environment since the focus of many organizations is to understand customers and to find ways to satisfy (or exceed) their needs with products and services. For example, companies such as Dell Computer, Southwest Airlines, and the Target Corporation have all done well in their respective industries because of their ability to satisfy customers' needs for value.

- **Competition.** Competition refers to other organizations that provide the same products and services to customers in a given industry. In many industries today, competition has become intense as new competitors emerge both domestically and globally. For example, in the personal digital assistant (PDA) market, PalmOne once owned over 80 percent of the market. However, as a slew of competitors has flocked to this market (such as Compaq, Sony, Dell, and Toshiba), Palm's market share has declined to less than 40 percent.

- **Technological factors.** Technological factors include methods and systems to automate production and to better manage information. For example, Amazon.com, the online book retailer, established itself as one of the first successful Internet companies through the use of highly efficient and cost-effective ordering and customer service systems. Likewise, airlines such as United Airlines have taken advantage of technology so that customers can check in and obtain their boarding passes without needing to see a ticket agent.

- **Laws and regulations.** Laws and regulations encompass a wide variety of issues, including trade, employment, finance, and consumer rights. For example, many employers need to plan carefully when they are contemplating the implementation of an employee layoff to take into consideration the Worker Adjustment and Retaining Notification Act that requires employers to give employees 60 days notification of a mass layoff under certain conditions.

- **Society.** Society can include a wide range of factors, including the demographics of the population and workforce (such as age, gender, education, and race/ethnicity) and the collective norms and values of the population as whole. Some significant societal factors facing organizations today include the "graying" of the workforce (i.e., the workforce is getting older) and greater diversity in terms of race and ethnicity in the general population. This diversity presents challenges for organizations in terms of tailoring their products and services to meet the needs of these customers.

- **Economic factors.** Economic factors refer to the state of the domestic and global economies in terms of whether they are contracting, becoming stagnant, or expanding. If the economy in a given country is in recession, it will likely reduce demand for many goods and services. Consumers will spend less on leisure (such as eating out and vacations) and focus more on essential items (such as paying bills, reducing debt, and saving). Conversely, if an economy is growing, consumers will be more likely to purchase "big ticket" items such as new cars and homes.

These factors shape the nature of the external environment that management must understand and adapt to if an organization is to survive in the long term.

Assessing Forces to Change for a Real-World Organization

Use a standard Internet browser (such as Internet Explorer or Netscape) to research business-oriented web sites (such as http://www.fortune.com and http://www.businessweek.com) in order to identify a real-world organization that is experiencing pressure (from internal or external factors) to change in some way. What are these factors and in what ways are they exerting pressure on the organization to change?

AN INTEGRATED FRAMEWORK FOR ORGANIZATIONAL CHANGE: DUNHAM'S SYSTEMATIC CHANGE PROCESS MODEL

Randy Dunham, an academic expert on organizational change, has developed a comprehensive process model for managing organizational change that describes the overall process for planning, implementing, and evaluating organizational change. This model, called the **Systematic Change Process Model**, is based on a model originally developed by Kotter and Schlesinger[1] and is shown in Figure 10-1. As you can see, the model involves four stages, each of which will be discussed in turn.

STAGE 1: IDENTIFY THE NEED FOR CHANGE AND THE NATURE OF THE CHANGE

Stage 1 of Dunham's Systematic Change Process Model is actually composed of two steps: (1) **Recognizing the Need for Change** and (2) **Identifying the Nature of the Change**. The objective of this stage is for management to determine that an organization needs to alter some aspect of its functioning. On the surface, it may seem like it would be easy for organizations to know when they need to change, but in the real world, this is not the case. In many organizations, emphasis tends to be placed on the positive, on what is going well. Because of this, problems and weaknesses in the performance of an individual, work unit, or organization are sometimes downplayed, denied, or overlooked. The result of this is that management may dismiss bad news about the performance of their organization and claim that there is no need for change.

The second step in this stage of change identification is to pinpoint the nature of the change that is needed. This requires management to develop a better understanding of *exactly* what type of change is needed in a given situation. This may be a strategy, process, policy, or system. It could also be a "people" issue such as the wrong person being in a certain job or an organizational culture that does not support the objectives of the organization as a whole. The identification of the specific nature of the change may be based on quarterly financial reports, an employee attitude survey, or a discussion at a business meeting.

Figure 10-1   Dunham's Systematic Change Management Model[2]

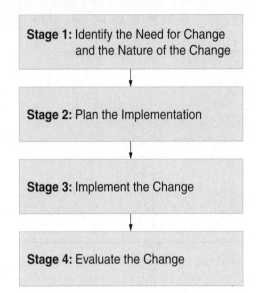
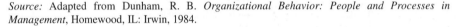

Source: Adapted from Dunham, R. B. *Organizational Behavior: People and Processes in Management*, Homewood, IL: Irwin, 1984.

It is important to note that the nature of the problem and the change that is needed may not be evident on first glance. Management needs to conduct an investigation of the problem and what type of changes might be most appropriate to address the situation. The key objective in identifying the nature of the change is to identify what type of change will be needed. That is, will the change involve a shift in people, specific processes or systems, the strategy of the organization, the introduction of a new technology, or a combination of all of the above?

STAGE 2: PLAN THE IMPLEMENTATION

Once the need for change has been addressed, the next stage in Dunham's Systematic Change Management Model involves the development of an overall **Plan for Implementing the Change**. This stage includes three basic steps: (1) *conducting a situational diagnosis,* (2) *selecting the general strategy,* and (3) *selecting support techniques.*

In the situational diagnosis step, management assesses the organizational and external environments in order to develop a solid understanding of how individuals who will be affected by the change are expected to react to the change. Will they be active supporters, neutral, or active resisters of the change? Based on the answers to this question, management formulates an overall plan for what actions they will take to implement the change and how these actions will be executed. Finally, when support techniques are selected, management develops another set of strategies to overcome resistance to change and to ensure that individuals who are affected by the change are given the resources they need to implement that change successfully. This support may come in the form of a budget, support staff, training, incentives to motivate people to embrace the change, and so on.

STAGE 3: IMPLEMENT THE CHANGE

The third stage in Dunham's Systematic Change Management Model involves the actual process associated with the execution of the plan designed in Stage 2. While the development of a good plan is obviously important, it is in this stage that the ultimate success of the change is largely determined. This stage integrates three stages from Lewin's force field analysis model: (1) *unfreezing,* (2) *changing,* and (3) *refreezing.*[3]

In the unfreezing phase, management takes action to foster a feeling among all members of the organization that there is a need for change. This can be a challenging task as some people in the organization may feel that there is nothing wrong with the status quo or that any problems that are the basis for justifying the change are exaggerated.

In the changing phase, management implements the change and provides the support that is required to enable it to be successful. This may involve the use of a variety of strategies. Table 10-1 displays some of the most commonly used strategies for overcoming resistance to change and for supporting the implementation of change.

Education and Communication—This strategy involves explaining what a given change involves, why the change is being made, and how it will affect the people who will be responsible for implementing the change. This is arguably the most important and effective strategy for overcoming resistance to change. Unfortunately, in the real

Table 10-1   Strategies for Overcoming Resistance to Change[4]

Strategy	Appropriate Situations	Advantages	Disadvantages
Education and Communication	When information is inaccurate or incomplete	Once persuaded, people will often help with implementation	Can be very time-consuming
Participation and Involvement	When initiators do not have all the information they need and others have considerable power to resist	People who participate will be committed, and information they have will be integrated into the change plan	Can be very time-consuming if participators design an inappropriate change
Support	When people are resisting because of adjustment problems	No other approach works as well with adjustment problems	Can be time-consuming, expensive, and still fail
Incentives	When someone will lose out in a change, and that group has considerable power	Sometimes it is a relatively easy way to avoid major resistance	Can be too expensive if it alerts others to negotiate for compliance
Manipulation and Co-optation	When other tactics will not work or are too expensive	Can be relatively quick and inexpensive	Can lead to future problems if people feel manipulated
Coercion	When speed is essential and the initiators possess considerable power	Speedy, and can overcome any kind of resistance	Can be risky if it leaves people mad at the initiators

Source: Adapted from Kotter, J. P., and L. A. Schlesinger. Choosing Strategies for Change, *Harvard Business Review,* Vol. 57, 1979, p. 106.

world, many managers make the mistake of simply announcing a change to employees without explaining the change to them. The result of this is employee confusion, frustration, and reduced effectiveness in implementing the change.

Participation and Involvement—Workers tend to be more supportive of a change in which they were involved. The means that managers need to seek the input of their employees and consider incorporating their ideas about what a change should involve and how it should be implemented into the design of the change.

Support—Managers need to take actions to make it possible for their employees to be successful in implementing a change. Support may take the form of providing direction regarding what employees need to do to adopt a change, training, emotional support (e.g., encouragement), financial resources, or support staff.

Incentives—In some cases, the use of rewards can motivate workers to accept a change. The key here is that the rewards (e.g., monetary bonuses, time off) must be positively valued by workers and the rewards must be linked to the effective implementation of a change.

Manipulation and Co-optation—This is not a recommended strategy in most cases. It may involve the use of deception of employees or giving them a role in designing a change that is purely symbolic. That is, there is no intention of actually using any of the employees' ideas. The involvement of employees is simply to obtain their support for the change.

Coercion—In some cases, coercion is an appropriate strategy for overcoming resistance to change. To apply this strategy, a manager needs to simply inform employees that they do not have a choice in the matter and that they must accept the change.

A key point here is that the management of organizational change should be viewed from a contingency perspective. That is, the most effective strategy for overcoming resistance to change depends on the nature of the situation. Again, the ultimate objective of the changing phase is for management to take actions that will make it possible for others in the organization to implement a change successfully.

The last stage, refreezing, involves management taking actions to ensure that the implemented change is reinforced so that it becomes an ongoing part of how things are done in the future. This is important because there is a tendency for people in organizations to regress to their default behavior (i.e., to go back to their old way of doing things) unless there are adequate forces and incentives to maintain the new behaviors associated with the change that has been implemented. For example, many U.S. companies fail to reap the long-term benefits of management approaches such as total quality management (TQM) because they do not take appropriate actions to sustain the implementation of TQM practices. How does this happen? The problem in these organizations is that TQM is viewed as a short-term "add on" or special program that is implemented and then largely ignored. The implicit assumption of management is that the program is complete after the initial implementation of change is rolled out. The result of this is often that these organizations initially experience some positive outcomes based on a TQM program (e.g., lower costs, better customer service), but these results deteriorate over time as management focuses on the next new business idea that will dramatically improve the performance of the organization, and employees do not have any incentives to continue to behave in ways that support TQM.

In order to support the refreezing stage, management must find ways to "institutionalize" the change (i.e., make it part of the system). Management can do this by integrating the change into the formal structure, processes, systems, and jobs in an organization. For example, if an organization is implementing a change to a new team-based approach to work, management would want to ensure that formal job descriptions explicitly state that many of the responsibilities of the job involve working in teams. Furthermore, the organization's performance appraisal and reward systems would also need to be redesigned so that at least part of the evaluation of an individual's performance is based on team results and that rewards such as recognition and merit pay increases are linked to team-level performance.

STAGE 4: EVALUATE THE CHANGE

The final stage of Dunham's Systematic Change Management Model is to **Evaluate the Change** in terms of the results achieved relative to the original objective(s) of the change that were specified earlier in the process. This stage involves three basic steps: (1) *collecting data,* (2) *evaluating data,* and (3) *using feedback.*

The first step, collecting data, refers to the process of systematically collecting empirical data that reflects key process and outcome measures of success related to the change. Depending on the change, this data may focus on costs, product and service quality, productivity, customer satisfaction, product development time, and so on.

The second step, evaluating data, involves analyzing the data to determine the degree to which the change has been successful in achieving its objective(s). Finally, the results of the evaluation of the change are used as feedback for the change identification stage at the beginning of the model.

APPLICATION & EVALUATION

Using the Systematic Change Management Model

Imagine that you work as an executive for a major department store that has been in decline over the past five years due to problems with high costs, boring merchandise, and a reputation for rotten customer service. Meanwhile, new competitors have emerged in the industry that are luring large numbers of customers from your stores. It is your task to devise a turnaround plan for your organization. The objective of this plan is to make your organization the number one department store in 10 years in terms of sales volume and customer satisfaction.

Based on this situation, *apply* Dunham's Systematic Change Management Model presented in Figure 10-1 to develop a comprehensive strategy to plan, implement, and *evaluate* appropriate changes in the organization. Be very specific and be sure to discuss how you would address each stage in the model.

**Using the Systematic Change Process
Model in a Real-World Organization**

Use a standard Internet browser (such as Internet Explorer and Netscape) to research business-oriented web sites (such as http://www.fortune.com or http://www.businessweek.com) to identify an article about a change in an organization. Use the Systematic Change Management Model to assess the effectiveness of the organization in planning, implementing, and evaluating the change.

**Linking the Systematic Change Process
Model with the Path-Goal
Theory of Leadership**

Organizational change and leadership are closely related topics since the actions of leaders play a critical role in designing and implementing change. The close relationship between these two topics offers a significant opportunity to link the major theoretical frameworks from these respective areas into a more comprehensive and powerful model. Given this, how can the Systematic Change Management Model discussed in this chapter be *synthesized* with the Path-Goal Theory of leadership discussed in Chapter 8. Now *evaluate* the new model you have created. What types of guidelines does your model offer that can help practitioners to be more effective as leaders and managers of change? Try to be as specific as possible.

PRACTICAL GUIDELINES

The following practical guidelines are offered to enhance the effectiveness of organizational change management in real-world organizations:

- Collect and analyze data in order to understand short- and long-term trends and environmental forces that may require some type of change.

- Foster an attitude in the organization that change is inevitable and that an organization must "change or die" in order to remain successful in the long term.

- Anticipate that at least some members of the organization will resist a given change and develop an action plan that will need to be implemented for responding to this resistance early in the change management process.

- Recognize that data will need to be presented clearly to leaders in the organization to show why a specific change will enhance the success of an organization and why change is needed in many situations.

- Be sure to provide the support for the implementation of a change so that organizational members have the tools and resources they need to make the change work successfully.

- Reinforce the change after it has been implemented so that organizational members will have the structure and incentives needed to motivate them to continue to engage in behavior that supports the change.

- Remember that the effective implementation of change requires a systems approach that recognizes that an organization is composed of inter-related parts (people, structures, systems, culture, and so on) that must all be managed so that they are consistent with or aligned with each other.

ORGANIZATIONAL CULTURE

Organizational culture can be defined as the shared values, beliefs, norms, rituals, symbols, and stories that shape the identity of an organization, its goals, and how it goes about achieving them. In a sense, the culture of an organization is its "collective personality" or its "way of doing things." When people refer to the "Disney Way" or the "Dell Way," they are talking about the culture of these organizations. Table 10-2 presents a summary of the elements of organizational culture.

It is important to note that every organization has some type of culture, although some organizations have stronger cultures than others. The strength of a culture can be seen in how much emphasis is placed on thinking and doing things in a certain way in the day-to-day operations of the organization. For example, in some organizations, there are executive parking spots and executive dining rooms. These things would suggest a stronger emphasis on valuing authority and status in the organization. Another organization may offer significant rewards to employees who engage in community service activities. This would indicate strong value placed on social responsibility in the organization.

Some skeptics might ask the question, "Why should we care about organizational culture?" The answer is that organizational culture can provide a mechanism to support the overall mission and strategic objectives of a company. For example, if an organization is seeking to become more customer service oriented, then having a culture that values, rewards, and reinforces positive attitudes toward customer service will be extremely valuable to the organization. Let's take another example. Say that an organization needs to enhance its ability to be flexible and responsive to changes in its external environment. However, the value system and set ways of doing things in the organization emphasize predictability and stability. This would be a situation in which the culture of the organization may inhibit the overall effectiveness of the company. In both examples, culture can be an important determinant of organizational performance.

Table 10-2   **Elements of Organizational Culture: A List of Definitions of Frequently Studied Cultural Forms**

Rite	A relatively elaborate, dramatic, planned set of activities that combines various forms of cultural expressions and that often has both practical and expressive consequences.
Ritual	A standardized, detailed set of techniques and behaviors that manages anxieties but seldom produces intended, practical consequences of any importance.
Myth	A dramatic narrative of imagined events, usually used to explain origins or transformations of something. Also, an unquestioned belief about the practical benefits of certain techniques and behaviors that is not supported by demonstrated facts.
Saga	An historical narrative describing (usually in heroic terms) the unique accomplishments of a group and its leaders.
Legend	A handed-down narrative of some wonderful event that has a historical basis but has been embellished with fictional details.
Story	A narrative based on true events—often a combination of truth and fiction.
Folktale	A completely fictional narrative.
Symbol	Any object, act, event, quality, or relation that serves as a vehicle for conveying meaning, usually by representing another thing.
Language	A particular manner in which members of a group use vocal sounds and written signs to convey meanings to each other.
Gesture	Movements of parts of the body used to express meanings.
Physical Setting	Those things that physically surround people and provide them with immediate sensory stimuli as they carry out culturally expressive activities.
Artifact	Material objects manufactured by people to facilitate culturally expressive activities.

Source: Adapted from Janice M. Beyer and Harrison M. Trice, "Studying Organizational Cultures Through Rites and Ceremonials" (*Academy of Management Review*, October 1984).

ANALYSIS & APPLICATION

Assessing the Culture of a Real-World Organization

Use a standard Internet browser (such as Internet Explorer or Netscape) to research the web sites of three companies in which you have an interest. Your task is to assess the culture of each organization, including its values, beliefs, rituals, norms, stories, and so on. Write a summary of each of the organization's cultures and compare them. How are they similar? How are they different? How is each culture unique?

APPLICATION & EVALUATION

Evaluating the Culture of *Fortune* Magazine's Best Companies to Work For

Visit *Fortune* magazine's listing of the Best Companies to Work For at its web site (http://www.fortune.com). Your task is to assess the cultures of the five best companies to work for as ranked on this web site. Write a summary of each of the cultures and compare them. How does the culture of each of these companies help to make it one of the best companies to work for?

SYNTHESIS & EVALUATION

Organizational Change and Culture

Discuss the relationship between organizational culture and the management of organizational change. Specifically, identify and describe where organizational culture would be an important factor in Dunham's Systematic Change Process Model discussed earlier in this chapter.

The next section will present various practical strategies for creating, maintaining, and changing organizational cultures based on the research of Trice and Beyer, two leading experts in this area.

TRICE AND BEYER: STRATEGIES FOR CREATING ORGANIZATIONAL CULTURES

Table 10-3 presents a summary of practical strategies for creating effective organizational cultures. These strategies help managers determine the culture of an organization and how to establish it effectively. Let's look at each of these strategies briefly.

Table 10-3   Practical Guidelines for Creating Organizational Cultures[5]

Discover and articulate distinctive ideologies.	Recruit like-minded people.
Devise and use distinctive cultural forms.	Socialize to instill and sustain ideologies.
Structure to influence subcultural formation.	Support innovative leadership.
Remain flexible enough to adapt.	Let go gracefully.

The first strategy is to *discover and articulate distinctive ideologies*. This involves managers creating a compelling and unique vision for the organization that is appealing and motivating to employees and then communicating this vision to employees.

The second strategy is to *recruit like-minded people*. This entails managers attempting to hire people whose personal ideologies are congruent with that of the organization.

The third strategy is to *devise and use distinctive cultural forms*. Managers need to creatively identify specific types of cultural elements such as symbols, stories, and rituals that communicate and reinforce the culture of a company in a compelling manner.

Fourth, an organization needs to *socialize to instill and sustain ideologies*. The objective of this strategy is to implement processes and practices that enable organizational members to learn, understand, and embrace the value and belief system of an organization. This can be accomplished formally through the use of systematic training (e.g., performance improvement plans, challenging assignments) and ongoing interaction and communication with more experienced members of the organization.

The fifth strategy is to *structure to influence subcultural formation*. The objective here is to decrease the emergence and influence of subcultures in the organization as they may weaken the culture of the overall organization. A subculture is an ideology that exists in one part of an organization that is somewhat different from the culture of the organization. For example, a marketing division in a company might have a culture that is very collaborative, quality-conscious, entrepreneurial and likes to take risks. However, the overall culture of the organization, while also collaborative and quality conscious, is more conservative and more averse to risk. The marketing division's culture is a subculture within the culture of the overall organization.

One strategy for discouraging an undesirable level of subculture formation is to cross-train members so that everyone can perform a wide range of jobs across different functional units. Another strategy is to emphasize to managers of specific units to make sure that their goals, strategies, and cultures are consistent or in alignment with those of the overall organization.

Sixth, organizations need to *remain flexible enough to adapt*. The concern here is that organizational members may embrace the current culture so much that they will have difficulty accepting a new ideology in the future. Organizations can build flexibility into their system by using decentralized structures and loose coupling that does not tie a given unit tightly with other units.

The seventh strategy is to *support innovative leadership*. This means that managers must be empowered to go out and recruit, hire, and develop other people who will buy-in to the culture and act to support it.

Finally, organizations should *let go gracefully*. The founders or the current top leadership in an organization are the keepers of the culture. It is their job to ensure that the culture lives on after they are no longer in their current positions. One way to do this is to engage in succession planning in order to have the time needed to identify and groom a replacement who will support the culture in the future.

ANALYSIS & APPLICATION

Creating an Effective Organizational Culture

Identify a new student organization that you would like to start at your college or university. Write down its basic mission, goals, and the type of students who would be interested in joining this organization. Now, using the strategies for creating an effective culture discussed above, develop an action plan that specifies what you would do to create an appropriate culture in your organization. Be very specific in formulating your action steps.

EVALUATION

Strategies for Creating Organizational Culture

Evaluate each of the strategies for creating an organizational culture discussed in this chapter. Which ones do you feel are most valuable? Do you disagree with any of them? If so, why? What are the most significant challenges associated with implementing these strategies? What could you do to overcome these barriers?

TRICE AND BEYER: STRATEGIES FOR MAINTAINING ORGANIZATIONAL CULTURES

Table 10-4 presents a summary of practical strategies for *maintaining* effective organizational cultures. Once an effective organizational culture has been established, managers must concern themselves with how to reinforce, reward, and sustain this culture on an ongoing basis. Let's look at each of these strategies for maintaining organizational cultures briefly.

The first strategy for maintaining organizational cultures is *don't assume continuity—work for it.* Managers need to recognize that they must focus on reinforcing the

Table 10-4   Practical Guidelines for Maintaining Organizational Cultures[6]

Don't assume continuity—work for it.	Respect the past, but adapt to the present.
Adapt existing ideologies to current challenges and crises.	Locate and reduce cultural disparities.
Manage the politics of subcultural relations.	Encourage the use of cultural forms.
Emphasize continuity in socialization.	Encourage and develop maintenance leadership.

desired culture and on driving it deeper into their work units. This can be done through ongoing communication and education, reward systems, formal statements of operating values for the company, and so on.

Second, managers need to *respect the past, but adapt to the present.* This can be tricky in some instances where the past culture of the company has become so sacred that it is extremely difficult to change it. Managers must work proactively to maintain the parts of the past that are still important and relevant to an organization today, but also to ensure that new elements can be integrated in the culture as the vision or external environment of the company changes.

Third, managers need to *adapt existing ideologies to current challenges and crises.* The key here is for managers to keep the ideological component of the organization's culture focused on its core elements, which should not change over time. This might be customer service, attention to detail, or quality, depending on the organization. So, while some elements of a culture can be allowed to change over time as the situation or business strategies of a company shift, the core elements must be protected by organizational leaders.

The fourth strategy is to *locate and reduce cultural disparities.* Managers should address this issue by conducting a "culture audit" of their organization. This is a systematic and formal process in which the elements of an organization's culture are assessed through surveys and interviews with managers and individual contributors in the company. This process helps management identify potential inconsistencies in its culture that need to be addressed. For example, one core value of an organization may emphasize teamwork and collaboration. However, the compensation system and the design of jobs may indicate an emphasis on individual contributions and performance.

Fifth, managers must *manage the politics of subcultural relations.* When an organization possesses one or more subcultures, management must engage in a political process using bargaining and negotiation with key players in the subculture units to ensure that acceptable arrangements or relationships can be agreed on to support the overall culture in the organization. This process requires ongoing communication and dialogue between all parties involved. The goal of this strategy is to integrate the interests of diverse subculture units with those of the overall culture.

Sixth, managers need to *encourage the use of cultural forms.* This strategy involves identifying specific things to do to communicate and reinforce a culture. Table 10-5 presents some examples of strategies for using rites to communicate the culture of an organization.

The seventh strategy for maintaining organizational cultures is to *emphasize continuity in socialization.* Integrating various rites (see Table 10-6) into organizational policies and practices is an effective strategy for socializing new organizational members into the overall culture of a company. These rites communicate and reinforce the culture of an organization to others in a way that is symbolic, powerful, and meaningful.

Finally, organizations must *encourage and develop maintenance leadership.* Maintenance leaders must serve as the "keepers and guardians" of an organization's culture. They must model appropriate behaviors that support the culture and take action to ensure that the core elements of the culture continue to provide a foundation for the organization. This is done through ongoing communication (e.g., newsletters, speeches, memos, annual reports, and so on) with members of the organization.

Table 10-5   **Trice and Beyer's Summary of Rites for Communicating Organizational Culture**[7]

Types of Rites	Example	Evident Expressive Consequences	Examples of Possible Hidden Expressive Consequences
Rites of passage	Induction and basic training, U.S. Army	Facilitate transition of persons into social roles and statuses that are new for them.	Minimize changes in ways people carry out social roles. Reestablish equilibrium in ongoing social relations.
Rites of degradation	Firing and replacing top executive	Dissolve social identities and their power.	Publicly acknowledge that problems exist and discuss their details. Defend group boundaries by redefining who belongs and who doesn't. Reaffirm social importance and value of role involved.
Rites of enhancement	Mary Kay seminars	Enhance social identities and their power.	Spread good news about the organization. Provide public recognition of individuals for their accomplishments; motivate others to similar efforts. Enable organizations to take some credit for individual accomplishments. Emphasize social value of performance of social roles.
Rites of renewal	Organizational development activities	Refurbish social structures and improve their functioning.	Reassure members that something is being done about problems. Distinguish nature of problems. Defer acknowledgment of problems. Focus attention toward some problems and away from others. Legitimize and reinforce existing systems of power and authority.
Rites of conflict reduction	Collective bargaining	Reduce conflict and aggression.	Deflect attention away from solving problems. Compartmentalize conflict and its disruptive effects. Reestablish equilibrium in disturbed social relations.
Rites of integration	Office Christmas party	Encourage and revive common feelings that bind members together and commit them to a social system.	Permit venting of emotion and temporary loosening of various norms. Reassert and Reaffirm, by contrast, moral rightness of usual norms.

Source: Adapted from Beyer, J. M., and H. M. Trice. Studying Organizational Cultures Through Rites and Ceremonials, *Academy of Management Review,* 1984.

ANALYSIS & APPLICATION   **Developing Strategies for Maintaining the Culture of a Real-World Organization**

Use a standard Internet browser (such as Internet Explorer or Netscape) to research the web site of one company in which you have an interest. Your task is to assess the culture of this organization in terms of its basic culture, including its values, beliefs, rituals, norms, stories, and so on. Write a summary of this organization's culture. Using material from this chapter, develop an action plan for maintaining this culture. Be specific and action-oriented.

EVALUATION   **Strategies for Maintaining Organizational Culture**

Evaluate each of the strategies for maintaining organizational culture discussed in this chapter. Which ones do you feel are most valuable? Do you disagree with any of them? If so, why? What are the most significant challenges associated with implementing these strategies? What could you do to overcome these barriers?

TRICE AND BEYER: STRATEGIES FOR CHANGING ORGANIZATIONAL CULTURES

Table 10-6 presents a summary of practical strategies for *changing* effective organizational cultures. These strategies are useful to real-world managers who are seeking to modify a culture that is not considered to be appropriate or in alignment with the current strategic focus of the organization or opportunities (i.e., something that an organization can take advantage of such as an unmet customer need or an emerging technology) and threats (i.e., something that can hurt an organization such as competition) that exist in the external environment.

Table 10-6   Practical Guidelines for Changing Organizational Cultures[8]

Capitalize on propitious moments.	Combine caution with optimism.
Understand resistance to cultural change.	Change many elements, but maintain some continuity.
Recognize the importance of implementation.	Select, modify, and create appropriate cultural forms.
Modify socialization tactics.	Find and cultivate innovative leadership.

The first strategy for changing organizational culture is to *capitalize on propitious (favorable or advantageous) moments*. Managers must take advantage of the right time and opportunity to change the culture of an organization. Typically, the best times to change an organizational culture are when there is a crisis, problem, or change in the situation facing a company. For example, when an organization is performing poorly and is seeking to turn itself around, it would be a good opportunity to change the organizational culture.

Second, managers need to *combine caution with optimism*. While it is important for leaders to express confidence to organizational members that a new culture can be created, they must also recognize that change will take time and that some dysfunctional and unintended consequences may occur.

The third strategy is to *understand resistance to cultural change*. Simply put, many people do not like change and they will resist it if at all possible. Some reasons people may resist a change to organizational culture include fear of the unknown, habit, lack of trust, and threats to people's power and influence. Managers need to understand the causes of resistance to a new culture and take action to address them. The discussion of strategies for overcoming resistance to change in this chapter will be helpful in developing appropriate strategies.

Fourth, managers need to *change many elements, but maintain some continuity*. Managers must again remember that in changing the culture of an organization, it is important that while they implement some new cultural elements and forms (e.g., values, beliefs, rites, and symbols), they also maintain a grounding in the core elements of the existing culture.

Fifth, managers must *recognize the importance of implementation*. The bottom line here is that the planning and design of an organizational culture is a complete waste of time, money, and resources if the execution of the strategies to implement the culture is sloppy or not systematic. This is a critical issue that must be treated very seriously.

The sixth strategy is to *select, modify, and create appropriate cultural forms*. Managers must identify new rites, symbols, values, and so on that can support and communicate elements of the new organizational culture. For example, this might involve changing the logo of a company or rewriting its formal statement of operating values.

Seventh, managers need to *modify socialization tactics*. Along with changing elements of the company's culture, management needs to develop and implement new processes to get organizational members to embrace the new culture. This may be done through a redesign of new employee orientation, management training programs, and communication mechanisms such as newsletters, town hall meetings, and so on.

Finally, organizational leaders must *find and cultivate innovative leadership*. Managers need to identify and develop leaders who can support the new culture in terms of vision, values, and leadership styles.

EVALUATION   **Strategies for Changing Organizational Culture**

Evaluate each of the strategies for changing organizational culture discussed in this chapter. Which ones do you feel are most valuable? Do you disagree with any of them? If so, why? What do you think are the most significant challenges associated with implementing these strategies? What could you do to overcome these barriers?

CONCLUSION

Organizations exist in rapidly changing external environments and managers must understand how to formulate and implement strategies to enable their companies to adapt to the opportunities and threats that they face. Dunham's Systematic Change Management Model provides a comprehensive approach to the process of establishing the need for change, overcoming resistance to change, supporting change, and reinforcing change so that it becomes a part of how the organization does things in the future. Organizational culture, or "collective personality," is related to change in that it is an important part of what needs to be modified or realigned in association with an overall change in an organization (e.g., strategy, goals, and business models). This chapter discussed a wide range of Trice and Beyer's practical strategies for creating, maintaining, and changing organizational cultures.

EXERCISES AND OTHER ACTIVITIES
■ *Experiential Exercise: In-Class 10-1*

IMPLEMENTING STRATEGIC CHANGE AT A HEALTH CARE ORGANIZATION[9]

The Organization

The American Developmentally Disabled Center (ADDC), located in Washington, DC, is a residential facility for individuals who have been diagnosed as having severe forms of mental retardation and other developmental disabilities. The center has over 600 individuals living in its complex.

The ADDC currently employs over 1,500 employees who develop and implement a variety of services and programs (e.g., nursing, direct care, and education) at the center. Although the overall ADDC workforce is committed to their work and the organization, there are a number of nursing and direct care jobs that are very routine and physically demanding, and they do not pay well. This has resulted in an annual turnover rate in excess of 100 percent for these jobs. In addition, increased competition from other facilities and increasing costs have exerted pressure on ADDC to find ways to remain competitive.

Figure 10-2   ADDC Strategic Framework

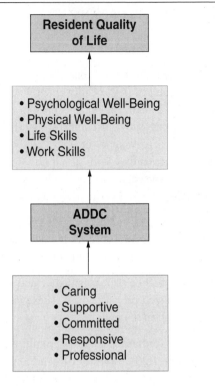

The Change

Recently, top administrators at ADDC held a week-long strategic planning meeting to discuss the future direction of the center. The result of this was the development of a new strategic framework for ADDC, which is shown in Figure 10-2. The model shows that "Resident Quality of Life" is the ultimate objective of the organization. The bullet points under Resident Quality of Life (e.g., psychological well being) show the specific measures that will be used to assess this dimension of the model. The "ADDC System" and the bullet points under it specify the elements of the system that the organization is seeking to support the achievement of Resident Quality of Life.

This framework was designed to focus everything that ADDC does on its customer, the resident.

Although the top administration was thrilled with the new strategic framework they had devised, they recognized that one of the most difficult challenges they would face would be getting the rest of the ADDC workforce (lower-level managers and supervisors and front-line employees) to understand it and to change their behavior to support it in the future.

Using Dunham's Systematic Change Management Model, develop an action plan for planning and implementing an effective change program for the strategic framework at ADDC. Be sure to address all elements of the model and focus on specific actions that the organization can take to implement your plan successfully.

■ *Experiential Exercise: In-Class 10-2*

ASSESSING AND EVALUATING THE ORGANIZATIONAL CULTURE AT GYMBOREE[10]

The Company

The Gymboree Corporation, started in 1976 by Joan Barnes, designs, contract manufactures, and retails a line of unique and high-quality apparel and accessories for children. The company operates more than 580 retail stores in the United States and Canada, the United Kingdom, and Ireland. The company's stores offer upscale, stylish apparel for children ages newborn to 9 years of age. Gymboree's retail stores are known for being "child and parent friendly." Each store possesses features such as full-length mirrors, child-sized chairs, toys, and various children's videos that make it easier for parents to shop. In addition to the Gymboree retail stores, the corporation's brands also include the following:

- **Gymboree Play & Music Programs:** These include parent and child classes that support the development of children from newborn to 5 years of age.

- **Janie and Jack Shops:** These shops offer distinctive and stylish clothing, accessories, and gifts for babies sized preemie to 3T. These items are sold in a boutique setting with great attention to detail.

In terms of recent financial performance, net sales from Gymboree's retail operations for the second fiscal quarter of 2003 were $110.4 million, an increase of 5 percent compared to net sales from the previous year. Comparable store sales for the second fiscal quarter increased 1 percent. Total net sales, including sales from Gymboree Play & Music operations, were $113.1 million, an increase of 5 percent over last year.

The Gymboree Vision Statement

The Gymboree vision statement reads as follows:[11]

> At the Gymboree Corporation, our customers are at the core of our business. We succeed by knowing them and exceeding their expectations for quality and service. We grow by drawing on the creativity, strengths and abilities of every member of the Gymboree Corp. team. We build our brand by constantly innovating to develop and deliver a unique array of products and services.

> We are committed to delivering stakeholder value, and to becoming the most respected specialty retailer in the world by embracing and encouraging innovation in all that we do.

Gymboree's Operating Values[12]

Gymboree's core values as a company include the following:

- **We are passionate about quality.** Gymboree Corp. represents quality. We are obsessed with exceeding our customers' expectations in our products and services. We build and respect our brand by maintaining stringent standards. We require authenticity in what we do. We continuously improve ourselves and look for new businesses to enhance the lives of our customers.

- **We are connected.** We are connected with our customers, employees, stores/shops, business partners, and shareholders. We are unified to achieve common goals and are committed to maximizing our profitability. We grow our business by removing roadblocks and respecting each other, while always remaining genuine to ourselves.

- **We are creative.** We create something from nothing. We harness the imagination, talent, and creative expression of our teams to bring the best products and experiences to our customers. We challenge our teams to search for unique solutions, we learn by doing, and we recognize success with creative rewards.

- **We are unique.** The Gymboree Corporation is unique. Simply stated, our customers deserve for us to give them the best possible products and services. We do this by providing the best environment for our employees so they can deliver the most innovative products and best service to our customers. We contribute to our Company by freely expressing our opinions and trusting each other.

- **We are playful.** We play with a purpose. As an organization, we are flexible and enjoy the challenge of change. We strive to enrich the lives of our customers and our employees by infusing the curiosity, laughter, and joy of being a child into all that we do.

Employee Benefits

The Gymboree Corporation seeks to hire and develop a diverse workforce. Employee benefits include the following:[13]

- Medical, dental, vision, life insurance and disability coverage

- Paid Flex-time off, holidays and parental

- 401(k) Savings Plan

- Funding of approved educational courses

- Employee Assistance Program

- Adoption Assistance

- Pager program for expectant parents

- Stock Purchase Plan

- Bonus Plan

- Direct Payroll Deposit

- Snack Time

- Sabbatical Program

- Employee Discounts

- Flexible Spending Account

The Challenge

One of the corporate values that has been central to the "Gymboree Way" is the "celebration of childhood." Given that the company is in the business of creating innovative and high-quality children's apparel, this is quite appropriate. In a nutshell, Gymboree Corp. management wanted to create a work environment that supported "playfulness," "creativity," and "spontaneity." The challenge was how to do it. What kinds of specific company policies, practices, procedures, and so on, would motivate employees to fulfill Gymboree's vision?

Management Strategies for Gymboree Corp. Employees

Gymboree Corp. management implemented a wide range of innovative employee policies and practices to motivate employees to "celebrate childhood" each and every day of work. Every Thursday at 3 p.m., employees take a "snack time" break by munching on root beer floats, chips and dips, and pretzels.

The company also implemented special benefits for employees who are pregnant or who have spouses that are expecting. Other benefits include on-site diaper-changing rooms and paternity or adoption leave for employees.

Finally, the company created a "GymCares" program that links employee volunteers from Gymboree with community service opportunities.

Discussion Questions

1. Evaluate Gymboree's strategies for *creating* an effective and appropriate organizational culture using Trice and Beyer's strategies for creating an organizational culture. Be as specific as possible.

2. Based on Trice and Beyer's strategies for *maintaining* organizational culture, develop an action plan for maintaining Gymboree's culture. Be as specific as possible.

3. Suppose that Gymboree management decided that they wanted to change the company's culture to emphasize speed, quality, and teamwork. Using Trice and Beyer's strategies for *changing* organizational culture, develop an action plan for handling this situation. Be as specific as possible.

4. What are the practical implications of this case for you as a future manager in a real-world organization?

■ *Experiential Exercise: Field 10-1*

FIELD PROJECT IN ASSESSING THE CULTURE OF A REAL-WORLD ORGANIZATION

Overview

Identify an organization that you are familiar with. This may be a company that you are working for in a part-time job or an internship. It may also be a company that you worked for in the past. If you know someone who works for a real-world organization and he or she is willing to help you out, this is fine as well.

Procedure

Step 1: Identify a manager who is willing to be interviewed for 30 to 45 minutes for this exercise.

Step 2: Meet with this manager and ask him or her the following questions:

a. How would you describe the culture of your work unit? Can you give me some specific examples of how you do things that reflect this culture?

b. In what ways is the culture of your work unit similar to or different from the culture of the overall organization?

c. What do you do to *create* the right kind of culture in your work unit?

d. What do you do to *maintain* the culture of your work unit?

e. Suppose that you determined that you needed to *change* the culture of your work unit. How would you approach this challenge?

f. What kinds of advice would you give students about how to manage organizational culture in real-world organizations?

Step 3: Write a summary of your report and present it to your class for discussion purposes.

REFERENCE NOTES

1. Kotter, J. P. and L. A. Schlesinger. Choosing Strategies for Change, *Harvard Business Review*, Volume 57, 1979, p. 106.

2. Dunham, R. B. *Organizational Behavior: People and Processes in Management,* Homewood, IL: Irwin, 1984, p. 484.

3. Lewin, K. *Field Theory in Social Science.* New York: Harper and Row, 1951.

4. Kotter, J. P., and L. A. Schlesinger. Choosing Strategies for Change, *Harvard Business Review*, 1979, p. 11.

5. Trice, H. M., and J. M. Beyer. *The Cultures of Work Organizations.* Englewood Cliffs, New Jersey: Prentice-Hall, 1993, p. 413.

6. Trice, H. M., and J. M. Beyer. *The Cultures of Work Organizations.* Englewood Cliffs, New Jersey: Prentice-Hall, 1993, p. 378.

7. Trice, H. M., and J. M. Beyer. How an Organization's Rites Reveal Its Culture, *Organizational Dynamics*, Volume 16, Issue 4, 1991, p. 5.

8. Trice, H. M., and J. M. Beyer. *The Cultures of Work Organizations.* Englewood Cliffs, New Jersey: Prentice-Hall, 1993, p. 399.

9. The name of the organization has been changed to protect its identity. The events described in this case are all true.

10. Hein, K. Gymboree, *Incentive*, January 1999, pp. 42–44.

11. Gymboree. *Vision Statement.* Retrieved September 2003 from http://www.gymboree.com.

12. Gymboree. *Our Values.* Retrieved September 2003 from http://www.gymboree.com.

13. Gymboree. *Benefits.* Retrieved September 2003 from http://www.gymboree.com.

APPENDIX 6A
Critical Evaluation of the Original Sets of Power Bases and Synthesis

Unlike every other integrated model, theory, or approach that is covered in *Organizational Behavior*, the integrated set of power bases that is presented in Chapter 6 was developed specifically for this textbook. Since an appropriately integrated model, theory, or approach was not available for this particular topic, a new one had to be created.

This appendix reviews, evaluates, and synthesizes the original research that served as the underlying foundation for the synthesized set of key individual power bases.

THE CLASSIC THEORY OF INDIVIDUAL POWER BASES

Several of the pioneering research studies on power[1] attempt to create theories of individual power based on clusters of commonly used power bases. A theory concerning the bases of social power, developed by French and Raven, has proven to be the most widely accepted of those pioneering attempts.

French and Raven posited the existence of five core bases of social power: reward power, coercive power, legitimate power, referent power, and expert power.[2]

Reward power is based on the powerholder's ability to give—or to influence the giving of—rewards to others who are dependent on a powerholder for such rewards (see also Chapters 3 and 9). The bigger the rewards and the greater the perceived ability to influence the giving of those rewards, the greater the reward power held. Rewards include both the giving of positive rewards (e.g., a pay raise) and the reduction or elimination of "negative valences" (e.g., having to work an unpopular shift, such as Saturday night or a holiday).

Coercive power deals with negative forms of "rewards" that can be anticipated if the dependent person fails to conform to the powerholder's wishes. In other words, coercive power is related to the perceived ability of the powerholder to punish others. The stronger the potential punishment and the greater the likelihood that it will be applied, the greater the coercive power held. An example is the ability to fire any worker who fails to meet minimum production standards.

A more complex power base is **legitimate power.** This results when the internal values of a particular individual are such that a certain holder of legitimate power is perceived to have the legitimate right to influence that individual. While this could well be due to the perceived authority[3] of the powerholder, it could also stem from internalized cultural norms, norms specific to a particular group, prescriptions for how to perform a particular group role (see Chapter 4), personal values stemming from one's childhood upbringing, and so on. Thus, while the manager of an accountant would clearly have legitimate power over him, so would a co-worker who reminds him of the need to follow generally accepted accounting principles, and so would a personal friend who tells him emphatically that it would not be right to "cook the books" in any way.

Referent power is based on the degree to which an individual identifies with the powerholder. In addition to identification, prestige and attraction[4] are other key aspects of referent power. The term referent power is derived from the concept of a reference group.

Expert power is based on the perceived extent of knowledge attributed to the powerholder. This can range from acceptance of medical advice from a highly educated and fully certified medical doctor to a willingness to follow directions given by a local inhabitant who appears to know what he is talking about.

MORE RECENT RESEARCH ON INDIVIDUAL POWER BASES

A more recent key contributor to the body of knowledge concerning power, Pfeffer, also developed a list of important individual power bases. These include formal authority, control over resources, control over information, and uncertainty reduction.[5]

Formal authority is similar to legitimate power, although it is narrower in scope. **Control over resources** may be viewed as an expanded version of reward power, since the resources controlled may be used for other purposes aside from providing rewards. **Control over information** is a new addition, reflecting the notion that knowledge is power. While some such knowledge can readily be linked to expert power, other knowledge derives more from one's location within the organizational communication network than it does from personal expertise. An interesting related research study found that having greater control over information could have a strong impact on a person's chances for obtaining a promotion.[6] **Uncertainty reduction** involves solving important problems faced by an organization, thereby reducing uncertainty for that organization. It seems clear that a person's ability to reduce uncertainty is usually likely to depend on the degree of expert power that individual has developed.

A major review of power in and around organizations by a researcher named Mintzberg led to the creation of a somewhat different general set of individual power bases. These include control of resources, control of a technical skill, control of a body of knowledge, exclusive rights or privileges to impose choices, and access to people who can rely on the preceding four power bases.[7]

Control of resources is a minor re-wording of control over resources. **Technical skill** and a **body of knowledge** are two important sub-categories of expert power, and thus a useful refinement of that power base. Incidentally, it is asserted that to truly provide power, the resources, technical skills, and bodies of knowledge must be essential to the functioning of the organization, concentrated in the hands of one person or a small number of people, and nonsubstitutable.

Exclusive rights or privileges to impose choices is a somewhat broader version of formal authority, although it is still narrower in scope than legitimate power. **Access to people who can rely on the preceding four power bases** is fundamentally a recognition of the old saying, "it's not what you know, it's who you know." However, note that to truly create a power base, the person with access must display the ability to *persuade* or influence a more powerful person to use his or her power bases to facilitate an action or decision outcome that the persuader desires. To make future references to this power base easier, it will henceforth be shortened to **"proven ability to persuade a powerful person."**

Another more recent effort to create a list of the most important individual power bases chose to accept the original set of five bases of social power[8] as being appropriate, but then contended that this list required expansion. Two organizational behavior researchers named Yukl and Falbe suggested three additional power bases: information power, persuasive power, and charisma power.[9]

Information power[10] is a minor re-wording of the control over information power base. **Persuasive power** involves the application of logical reasoning, with relevant supporting facts, to persuade another person or group to do something. This appears to be a political skill rather than a power base. The political skill known as reasoning quite similarly identifies and applies facts and data to make logical, rational presentations of ideas.[11] However, persuasive power also is similar to the proven ability to persuade a powerful person, with its focus on persuading a powerful person to use her power to create outcomes desired by the persuader. **Charisma power** shares many characteristics of referent power, but in a more extreme form.

One other more recent in-depth overview of power—also by Pfeffer—provides additional insight into the question of the primary individual power bases.[12] This review makes a very convincing case that **being in the "right" subunit** will greatly strengthen an individual's formal authority, control over resources, and control over information power bases. Thus, individual power is substantially affected by the relative power of the subunit in which the individual is located. However, personal characteristics such as **being articulate, sensitive, and socially adept** are also viewed as contributing to overall power, along with **personal knowledge and skills.** The former link directly to referent power and charisma power, whereas the latter are clearly another way of discussing expert power.

Now that these more recent contributions to the research on individual power bases[13] have been presented and preliminarily critiqued, the evaluation process can be extended in an effort to integrate these power-related ideas into a new synthesized set of key individual power bases.

CRITICAL EVALUATION AND SYNTHESIS

It is apparent from the previous section that there is a significant amount of overlap in the various research efforts to develop a list of the most important individual power bases. With the single exception of coercive power, the original five power bases described by French and Raven seem to re-appear frequently in more recent research efforts, though often in slightly different form. Thus, these power bases form a rather firm foundation for a synthesized set of key individual power bases.

Reward power and *coercive power* both appear to have their roots in reinforcement theory[14]—specifically, in positive and negative reinforcement plus punishment, respectively. As was indicated in the previous section, *control over resources* is essential for providing positively reinforcing types of rewards, but is broader than *reward power* because those resources can be used in other ways than providing rewards. This suggests that *control over resources* is a better overall choice for labeling that particular cluster of fairly similar power bases. Negatively reinforcing types of rewards, such as not making a subordinate work on a Saturday night, do not appear to be a form of resource. However, they are typically something that a manager would control based on her *formal authority* or *exclusive rights or privileges to impose choices.*

While *coercive power* might conceivably at times be based on the ability to physically intimidate someone, it depends primarily on having the *right* to punish people. Therefore it is based largely on *legitimate power*[15] or *formal authority* or the *exclusive rights or privileges to impose choices.* For example, a manager might use his *formal authority* to coerce a subordinate into working overtime when the subordinate has no desire whatsoever to work overtime. This example brings up an interesting point: a manager could certainly use his *formal authority* to coerce a subordinate into working overtime, but is this legitimate? Perhaps *formal authority* is therefore a better overall choice than *legitimate power.*

Formal authority also has the advantage of being more readily understood as a concept. While the meaning of *legitimate power* extends beyond *formal authority* (e.g., reminding others of group or cultural norms), *formal authority* likely accounts for the most significant applications of *legitimate power* in most organizations. The *exclusive rights or privileges to impose choices* is broader and more accurate than *formal authority,* but it is a fairly similar concept—as well as being quite a mouthful for describing a frequently used power base. Finally, as suggested in the previous paragraph, the right or ability to provide negatively reinforcing types of rewards can also be subsumed under the concept labeled *formal authority.*

Expert power and *uncertainty reduction* both have strong points as potential labels for the knowledge and skills cluster of similar power bases. *Expert power* focuses more on having the requisite knowledge and skills to *be able* to solve problems, whereas *uncertainty reduction* focuses more on having *actually used* that knowledge and those skills to solve important problems. Overall, *expert power* is a little broader and easier to comprehend. The concepts of *control of a technical skill* and *control of a body of knowledge* are useful re-wordings of plain *"knowledge and skills"* that can help in focusing on more specific types of expertise.

Referent power—power that is based on identification, prestige and attraction—can encompass *being articulate, sensitive, socially adept,* and other similar positive personal characteristics. As was stated earlier, *charisma power* is a narrower, more extreme form of *referent power,* leading to a very high degree of identification, prestige, and attraction. In addition, recent research suggests that an individual's charisma may depend significantly on the situation that individual happens to be in, as opposed to an individual having a charisma power base that applies in all situations.[16] Thus, *referent power* appears to be the best overall choice for this cluster of factors.

Control over information, an important element appearing in several of the more recent research efforts looking at individual power, appears to have good support for adding it to the Synthesized Set of Key Individual Power Bases. Choosing *control over information* instead of *information power* can be justified by noting that the former term serves as a reminder that filtering of information is an important underpinning of this particular power base,[17] whereas *information power* is comparatively vague.

The power base labeled as the *proven ability to persuade a powerful person* has a fair amount of support for adding it to the Synthesized Set of Key Individual Power Bases—not the least of which is that the expression "it's not what you know, it's who you know" makes a great deal of sense to most people. The *proven ability to persuade a powerful person* is preferred over *persuasive power* because of the previously noted concern that the latter is more of a political skill than a power base, whereas the former focuses on using persuasion to *indirectly* exercise *control* over another person's key power base. In addition, *the proven ability to persuade a powerful person* more broadly encompasses the important exchange-of-favors aspect as well as aspects that appear to be related to *expert power* and *referent power.*[18] Because the *proven ability to persuade a powerful person* power base is more indirect than the other five power bases synthesized previously, it could be argued that it is generally a less potent power base than the other five.

A strong case has been made that *being in the "right" subunit* greatly strengthens an individual's *formal authority, control over resources,* and *control over information* power bases. Thus, a truly thorough analysis of individual power should take the power of subunits into account as well. However, the requirement to scrutinize the power of subunits as well as individuals makes what is already a fairly complex analysis into a much more complicated one. Readers interested in pursuing this even more advanced approach are encouraged to consult sources that discuss the Strategic Contingencies Model[19] and the Resource-Dependency Model[20] of subunit power, as well as the importance of *being in the "right" subunit.*[21]

REFERENCE NOTES

1. French, J. R. P., Jr., and B. Raven. The Bases of Social Power. In D. Cartwright (ed.), *Studies in Social Power*. Ann Arbor, MI: University of Michigan Institute of Social Research, 1959, pp. 150–167. Mechanic, D. Sources of Power in Lower Participants in Complex Organizations. *Administrative Science Quarterly*, Vol. 7, 1962, pp. 349–364.

2. French, J. R. P., Jr., and B. Raven. The Bases of Social Power. In D. Cartwright (ed.), *Studies in Social Power*. Ann Arbor, MI: University of Michigan Institute of Social Research, 1959, pp. 150–167.

3. Weber, M. *The Theory of Social and Economic Organization*. New York, NY: Free Press, 1947.

4. French, J. R. P., Jr., and B. Raven. The Bases of Social Power. In D. Cartwright (ed.), *Studies in Social Power*. Ann Arbor, MI: University of Michigan Institute of Social Research, 1959, pp. 150–167. Mechanic, D. Sources of Power in Lower Participants in Complex Organizations. *Administrative Science Quarterly*, Vol. 7, 1962, pp. 349–364.

5. Pfeffer, J. *Organizational Design*. Arlington Heights, IL: AHM Publishing Company, 1978.

6. Brass, D. J. Being in the Right Place: A Structural Analysis of Individual Influence in an Organization. *Administrative Science Quarterly*, Vol. 29, 1984, pp. 518–539.

7. Mintzberg, H. *Power in and Around Organizations*. Englewood Cliffs, NJ: Prentice-Hall, 1983.

8. French, J. R. P., Jr., and B. Raven. The Bases of Social Power. In D. Cartwright (ed.), *Studies in Social Power*. Ann Arbor, MI: University of Michigan Institute of Social Research, 1959, pp. 150–167.

9. Yukl, G., and C. M. Falbe. Importance of Different Power Sources in Downward and Lateral Relations. *Journal of Applied Psychology*, Vol. 76, 1991, pp. 416–423.

10. Not to be confused with the earlier version of Informational Power presented by Deutsch & Gerard (1955), which French and Raven (1959) view as being equivalent to their Expert Power base. Deutsch, M., and H. B. Gerard. A Study of Normative and Informational Influence upon Individual Judgement. *Journal of Abnormal and Social Psychology*, Vol. 51, 1955, pp. 629–636. French, J. R. P., Jr., and B. Raven. The Bases of Social Power. In D. Cartwright (ed.), *Studies in Social Power*. Ann Arbor, MI: University of Michigan Institute of Social Research, 1959, pp. 150–167.

11. Kipnis, D., S. M. Schmidt, C. Swaffin-Smith, and I. Wilkinson. Patterns of Managerial Influence: Shotgun Managers, Tacticians, and Bystanders. *Organizational Dynamics*, Vol. 12, 1984, pp. 58–67.

12. Pfeffer, J. *Managing with Power*. Boston, MA: Harvard Business School Press, 1992.

13. One other more recent contribution to the research on individual power bases is provided by Finkelstein (1992). However, because Finkelstein's typology focuses very narrowly on the power bases of top managers, its two unique contributions are not generally applicable. While structural power is very much the same as formal authority, and while expert power is expert power, ownership power is essentially based on number of shares held, and prestige power is essentially based on the number of different boards on which a top manager serves. Finkelstein, S. Power in Top Management Teams: Dimensions, Measurement, and Validation. Academy of Management Journal, Vol. 35, 1992, pp. 505–538.

14. Skinner, B. F. *Contingencies of Reinforcement*. New York, NY: Appleton-Century-Crofts, 1969.

15. Podsakoff, P. M., and C. A. Schriesheim. Field Studies of French and Raven's Bases of Power: Critique, Re-Analysis, and Suggestions for Future Research. *Psychological Bulletin*, Vol. 97, 1985, pp. 387–411.

16. Roberts, N. C., and R. T. Bradley. Limits of Charisma. In J. A. Conger, R. N. Kanungo, and Associates (eds.), *Charismatic Leadership*. San Francisco, CA: Jossey-Bass, 1988.

17. Pfeffer, J. *Organizational Design*. Arlington Heights, IL: AHM Publishing Company, 1978.

18. Podsakoff, P. M., and C. A. Schriesheim. Field Studies of French and Raven's Bases of Power: Critique, Re-Analysis, and Suggestions for Future Research. *Psychological Bulletin*, Vol. 97, 1985, pp. 387–411.

19. Hickson, D. J., C. R. Hinings, C. A. Lee, R. E. Schneck, and J. M. Pennings. A Strategic Contingency Theory of Intra-organizational Power. *Administrative Science Quarterly*,

Vol. 16, 1971, pp. 216–229. Hinings, C. R., D. J. Hickson, J. M. Pennings, and R. E. Schneck. Structural Conditions of Intraorganizational Power. *Administrative Science Quarterly*, Vol. 19, 1974, pp. 22–44.

20. Salancik, G. R., and J. Pfeffer. The Bases and Use of Power in Organizational Decision Making: The Case of a University. *Administrative Science Quarterly*, Vol. 19, 1974, pp. 453–473.

21. Pfeffer, J. *Managing with Power*. Boston, MA: Harvard Business School Press, 1992.

INDEX